# Diocletian and the Tetrarchy

# DEBATES AND DOCUMENTS IN ANCIENT HISTORY

GENERAL EDITORS

Hugh Bowden, *King's College London*, and
Shaun Tougher, *University of Cardiff*

Focusing on important themes, events or periods throughout ancient
history, each volume in this series is divided into roughly equal parts.
The first introduces the reader to the main issues of interpretation.
The second contains a selection of relevant evidence supporting
different views.

PUBLISHED

*Diocletian and the Tetrarchy*
Roger Rees

IN PREPARATION

*Roman Imperialism*
Andrew Erskine

*Julian the Apostate*
Shaun Tougher

# Series Editors' Preface

*Debates and Documents in Ancient History* is a series of short books on central topics in Greek and Roman history. It will range over the whole period of classical history from the early first millennium BC to the sixth century AD. The works in the series are written by expert academics and provide up-to-date and accessible accounts of the historical issues and problems raised by each topic. They also contain the important evidence on which the arguments are based, including texts (in translation), archaeological data and visual material. This allows readers to judge how convincing the arguments are and to enter the debates themselves. The series is intended for all those interested in the history of the Greek and Roman world.

In this book Roger Rees focuses on a seminal period in the history of the Roman empire, the reign of Diocletian (AD 284–305). This is usually taken as a turning point in the history of the empire, and the reforms attributed to Diocletian are thought to mark the transformation of the Roman world in to the world of Late Antiquity. But is this correct? Was Diocletian an original thinker or was he merely developing extant trends? Did his reforms follow a systematic plan or were they executed *ad hoc*? Does Diocletian deserve to be seen as the saviour of the Roman empire, or did he in fact set it on a course towards its ultimate decline? No major narrative history of this period survives, but there is no shortage of evidence from which a picture of the reign of Diocletian and his colleagues can be drawn, such as speeches, inscriptions, Christian tracts, statues and coins. Roger Rees draws on the range of evidence to provide a thoughtful and balanced consideration of Diocletian and the Tetrarchy.

Hugh Bowden and Shaun Tougher
January 2004

# Preface

When we look into the eyes of the famous porphyry bust in the Worcester Art Museum (below Part II 48), we might well wonder what Diocletian was like – unusual, inscrutable, severe perhaps, determined. I sometimes think I can see a tired man. But no matter how we see it, in all honesty we cannot even be thoroughly confident the bust *is* of Diocletian. Other sources might promise to get us nearer to him: for some of his contemporaries he was a saviour, the man who restored stability to the Roman world and brought a golden age of peace and prosperity; but then others thought him evil, a man who brought the empire to its knees with his greed and cruelty. Seventeen centuries after his death, historians are still looking, following up new lines of enquiry, reopening old ones, applying different procedures and techniques. The search for Diocletian goes on, as this book consisting of evidence and inquiry is intended to show.

The late third and early fourth centuries may be unfamiliar to some, so Part I (Debates) opens with a narrative for the years 284 to 313 and consideration of how that narrative can be written; this involves the book's first cross-referencing to primary sources in Part II (Documents). Throughout Part I cross references to Part II, indicated by bold type in brackets, direct the reader to the sources under discussion: for example, the reference (II 7) indicates the seventh item in Part II; likewise, a more specific reference such as (II 6 7.4) indicates a particular subsection (7.4) of the sixth item in Part II. The few references to primary sources not in bold type indicate material not in Part II. References to secondary literature, by author and year of publication, can be followed up in the bibliography. Maps (pp. xii–xiv), a chronology (pp. 197–8) and a glossary (pp. 214–15) should provide further points of reference.

Each of the subsequent six chapters in Part I is dedicated to a theme of central importance to government or society under Diocletian and his colleagues in office; in each case, I have tried to introduce the relevant sources and discuss their value and interpretations. I hope a constructive dialogue will be set up between the Debates and the Documents, which encourages each relevant source and interpretation to be considered and evaluated in relation to each other.

Inevitably, I have had to make sacrifices in both parts of the book, but I hope the guides to further reading and internet resources which follow Part II will make good any disappointment. With the exception of the Panopolis papyri, translations of texts are my own. I would like to record my sincere thanks to the late Dr T. C. Skeat for his permission to reproduce his versions of the papyri (with minor alterations); and my debts to translators and commentators who have gone before me and whose scholarship has helped me.

My thanks to John Davey and James Dale of Edinburgh University Press, and to the series editors Hugh Bowden and Shaun Tougher for their patience and help; to Colin Adams, Nic Fields, Andy Hart and Bill Leadbetter, for advice, correspondence and offprints; to students of Diocletian at Trinity College, Dublin and Edinburgh, for their indulgence; but most of all to Aileen, who has lived with Diocletian longer than she has lived with me.

R.D.R.
Fife, September 2003

# Acknowledgements

Grateful acknowledgement is made to the following sources for permission to reproduce material previously published elsewhere. Every effort has been made to trace the copyright holders, but if any have been inadvertently overlooked, the publisher will be pleased to make the necessary arrangements at the first opportunity.

II 26    MS. Canon. Misc. 378, fol. 153v, Bodleian Library, University of Oxford

II 34    MS. Wilkinson dep. d. 34, pp. 51–2. Bodleian Library, University of Oxford

II 35    Source: *Roman Architecture*, F. Sear, 1982, BT Batsford (plate 173)

II 36    J. J. Wilkes

II 37    Source: *Roman Architecture*, F. Sear, 1982, BT Batsford (plate 172)

II 38    J. C. N. Coulston

II 39    J. C. N. Coulston

II 40    Nic Fields

II 41    J. C. N. Coulston

II 42    J. C. N. Coulston

II 43a, b  J. C. N. Coulston

II 44    © copyright the Trustees of the British Museum

II 45    Musée d'Arras

II 46    Ian McAuslan

II 47    Vatican Library

II 48    Worcester Art Museum, Worcester, Massachusetts, Alexander H. Bullock Fund

II 49    National Museum, Cairo

II 50    National Museum Belgrade

# Abbreviations

*Primary Sources*

A.E.        *L' Année Epigraphique*
I.L.S.      *Inscriptiones Latinae Selectae*, H. Dessau (ed.), 3 vols (Berlin
            1892–1916)
R.I.C.      *Roman Imperial Coinage*, London 1923: Spink

*Secondary Sources*

A.T.        *Antiquité Tardive*
B.A.S.P.    *Bulletin of the American Society of Papyrologists*
C.A.H.      *Cambridge Ancient History*
Cl.A.       *Classical Antiquity*
C.Ph.       *Classical Philology*
C.Q.        *Classical Quarterly*
D.O.P.      *Dumbarton Oaks Papers*
G.&R.       *Greece and Rome*
G.R.B.S.    *Greek, Roman and Byzantine Studies*
H.Th.R.     *Harvard Theological Review*
J.R.A.      *Journal of Roman Archaeology*
J.R.S.      *Journal of Roman Studies*
J.Th.S.     *Journal of Theological Studies*
NC          *Numismatic Chronicle*
O.C.D.³     *Oxford Classical Dictionary* (3rd edn), S. Hornblower and
            A. Spawforth (eds), Oxford 1996: Oxford University Press
P.L.L.S.    *Proceedings of the Leeds Latin Seminar*
P.L.R.E.    A. H. M. Jones, J. R. Martindale, J. Morris, *Prosopography
            of the Later Roman Empire 260–395 AD*, Cambridge 1971:
            Cambridge University Press
TAPA        *Transactions of the American Philological Association*
Z.P.E.      *Zeitschrift für Papyrologie und Epigraphik*

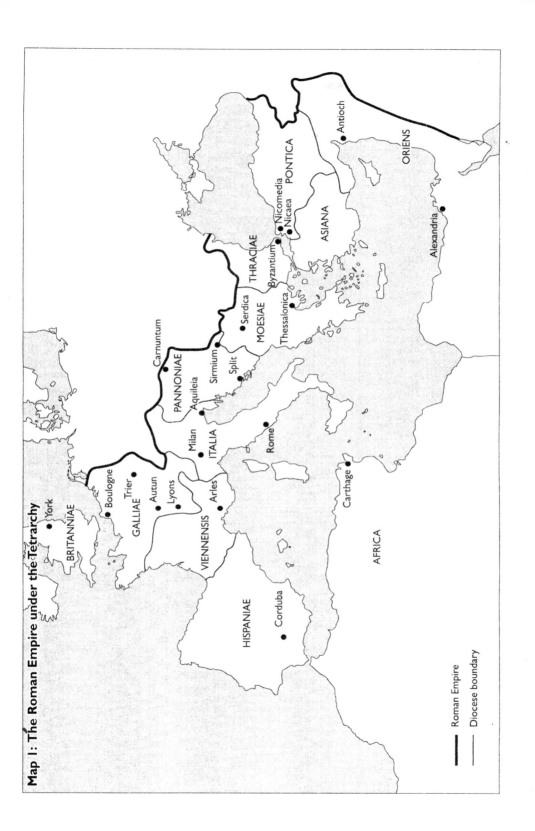

Map 1: The Roman Empire under the Tetrarchy

Roman Empire
Diocese boundary

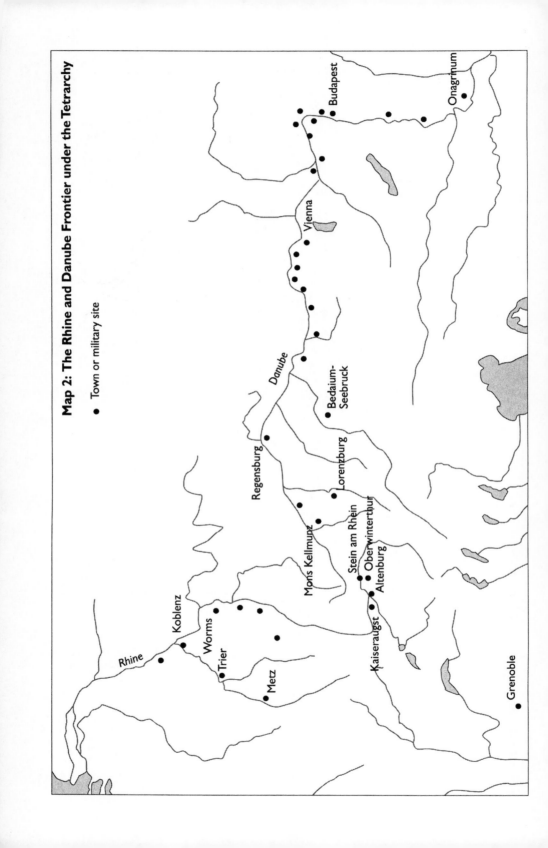

Map 2: The Rhine and Danube Frontier under the Tetrarchy

• Town or military site

Rhine
Koblenz
Trier
Worms
Metz
Mons Kellmunz
Regensburg
Danube
Lorenzburg
Stein am Rhein
Oberwinterthur
Altenburg
Kaiseraugst
Bedaium-Seebruck
Vienna
Budapest
Onagrinum
Grenoble

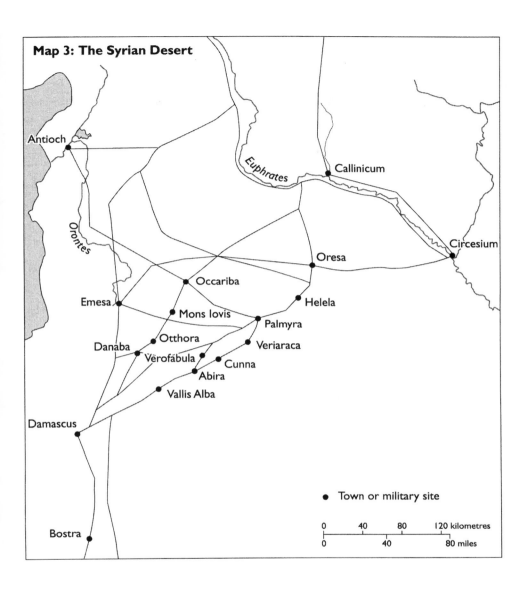

**Map 3: The Syrian Desert**

Antioch

*Euphrates*

Callinicum

*Orontes*

Circesium

Oresa

Occariba

Helela

Emesa

Mons Iovis

Palmyra

Otthora

Veriaraca

Danaba

Verofábula

Cunna

Abira

Vallis Alba

Damascus

● Town or military site

```
0        40       80      120 kilometres
├────┼────┼────┼────┼────┼────┤
0              40              80 miles
```

Bostra

# Part I

# Debates

# INTRODUCTION

# History and Narrative

## 1. Historiography

No large scale historiography in the manner of Thucydides or Tacitus survives for the reign of Diocletian and his immediate successors. The work of Ammianus Marcellinus, written in the late fourth century, covered the years from Nerva (96) to his own lifetime, but the surviving books cover only the period after 353; Ammianus' references to Diocletian are illuminating but infrequent (**II 7**). Books 8 and 9 of the *History of the Church* (c. 324–5) by Eusebius offer a vivid narrative of the fortunes of the Christian faithful under Diocletian and his colleagues, circumstances in which Eusebius himself shared (**II 8**). However, Eusebius, bishop of Caesarea (c. 260–339) radically departed from the conventions of classical historiography, and his consuming interest in ecclesiastical affairs left almost no room for other matters.

The lack of an heir to Livy or Tacitus puts a great premium on the historiography that does survive. What we have is not large scale – quite the opposite in fact, and in several cases, deliberately so – but authors such as Aurelius Victor, Eutropius, Festus, and other texts such as the anonymous *Epitome* and *Valesianus* are nonetheless valuable if curious sources for the reign of Diocletian (**II 4, 5**). At once, they weave into concise and fluent accounts many aspects of constitutional, military, biographical, economical and administrative history. But they are not unproblematic.

Sextus Aurelius Victor was born soon after 320, in north Africa. A good education was followed by a successful career in government bureaucracy, including most notably his appointment as the consular governor of the province of Pannonia Secunda (c. 361–4), and later as urban prefect at Rome in 388–9. His *Book of the Caesars*, a political history of the Roman Empire in forty-two chapters, was published in c. 361 (**II 1**). Although brief, the work is characterised by digressions reminiscent of the manner of the Republican historian Sallust; Aurelius Victor's main source is thought to be a work now lost, known after its existence was posited by a German scholar in the nineteenth century, as the *Kaisergeschichte*. The same *Kaisergeschichte* is generally held to have been the main source for the sections covering the imperial period of the *Breviarium* of Eutropius, published in c. 369–70 (**II 2**). Like Aurelius Victor, Eutropius worked in administration, and was secretary of state for petitions at the time of publication. The *Breviarium*, detailing Roman political affairs from 753 BCE to 364, is divided into ten books of unequal coverage; in style if not in content, the work is unambitious. Stylistically plain and also termed *Breviarium*, but briefer still, is the work of Festus, usually thought to have been published shortly after Eutropius' (**II 3**). Festus, like Eutropius a secretary of state for petitions, is most interested in the history of the political relations between Rome and Persia.

In Aurelius Victor, Eutropius and Festus, writing within a decade of each other, we have densely detailed but widely accessible accounts of Roman political and constitutional affairs. (This characterisation has given rise to the suspicion that the texts were written to serve as manageable but intensive introductions to Roman affairs of state, for consumption by the new, often non-Roman military elite of the mid-fourth century.) Writing two generations after his death, the texts provide reasonably consistent versions of such matters for the reign of Diocletian and his colleagues in office. But a lack of uniformity in some details – for example, the initial imperial position held by Maximian – and the occasional tendency to compress chronologies, necessarily raise the question of the texts' reliability. Similarly, the fondness for melodramatic detail of the anonymous *Epitome about the Caesars* (**II 4**) (probably dating to the last years of the fourth century) or the extreme pro-Constantinian bias of the *Anonymous Valesianus* (**II 5**) urge caution. Perhaps of a similar date but even more untrustworthy is the *Historia Augusta* (also known as the *Scriptores Historiae Augustae* or *S.H.A.*). This series of imperial biographies from Hadrian to Numerian in the style of Suetonius purports to have been written in the time of Diocletian and Constantine by six different authors. It has some interesting points about Diocletian and his colleagues, but it has been very widely accepted since the seminal proposition by Dessau in 1889 that in fact the work dates to much later in the fourth century, and was penned by one author. If the motivation for the deception remains one of classical scholarship's great mysteries, it certainly calls into question the text's reliability.

Reliability is also the key battleground in modern appreciation of Lactantius' *On the Deaths of the Persecutors* (**II 6**). Lactantius was a contemporary of Diocletian, and appointed by the emperor as a teacher of rhetoric in Nicomedia – he was therefore an eye-witness to many of the events and developments his work covers. However, the important testimony his *On the Deaths* constitutes is compromised by Lactantius' Christian faith. Lactantius covers most of the important constitutional and political affairs of the time, but focuses on the persecution of the Christians. This policy rendered Diocletian and his persecuting colleagues intolerable to the Christian Lactantius and informs the entire work – Lactantius' decision to cast the persecuting emperors' deaths as the deserved punishment of a Christian justice at work can be seen as deeply held religious prejudice overriding the exercise of balanced historical judgement. The work, published c. 315, is difficult to classify: covering a wide range of imperial persecutors from the first century to the fourth, it is a curious combination of political and religious history; at the same time, its aggressive moralising and polemical tone have the air of invective. Addressed to a Donatus, who had suffered in the Diocletianic persecution, *On the Deaths* could also have had a proselytising ambition.

But if the surviving narrative texts for the reign of Diocletian present certain challenges both in specific details and in broader philosophies of historical causation, taken together they do permit reasonably confident reconstruction of the key political and constitutional developments for the reign of Diocletian (see Chronology, below). These developments were far from uncomplicated.

## 2. Roman Politics 284–305

Gaius Aurelius Valerius Diocletian was born in Dalmatia about 240. Known then simply as Diocles, the future emperor was from a poor family. He worked his way through military service, perhaps in Gaul. When on the elite bodyguard for the emperor Carus, he was granted the consulship in 283. Carus died in suspicious circumstances soon after a campaign had been launched against the Persians; his sons Numerian and Carinus succeeded him, but Numerian died soon afterwards, the victim it seems of assassination. Troops loyal to the late emperor promoted Diocletian to the throne (**II 18 Carus 13.1**); the following spring, Carinus was killed by one of his own men, leaving Diocletian, the career soldier from humble non-Italian stock, sole Augustus. By the standards of the preceding few decades of the turbulent mid-third century, this accelerated elevation to absolute power might not have seemed particularly noteworthy.

Likewise, Diocletian's appointment of an imperial colleague in 285 might not have caused surprise – the second and third centuries had both seen collegiate governments. What was perhaps more arresting was that Diocletian's choice was no relation. Marcus Aurelius Valerius Maximian was a man of ignoble origins (in Sirmium, Pannonia) and considerable military record. This collegiate government is known now by the convenient term 'Dyarchy'. As Diocletian turned his mind to the Sarmatians and further east to the Persians, Maximian was dispatched to Gaul to deal with the rebels known as the Bagaudae, a mission he achieved quickly (**II 1 39.17, 2 9.20**) – the Dyarchy, it seems, came into being so that the imperial government could face challenges in two different areas at the same time without compromising unity. Circumstances were such that they could rarely meet – in 288, and again in the winter of 290–1 at Milan, there was an imperial conference. Otherwise, Diocletian based himself for the next decade or so in Sirmium and Nicomedia; meanwhile, Maximian's base was at Trier (Barnes 1982: 49–60).

The prevailing opinion amongst moderns is that Maximian's original imperial rank was Caesar, that is, unmistakably subordinate to Diocletian with his rank of Augustus; and that Maximian was promoted to the position of Augustus in 286 (Leadbetter 1998a). The issue is important because it raises questions about Diocletian's vision for efficient government of the empire, and the ambitions others might have entertained for high office. At this early stage, had Diocletian devised a hierarchical system of imperial probation and promotion, or was he improvising in the face of new threats? Did Maximian insist upon the rank of Augustus, his confidence high after his successes in Gaul?

About 287, the Augusti adopted *signa*. A *signum* was an appellation which typically implied a relationship between the claimant and a second party. The Dyarchs took theophoric *signa*, Diocletian 'Jovius', recalling Jupiter, and Maximian 'Herculius', recalling Hercules (**Chapter 4.3**). Jupiter's (paternal) authority over Hercules might have inspired appreciation of a similar hierarchy between Diocletian Iovius and Maximian Herculius; but ancient testimony for a symbolic father–son relationship between the Dyarchs can be dismissed (Nixon and Rodgers 1994: 45–6). Lactantius and other sources speak of a brotherhood between the men (**II 6 8.1; Chapter 6.1**).

A further complicating factor in the matter of the constitutional changes of the mid-280s (and which might also have inspired the adoption of the *signa*), is that when from about 286 Diocletian and Maximian attended to manoeuvres and negotiations on the Syrian and German frontiers respectively, a man called Carausius abandoned his responsibilities to rid the English Channel of pirates for the Romans, and taking troops and resources with him, declared himself emperor in Britain. Carausius was not overtly aggressive to the Dyarchs, but they were not prepared to tolerate him (**Chapter 6.3**). A campaign by Maximian to recover Britain in 289 failed. Carausius' murder in 293 did not end the separatist regime, as he was succeeded as emperor by his assassin Allectus. By the time Allectus was crushed and Britain recovered, in 296, further major constitutional changes had taken place.

On 1 March 293 the Dyarchy was replaced by what is now known as the Tetrarchy, with the appointment to the position of Caesar of Constantius and Galerius (**Chapter 6.2**). The Caesar to Maximian, Flavius Valerius Constantius, was born to Illyrian parents in the mid-third century; his successful military career included the governorship of Dalmatia, and it seems, his appointment as praetorian prefect under Maximian. Diocletian's Caesar, Gaius Galerius Valerius Maximianus (in some sources referred to as Maximian, to confusing effect), was born into a peasant family at Romulianum on the Danube. As a career soldier, he perhaps too attained the position of praetorian prefect (under Diocletian).

Constantius assumed the *signum* Herculius, Galerius Jovius. Aurelius Victor (**II 1 39.24–5**) and Eutropius (**II 2 9.22**) claim that marriage alliances were forged to seal this imperial college, with Constantius divorcing his first wife (Helena) to marry Maximian's daughter (or step-daughter) Theodora, and Galerius marrying Diocletian's daughter Valeria. In fact, the dating of these marriages to 293 might well be a convenient assumption, made in error by unquestioning reliance on the *Kaisergeschichte* (Barnes 1982: 37–8, 125–6; Leadbetter 1998b: 75). Again, the question is important because it concerns political motivation – if it is right that the Augusti appointed as their Caesars their sons-in-law, whom presumably they had been able to observe at close quarters in the years since their marriages, why did the *Kaisergeschichte* get such a founding principle wrong? Or did Diocletian and Maximian use new marriages in 293 as a means of guaranteeing harmony amongst the new Tetrarchy? What is certain is that dynastic succession was not the determining principle in Tetrarchic appointment. Diocletian had no son he could appoint, but Maximian did, in Maxentius, then a boy of about 10 years (**Chapter 6.2**).

In 293 Maximian moved his base to north Italy, at Milan and Aquileia, leaving Trier for Constantius. Galerius' location is less well-attested, but he was probably based at Antioch, then from 299 at Thessalonica. But all four emperors were busy. If Aurelius Victor's understanding of the dates of various campaigns in the 290s is demonstrably wrong (II 1 **39.23**; Barnes 1982: 12), nonetheless he is doubtless correct to infer that the 'mass of wars' demanding imperial attention (**39.30**) might have inspired the creation of the Tetrarchy. Civil and foreign wars and campaigns in Britain, the Rhine and Danube frontiers, Spain, North Africa, Egypt and Syria took place between 293 and 299; they were conducted with considerable success (**Chapter 1.1**). The fundamental motivation for the establishment of Tetrarchic rule seems to have been to allow more emperors to police the empire in its critical zones. Despite their bias or ignorance, Lactantius and the fourth-century historians reveal in their biographical details that the qualifications for imperial office under Diocletian were not dynastic, much as the harmony and integrity of the governing colleges of Dyarchy then Tetrarchy may have been promoted and celebrated through conventional familial alliances and terminology (**Chapter 6.1**). Instead, military problems required military solutions (II 1 **39.26–8**; 2 **10.2**; 4 **40.15**). In each of his three colleagues, Diocletian had appointed a known and trusted Balkan soldier of high military calibre and hard-won experience. If this power-sharing executive put more store in meritocratic appointment than did the vagaries of dynastic succession, it would be naïve to assume Diocletian looked simply for the best men (however defined) to take office. He clearly only looked to a very small circle of candidates.

### 3. Roman Politics 305–7

In addition to the military successes, Diocletian stands out for extraordinary policies in economics, administration and religion, to be discussed below (**Chapters 2, 3 and 5**). But in the context of Roman imperial traditions, perhaps his most surprising innovation was his retirement. In parallel ceremonies at Nicomedia and Milan on 1 May 305, Diocletian and Maximian resigned their imperial power and retired, Diocletian to his palace in Split, Maximian to Italy. Constantius and Galerius replaced them as Augusti, and new Caesars were appointed in Flavius Valerius Severus and Gaius Galerius Valerius Maximinus, also known as Maximinus Daia. Each member of this second Tetrarchy was allocated specific regions to rule, it seems (II 1 **40.1**; 2 **10.1**; 5 **3.5**).

Retirement from imperial office was unprecedented, and its motivation has caused intrigue from antiquity on. While Eutropius commends the action (**II 2 9.27–8**), Aurelius Victor is more sceptical (**II 1 39.48**). Had Diocletian and Maximian intended to retire, or did they do so against their will? If the retirement was planned, when were those plans formulated, what inspired them, and who knew of them?

Lactantius' *On the Deaths* is a most revealing source here, although perhaps it reveals more about its author's reliability than it does about Tetrarchic policy (**II 6 18.2–15**). The scene is an interview in spring 305 between an ageing and increasingly frail Diocletian and an aggressive, bullying, power-hungry Galerius. At the outset of the dialogue, Diocletian is not entertaining thoughts of retirement, although he is urged to do so by his junior colleague. On the one hand, as a teacher of rhetoric in Nicomedia by imperial appointment, it is not impossible, though by no means likely, that Lactantius was privy to aspects of Diocletian's political planning, so his image of the Augustus intending to continue in his role may have some basis in fact; on the other hand, if as is generally assumed, the Christian Lactantius fled Nicomedia soon after the outbreak of the persecution of the Christians in 303, his contact with intimate matters of state must have broken off some two years before the dramatic date of the interview he purports to be putting on record. But apart from the serious vulnerability of Lactantius' general authority for the transcript of the dialogue, some of its details too require close scrutiny. In the exchange, Diocletian is weak and irresolute (**18.7, 12, 14**) – is this psychological profile convincing for a man with his experience and achievements? Again, how persuasive is Lactantius' claim that in the face of Galerius' intimidation Diocletian wanted the reigning Caesars to become the Augusti and have Maximian's son Maxentius and Constantius' son Constantine appointed as Caesars? Of course, it is not impossible that Diocletian's opinions about the necessary qualifications for imperial office had undergone a *volte face* since the creation of the Tetrarchy twelve years earlier, but a return to the principles of dynastic succession might seem inherently unlikely when it had been avoided thus far: Diocletian's alleged proposal to Galerius would see Maximian's son-in-law Constantius Augustus and Constantius' son Constantine and Maximian's son Maxentius Caesars. Such an arrangement would provide an ideal basis for the re-establishment of dynastic succession through the allied houses of Maximian and Constantius. Would Diocletian really have recommended to Galerius a system which all but guaranteed they themselves would both be marginalised? When some of Lactantius' claims are tested, it may seem that in his desire to present Galerius as a selfish and vicious megalomaniac, his lively but rather fanciful historical imagination has come to dominate the narrative.

As it happened, whatever its motivation and the selection of its personnel, the 'second' Tetrarchy was short-lived. Constantius died at York on 25 July 306. At his side was his son Constantine, who, according to some sources had managed to evade the wily schemes of Galerius to reach Britain to be with his father (**II 1 40.2–4; 5 2.2, 2.4; 6 24.3–25.5**). Constantius' troops heralded Constantine emperor, the position for which he had been passed over the previous year. Although sources show Constantine showing a diplomatic regard for political decorum in seeking the approval of Galerius for this promotion (and winning it, although to the rank of Caesar with Severus filling the vacancy of Augustus), the role the army had assumed as kingmaker might be seen as potentially fatal to the continuing integrity of the imperial college.

The college even survived the proclamation of another man as emperor. On 28 October 306, Maxentius who like Constantine was an emperor's son who had been passed over for imperial appointment (himself twice, in 293 and 305), staged a coup with the praetorian guard at Rome and declared himself *princeps* ('prince') (**Chapter 6.3**). Galerius' response was to send his co-Augustus Severus to crush Maxentius; Severus marched with the army he had inherited from Maximian. As Lactantius implies, Maxentius was alert to the possibilities of this fact when he invited his father Maximian to give up retirement and resume imperial office with him at Rome (**II 6 26.6–7**). The tenuous loyalty of his army and the imposing new 'Aurelian' wall at Rome, built only thirty years previously, were too much for Severus who took flight and died soon afterwards in captivity.

Galerius was now moved to challenge Maxentius himself, in the summer of 307. Before Galerius reached Rome, Maximian went to Trier to forge an alliance with Constantine by giving him the hand of his daughter Fausta in marriage. But even without the reassuring presence of Maximian, the troops at Rome were too powerful for Galerius, who had underestimated the city's strength (**II 6 27.1–2**). He too had to back-pedal, leaving Maxentius in firm control over Italy, Sicily, Corsica, Sardinia and some of North Africa; this was challenged by an ill-fated usurpation by Domitius Alexander in 308–9.

## 4. Roman politics 308–13

If hopes of re-establishing collegiate harmony were fading fast, even ruling families were imploding. In the spring of 308 Maximian and his son Maxentius fell out with each other in dramatic fashion at Rome and Maximian fled to his son-in-law Constantine in Gaul. Although now brothers-in-law Constantine and Maxentius showed little interest in each other, neither threatening war nor celebrating peace. In November 308 Galerius organised an imperial conference at Carnuntum; the occasion is not well attested, and Lactantius suggests that, when Maximian turned up, Galerius had summoned Diocletian to give his authority and consent to the appointment of Licinius directly to the position of Augustus left vacant by Severus' death (**II 6 29.1–2**). Licinius, born in Dacia about forty years before, was a soldier and close friend to Galerius. It seems that not only was Licinius' appointment approved, but Maximian was persuaded to step down as Augustus, although Lactantius' remark that there were then six emperors in office at one time remains enigmatic – from Diocletian, Maximian, Galerius, Maximinus Daia, Constantine, Licinius and Maxentius, one must drop in Lactantius' accounting, but it is not clear which. If, however, we refer to Diocletian and Maximian as 'senior Augusti' at this stage, and Maxentius as a usurper, then regardless of the ranks they claimed for themselves or recognised for each other, initially the remaining four emperors can still be seen as constituting a college of sorts. But by 310, coins and inscriptions make it quite clear that nobody was prepared to accept the junior rank of Caesar.

It seems Maximian made one final bid to regain imperial power, but his attempt to use his daughter Fausta to help assassinate Constantine failed, and he was forced to kill himself in 310. Galerius died a natural though agonising death in May 311, the nature of his demise an intrinsic touchstone for the Christian theodicy of his detractors Lactantius and Eusebius (**II 6 33.1–35.3; 8 8.16.4 – Appendix 1**). Licinius assumed Galerius' European territory, with Maximinus claiming the Asian. Constantine successfully challenged Maxentius' authority in Italy in 312, culminating in his decisive victory at the Battle of the Milvian Bridge on 28 October. The following spring saw Licinius defeat Maximinus Daia. Maximinus' subsequent suicide left only Constantine and Licinius, by now brothers-in-law, on the throne.

The least well-attested death is that of Diocletian himself. The date is obscure, but is generally put at 311 or 312 (Barnes 1982: 31–2; Corcoran 1996, 2002[2]: 7). But despite their ignorance of Diocletian's biographic particulars, some of these narrative authors did not shy clear of forming judgements about his rule – and in this regard they diverge dramatically. Lactantius is most caustic: Diocletian is damned for his economic and administrative policies, and his building schemes, which together destroyed the world (**II 6 7.1–11**); yet in a revealing concession, Lactantius concedes that he reigned very successfully until he launched his persecution (**9.11**). That the persecution began nearly twenty years after Diocletian had taken office and only two years before he retired is glossed over, subordinated to Lactantius' emphatically Christian understanding of historical causation. In contrast, the *Historia Augusta* is only complimentary about Diocletian (**II 18 Carus 13.1; Elagabalus 35.4**), although such a position might be part of the text's pretence to be addressed in part to him. In their assessments, notably silent on religious affairs as was presumably the *Kaisergeschichte*, Aurelius Victor and Eutropius achieve a balance, their generally positive comments offset by observations about Diocletian's conceit (**II 1 1.39.1–8; 2 9.26–8**).

It is clear then that Diocletian's reign provoked strong feelings, but when we have judgements preserved in the narrative sources, we usually have compelling reasons to be sceptical – their levels of bias and confusion must be acknowledged. Between them, they do make possible reasonably confident and detailed reconstructions of events; but if they broadly tell us what happened, they are hardly reliable on the question of why, even less how. On crucial matters of political motivation and ideology, of the practical machinery of government administration, of life as it was lived, they can tell us little. To begin to address these questions it is necessary to look elsewhere.

# CHAPTER 1

# The Military

## 1. Tetrarchic campaigns

We have noted that whatever their other strengths or weaknesses, the Tetrarchs' essential qualifications for office were military (**II 1 39.26–8**). Without exception, they were all successful soldiers, from similar backgrounds in the Balkan lands. A distinguished military reputation had long been a strong card in seeking imperial office, with men such as Augustus, Vespasian and Trajan excellent examples. This was accentuated in the mid-third century, when no imperial dynasty managed to assert itself, as respect for constitutional procedure evaporated. Senators largely looked on helplessly as soldier-emperor succeeded soldier-emperor, each new man elevated to power by his army, and in the end most falling victim to assassins or dying in civil war. Meantime, foreign threats were considerable, in particular the Persians on the eastern frontier. In 260 Rome suffered one of her bleakest defeats when the emperor Valerian was taken in battle against Shapur I; Shapur kept Valerian in humiliating captivity until his death, and even extended the torment by having the emperor's corpse skinned (Lactantius *On the Deaths of the Persecutors* 5). In this bruising context, the rise to power of Diocletian and his appointment of Maximian were hardly extraordinary.

The Tetrarchy enjoyed many military successes. The most conspicuous was the hard won victory over the Persian Narses in 298. No doubt the memory of Valerian's death rankled amongst his successors, and the emperor Carus had planned and begun a campaign against Persia in the early 280s. Details are hazy, but it is possible that a treaty between Diocletian and king Bahram II was forged in 287, and that the terms favoured Rome (Nixon and Rodgers 1994: 64–9). About the same time it seems, Diocletian reorganised the eastern frontier, although the source Ammianus is vague about the date and extent of the changes (**II 7 23.5.2; map 3**). It does seem, however, that Diocletian was wise to be sceptical about the chances of a lasting peace. According to

13

Lactantius, the new king Narses came to power about the same time as the Tetrarchy came into being, and had designs on Roman territory (**II 6 9.5**). Galerius campaigned against Persia, but significantly outnumbered in his first engagement, suffered a defeat north of Callinicum in Syria in 297 (**II 1 39.34; 2 9.24; 3 25; map 3**). A tradition built up among later writers that Diocletian shamed Galerius for this defeat by making him walk in front of his carriage (**II 2 9.24; 3 25; 7 14.11.10**); but if such a procession happened at all, it is possible that it was simply the conventional way for a Caesar to show his deference to his Augustus. However, Galerius augmented his army with reinforcements from the Balkans, and secured immediate gains in Armenia; a crushing victory over Narses was to follow, including capture of the king's harem. By the spring of 298, Galerius had captured Ctesiphon, deep in the Tigris valley. Narses sued for peace, and the treaty which followed established further territorial gains for Rome around the upper Tigris; this treaty, which was to hold reasonably secure for about four decades, finally laid the distracting memory of Valerian to rest after thirty-seven years (Blockley 1984).

The surviving literary texts record the victory in varying degrees of detail. The best evidence for the imperial reaction to the victory is Galerius' arch at Thessalonica. Thessalonica was Galerius' base for several years from 299, and his palace complex there incorporated the triumphal arch connecting a colonnaded walkway leading to the emperor's mausoleum with the city's main thoroughfare, the *via Egnatia* (Barnes 1982: 61–2; Ward-Perkins 1981: 449; Sear 1982). Some scenes on the arch's panel reliefs depict stages in the war against Narses. A particularly well preserved example shows Galerius on horseback in the thick of battle, trampling Persians underfoot (**II 40**). Elsewhere, the Persian harem is seen led into captivity (Pond Rothman 1977). According to regular Tetrarchic practice, all four emperors assumed the victory title *Persicus maximus* (the Augusti for the second time – **II 20 I.L.S. 640**), and proudly displayed this on inscriptions (**II 19**).

Other victory titles preserved on inscriptions can be matched with the literary record to reconstruct a reasonable chronology for the considerable range of the Tetrarchs' other military successes (Barnes 1982: 27, 254–6). Not all the confusion apparent in the mid-fourth century literary record has been cleared up (e.g. **II 1 39.22–3; 2 9.22–3; 4 39.4**). The chronologies for the suppression of Carausius and Allectus in Britain and Domitius Domitianus in Egypt have proved particularly controversial (Casey 1994; Thomas 1976; Barnes 1996); in the latter case, Domitius Domitianus' revolt in Egypt distracted Diocletian from events on the frontier with Persia, the precise dating of which has also proved elusive. While the dramatic narratives of these campaigns, such as the anonymous orator's account of the recovery of Britain (**II 13** 12–19) or Eutropius' reference to Diocletian's brutal campaign in Egypt (**II 2 23**) are certainly engaging, their general focus is biographical and they tend to reveal little about defensive policies or military strategies. For example, Lactantius' claim that Diocletian's fear of Galerius led him to send the Caesar east to confront Narses is entirely in keeping with the text's general psychological profile of these two persecuting emperors – but its limited vision and manifest prejudice must call into question its reliability (**II 6 9.3–7**).

What is undeniable is that these military emperors fought a great number of wars. Before the creation of the Tetrarchy, Diocletian had fought two major campaigns against the Sarmatians; Maximian meantime crushed the Bagaudae in Gaul, successfully confronted Germans on the Rhine frontier, and unsuccessfully challenged Carausius. Soon after his appointment as Caesar in 293 Galerius crushed revolts in the Egyptian cities of Busiris and Coptos, before moving to the Syrian frontier to face Narses (Leadbetter 2000). Diocletian won a victory over the Carpi on the Danube frontier before himself moving against the usurpers in Egypt in 297. On his appointment in 293 Constantius forced Carausius back to Britain from his holdings in mainland Europe. Constantius then quickly crushed rebels in the Low Countries before, in 296, Britain was recovered; Constantius kept his base at Trier and won victories over Franks and Germans before his final campaign, against the Picts in 305. After his success against Narses, Galerius turned to the north where, over the next ten years, he campaigned against the Marcomanni, the Carpi and the Sarmatians. As a Tetrarch, Maximian fought successful campaigns in Spain and North Africa. After the retirement of Diocletian and Maximian in 305, the Tetrarchy fought fewer campaigns against foreign enemies, although Maximinus Daia engaged with the Persians and Armenians (Barnes 1981). Perhaps in the years immediately after 305 foreigners posed less of a threat to the empire, cowed or weakened by the Tetrarchy's earlier successes; or perhaps the internal struggles such as the usurpations by Maxentius in Rome and Domitius Alexander in North Africa demanded the devoted attention of the imperial college.

Overall this catalogue reveals that Diocletian and his colleagues had to deal with two sorts of military challenge – foreign threats on the frontiers and rival claimants to the throne. There is no indication of any ambition to secure new gains and extend the empire, suggesting that

Tetrarchic military policy was defensive rather than offensive – although in the case of Narses or, on occasion, Germans on the east bank of the Rhine, attack was to prove the Tetrarchs' best form of defence. On the one hand, such a policy of consolidation, if conducted successfully, could hope to meet the needs of the time and end the chronic problems of the mid-third century – the rapid and violent turn-over of emperors, separatist regimes (Eutropius *Breviarium* 9.9–13) and the debilitating effects of barbarian incursions (**see Conclusion**). On the other hand, the policy would generate relatively few large-scale victories. Spectacular triumphs would be rare, and not much booty would flow into the imperial purse. There would be little in the way of glamour in this policy for writers with a strong biographical interest to relish. For the question of how Diocletian pursued his military ambitions, we have to look to other sources.

## 2. The *Notitia Dignitatum*

Although bewildering and mercurial, the documentary source known as the *Notitia Dignitatum* makes a vital contribution to modern under-standing of the late Roman army (**II 25**; Brennan 1995). It is an illustrated list of high civilian and military officials detailing in each case responsibilities and subordinates (**II 26**). The document is divided into Eastern and Western halves, and subdivided into chapters for each office. The first item in each of the two geographical halves of the document serves as an index for the rest, essentially listing all the offices the document covers. Insignia are attached to many of the offices, representing the associated responsibilities. Thus, for example, the chapter for the office of the count of the sacred treasuries in the east (**II 25 East 13**) lists that official's subordinates and then the (bureaucratic) staff attached to his office; the chapter for the master of the military in the [emperor's] presence (i.e. attendant on the emperor) (**II 25 East 5**) lists the various units under his direct command. The value of the *Notitia Dignitatum* is that it allows a reconstruction of the distribution and hierarchies of civilian and military command in the late empire; and because firmer understanding of these superstructures prompts conclusions about the ambitions which underlay their original intro-duction, the *Notitia Dignitatum* is a more promising source for Tetrarchic military policy than much of the historiographical narratives.

However, there are problems. The *Notitia Dignitatum* catalogues the offices and does not record the names of office holders. Details of troop-unit names such as 'The First Theodosians' (after Theodosius, the emperor 378–95) (**II 25 East 5**) dates the composition of the chapters from the eastern half to about 395, the year in fact when the empire was split formally east and west. The western half contains later revisions and so dates to about thirteen years later. Thus the *Notitia Dignitatum* is not a snap-shot of the military and civilian hierarchies at any given time, and is certainly almost a century later than the Tetrarchy. The discrepancy in dates between the two halves suggests that the list underwent regular revisions when it had to be updated according to changes in the offices. It seems then that the list evolved over time, a fact which makes very difficult the process of establishing a definitive picture of the situation at any given time before the composition of the list as it survives. It is broadly accepted that on his accession in 284 Diocletian inherited an army which was much like that of Septimius Severus some seventy years earlier; this was based on legions, over thirty in number, and a comparable mass of auxiliary troops. Most of these soldiers were concentrated on the frontiers. The evidence of the *Notitia Dignitatum* reveals that by the early fifth century there were more, new units, and that while there were still forces on the frontiers, other units had different responsibilities. The extent of Diocletian's contribution to these changes can be difficult to gauge.

### 3. Troops and Armour

Lactantius criticises Diocletian for increasing the number of troops in the army (**II 6 7.2**), even implying that the growth was fourfold. Although this is clearly a huge exaggeration, numbers did increase. There is a general consensus that by the end of Diocletian's reign there were some fifty legions or more, a considerable increase on the Severan position (Parker 1933); some of the new legions are identifiable in the *Notitia Dignitatum* by their names Jovian or Herculian (**II 25 East 5**). However, the *Notitia Dignitatum* gives no indication of the troop numbers in the units it catalogues. The Byzantine author John Lydus (*de mensibus* 1.27) put Diocletian's army at 389,704 men, with a further 45,562 in the fleets; his precision is extraordinary and has been greeted variously with admiration (by those who assume Lydus had access to documentary evidence) and derision (by those who doubt his authority). From Lactantius' hyperbole, Lydus' questionable precision, and the names and distribution of legions in the *Notitia Dignitatum*, the consensus has emerged that Diocletian's army numbers represented a significant increase on the c. 350,000 under Septimius Severus; that new legions were created by Diocletian; but that legions were now smaller in size than they had been before (Duncan Jones 1990: 105–17).

The growth in numbers must have increased the burden on the process of recruitment. Recruitment from the citizen body seems to have been conducted by three methods. Some men joined up voluntarily; a greater number, as sons of active or retired soldiers, were obliged to serve if physically able, according to a law in effect in 313 which might refer to a similar edict passed under Diocletian (**II 29 7.22.1**); more citizen-recruits still were conscripted through a tax on landlords' estates (Ammianus Marcellinus 31.4.4). Recruits had to be a minimum of five foot ten inches tall, and were tattooed for identification. Soldiers and veterans enjoyed some legal privileges (**II 30**). Auxiliary units seem also to have been recruited from barbarian populations by Diocletian (**II 13 21.1** and Nixon and Rodgers 1994: 141–3).

Appreciation of the fabric and culture of military life under Diocletian is in some respects quite detailed, and again attests significant changes from the earlier empire (Coulston 2002). Typical armour for infantrymen included a metallic cuirass, an innovative style of helmet, and round or oval shields, with blazons to distinguish units (if the evidence of the Arch of Galerius (**II 40**) and the *Notitia Dignitatum* illustrations is accepted at face value). The *gladius*, the short-sword of the earlier Empire, was replaced in Late Antiquity by the long *spatha*, suggesting a change in fencing style. The *Notitia Dignitatum* indicates a separation in command of infantry and cavalry units, and perhaps an improvement in the status the cavalry enjoyed in relation to the infantry. The Arch of Galerius and literary accounts of the battle of the Milvian Bridge (*Panegyrici Latini* IV(10)22.4) demonstrate the effective use of (armed) horses in battle.

To meet the needs of this bigger army, Diocletian established arms factories at key strategic points. Lactantius bemoaned their introduction (**II 6 7.9**) but by the time of the *Notitia Dignitatum* they were clearly an established part of the military infrastructure, part of the responsibilities of the master of offices (**II 25 West 9**). Many of the letters from the *strategos* of Panopolis relate to matters of supply for the army; in one the smith Nilus appears to have been evading his responsibilities at the arsenal (**II 21 1.213–16**). His duties seem to have been well understood by all concerned, suggesting the infrastructure for supply was firmly established, if not exactly popular.

## 4. Frontier Archaeology

The *Notitia Dignitatum* provides some indication of how and where the various components of the late Roman army were employed, but for specifically Tetrarchic practice, material remains have much to tell us. The emperor Probus (276–82) had begun to fortify towns in Gaul, presumably to equip them to resist barbarian incursions or civil uprising. Diocletian seems to have continued this strategy; towns in Gaul and sites in the mining areas of Spain are good examples, but the focus of scholarly interest here has been on frontier archaeology. The interpretations have proved very controversial.

The contemporary orator Eumenius (**II 14 18.4**) and the chronicler John Malalas, writing much later and from a Christian perspective (**II 9**), write of camps or forts being built on frontiers under Diocletian. Eumenius' observation that the camps were 'restored' (*restituta*) suggests a resurrection under the Tetrarchs of a lapsed system of fortification, perhaps that of Aurelian or Probus, but there can be no doubt that many sites on or near frontiers were fortified or built by the Tetrarchs (Johnston 1983). This can be illustrated by brief consideration of three frontier regions, the Syrian desert, the Rhine and Danube rivers, and the south-east coast of England.

Unlike rivers and coasts, the Syrian desert did not constitute a natural frontier between the Romans and Persians. A series of forts and fortified towns from Bostra to Palmyra and beyond towards the Euphrates was connected by a road known after inscriptions (*A.E.* 1931: 85, 101–10) as the *strata Diocletiana* (**map 3**). This title not only decisively dates the system but also suggests some strategic intent in the emperor's mind. The forts along the road were of the type which were characteristic of the later empire: put simply, unlike early imperial forts, planned axially, typically with four gates and surrounded with thin walls and a narrow ditch, from the late third century fortress architecture featured smaller installations, with a single heavily defended gateway, thick walls, wide ditches and prominent bastions. These later 'hard' fortresses, forerunners in many ways to mediaeval structures, could accommodate fewer men, but were designed, it seems, to be more resistant to attack. Epigraphy confirms that several forts in the region were Tetrarchic in origin, attesting to a marked increase in building activity. The network of Roman roads inside the frontier allowed another route between Damascus and Palmyra (via Danaba). A Tetrarchic camp at Palmyra was the base for the legion I Illyricorum (Isaac 1992: 163–5).

Between them the Rhine and Danube rivers constituted a natural frontier from the North Sea to the Black Sea (**maps 1** and **2**). This frontier had been particularly vulnerable in the third century, penetrated by Franks, Vandals, Alemanni, Iuthungi, and Sarmatians. An orator in Trier in 289 makes the Rhine the subject of a section of his panegyric to Maximian – by crushing the barbarians beyond the river, the emperor had effectively rendered superfluous nature's provision of a frontier (**II 11** 7.3–7). The flighty rhetoric betrays a genuine anxiety amongst the towns of north-east Gaul. Archaeology of the Rhine–Danube frontier reveals concerted activity by the Tetrarchs. Typically 'hard' forts feature along the length of the rivers either refortified or newly built; defensive walls were added to frontier towns, just as they were to some towns in the interior (**Map 2**; von Petrikovits 1971).

Along the natural frontier of the coast of south-east England, known as the Saxon Shore after the catalogue entry for its commanding officer in the *Notitia Dignitatum*, was a series of forts (**II 25, 26**). Although the names listed do not correspond precisely to the given names of the sites on the ground, the *Notitia Dignitatum* entry reveals that there was a system in operation at some point in that region before the beginning of the fifth century; however, archaeology complicates the picture significantly. The forts can all be characterised as 'hard', perhaps the best example being Portchester (**II 38**) with its imposing walls and bastions; however, architectural typology and coin finds suggest that foundation dates for the forts range from the mid-third century to the 340s (Cunliffe 1977). Coin finds indicate that Portchester was built during the reign of Carausius, and the difficulty the central imperial college had in recovering Britain from Carausius and Allectus might indicate that the Saxon Shore installations proved an efficient defensive system; likewise the Rhine–Danube frontier installations and the *strata Diocletiana* seem to have been successful.

## 5. Strategy

The comments of Malalas on the frontier between Egypt and Mesopotamia – a stretch which would include the *strata Diocletiana* – combine military installations and soldiers (**II 9**). He identifies a frontier of forts with dedicated troops in them; in addition a considerable force of reserve troops was ready to move as required. This description does not quite square with that of the late fifth-century historian Zosimus, who writes in general terms about the empire as a whole but makes no mention of a mobile reserve (**II 10**). Ammianus Marcellinus' observations on Cercusium (on the Euphrates, **map 3**) imply a zonal defensive system protecting Syria from enemy invasion, although he does not refer to troops at all (**II 7 23.5.1–2**). In sum, there is no consistency in the few brief (and late) texts which comment on the Tetrarchic frontiers. And despite the overview which the *Notitia Dignitatum* grants, neither literary nor documentary sources yield an explicit statement about defensive strategy. However, to considerable controversy, an integrated defensive model has been posited for Diocletian.

Edward Luttwak's proposal is referred to as a strategy of zonal defence (1976). According to Luttwak, this was the third and final model of defence in a distinctive series of three from the late republic until the fall of the empire in the west. Luttwak's model, known by the shorthand descriptor 'defence in depth', replaced the early imperial frontier strategy of a fixed line providing preclusive defence. The weaknesses of this so-called 'Hadrianic' strategy were exposed in the fraught third century – and the huge protective walls built for Gallic cities by Probus and for Rome by Aurelian indicate both the anxiety of the times and the realisation that the 'fixed line' was vulnerable. The 'defence in depth' model proposed a drastic reorganisation of resources. A systematic provision of 'hard' defences on the frontier, each continuously manned by second-grade troops known as *limitanei* ('border troops'), would offer significant obstruction to any invading force; meanwhile, in a zone behind the frontier, well served with a network of roads, mobile forces of high grade infantry and cavalry would be ready to operate at short notice wherever they were needed. If the enemy bypassed the 'hard' points to cross the frontier, they would find themselves in an uncomfortable situation, with crack troops ahead and at the rear their own supply lines exposed to attack from the forts. Thus, 'defence in depth' comprised militarised zones on the frontiers, with troops of different calibre with their own lines of command (**Chapter 2**) allocated specific responsibilities. Redrawing of some boundaries indicates the ambition to maximise the advantage of natural frontiers such as mountains and rivers, and inevitably resulted in some regional variety, but essentially this zonal system was proposed as a consistent and integrated strategy.

The 'defence in depth' model has met with mixed response. Accepting the model wholesale, Williams (1985) saw it as a major example of Diocletian's originality; he presents Diocletian as a far-sighted and daring strategist. In answer to some of Luttwak's critics, Nicasie (1998) reprised the model, arguing that it makes better sense of the evidence than any alternative interpretation. Furthermore, both Williams and

Nicasie accommodate this defensive strategy within the broader raft of policy undertaken by Diocletian, including administrative re-organisation (**Chapter 2**) and economics (**Chapter 3**). This positivist interpretation goes beyond Luttwak to the totality of government.

The 'defence in depth' model has been criticised at a conceptual level and for its interpretation of particular evidence (Mann 1979; Isaac 1992; Whittaker 1994). At a fundamental level, the claim that the contemporary realities of military and political communication and awareness allowed a unified strategy to be articulated and prosecuted can be challenged; or even that a consistent defensive strategy such as Luttwak's model was either desirable or possible in the face of the variety of challenges the Tetrarchy faced along the extent of the frontiers. All available evidence supports the claim that material and troop resources were intensified on the frontiers. However, while the evidence from the desert regions can be used to support the 'deep' reserve component of the model, for its empire-wide application to be assumed, an *argumentum ex silentio* has to be accepted for the hinterland of the Rhine–Danube frontiers, where no evidence has been found. More critical still is the rejection of the 'defence in depth' model at any point on the frontier, with counter arguments claiming that Diocletian's 'hard' point perimeter defence is not markedly distinctive from earlier systems, or that a model of a frontier as a fluid medium of cultural and economic exchange is more appropriate. In the former case, for example, the *strata Diocletiana* has been seen by some to be a heavily garrisoned road (Isaac 1992: 171); in the latter, the settling of veterans and especially of foreigners in frontier areas (such as Gaul) depopulated by the depredations of earlier decades need not be interpreted as an essentially 'military' policy (**II 13 21; 16 5.3**).

Clarification of certain dating controversies would advance the debate. The vast majority of surviving references to the foreigners settled on the Gallic borders, for example, date to the fourth century, rendering speculative any estimates about the date and extent of the original policy (Nixon and Rodgers 1994: 142–3). A similar inability to differentiate with absolute authority between Tetrarchic and Constantinian innovations (such as the use of a mobile field army) is characteristic of interpretation of the *Notitia Dignitatum*. Finally, the rather hazy picture the sources provide of developments in the mid-third century (such as the extent of the cavalry's role in the army) further compromises appreciation of the nature of Diocletian's con-tribution. Was Diocletian a visionary radical with an infrastructure to hand to realise his ambitions? Or were perhaps his policies more measured, his reign a conservative but vital stage in a process of evolution in the late Roman army? These ideological questions take us a long way from the intricacies of campaigns and tactics, and move towards consideration of other aspects of Diocletian's rule.

CHAPTER 2

# Administration

## 1. Provinces and the *Verona List*

There is no evidence to suggest that when in 285 Diocletian appointed Maximian emperor and sent him to face the Bagaudae in Gaul the empire was to be considered split between the two colleagues, east and west. An orator in 289 speaks of the east petitioning Diocletian in a way which might prompt understanding of such a system; but earlier in the speech he is absolutely clear that the empire is undivided (**II 11 11.2, 14.4**). What can perhaps be detected here is the difference between the constitutional realities of a political hierarchy in which responsibilities are delegated and the rhetorical representation of that college by a man with regional loyalties to articulate (Leadbetter 1998a; Rees 2002: 66–7). Sources are little more forthcoming about any subdivision of the empire on the creation of the Tetrarchy in 293: Lactantius says the empire was divided four ways, and later mentions some of Maximian's allocation (**II 6 7.2, 8.3**); Aurelius Victor also states that the empire was divided into four but then details a scheme of regionalised authority (**II 1 39.30**). However, claims for any schematic division must be treated with caution: the Caesars Constantius and Galerius (in Gaul and the Danube provinces respectively, according to Aurelius Victor) were not at complete liberty to pursue their own agendas, as they were in some important respects answerable to their Augusti; similarly, the empire's military needs in particular occasionally demanded an emperor to cross over divisional boundaries to assist a colleague. A degree of territoriality can be detected in imperial administration in these years, but should probably be understood flexibly (Barnes 1982: 195–200; Corcoran 1996, 2000[2]: 266–74).

However, fundamental changes to the administrative map of the empire certainly took place (Jones 1964: 42–52). Laying aside his typically polemical tone, Lactantius' separate observation that Diocletian fragmented the provinces can be tested against an unusual

24

documentary source (**II 6 7.4**). The *Verona List* is a seventh-century manuscript which catalogues the Roman provinces of late antiquity (**II 27**). As with the *Notitia Dignitatum* (**II 25**), the *List*'s nature and date have been subjects of scholarly controversy, (compounded in part by some of its transmission errors); Barnes summarises the history of the scholarship and concludes that the *List* details eastern provinces as they were between 314–15 and 324, and the western provinces as they were slightly earlier, from 303 to 314 (Barnes 1982: 203–5). This important conclusion already alerts us to the fact that provincial organisation was subject to more than one change over the period; however, this need not force the assumption that reorganisation under Diocletian was a process and not a single event (Anderson 1932; Adams 2004). We do not know.

Without extending the limits of empire, the *List* establishes that Diocletian almost doubled the number of provinces. How the geography of the new provinces was decided is a matter for speculation – while conceding regional variety, for example, Williams proposes an underlying military motivation (Williams 1985: 104–5). From the time of Augustus, provincial governorships were either senatorial (open only to the senatorial class, and generally in non-combat zones and therefore without significant military responsibility) or imperial (appointed by the emperor himself from the equestrian class). The governors of Diocletian's new provinces were equestrian; in this and other respects, senators had no place in the government structures. Each governor (*praeses* in Latin) was responsible for judicial and fiscal affairs in his province, for ensuring that town-councils fulfilled their roles, and for maintaining the postal system (Corcoran 1996, 2000[2]: 234–53). The *Notitia Dignitatum* gives details of the staff at the disposal of the provincial governor (**II 25 West 45**).

The *Verona List* also provides excellent evidence for the innovative tier of organisation known as dioceses – under Diocletian, the empire was divided into twelve dioceses, each consisting of several provinces (**map 1; II 27**). A new position was created to head each diocese – the *vicarius*, as can be seen in the *Notitia Dignitatum* (**II 25 East 1, West 1**). As with the provinces, the date for the creation of the dioceses and *vicarii* (also drawn from the equestrian rank) is not established beyond doubt: support has been found for proposals both for piecemeal and wholesale implementation (Anderson 1932; Barnes 1982: 224–5). The earliest attestation for a *vicarius* dates to 298; the diocese of Britain could hardly have come into being until the island was recovered from Allectus in 296, and the usurpation by Domitius Domitianus in Egypt in 297 will have put on hold any of Diocletian's plans for administrative change there. The jockeying between claims for piecemeal and whole-sale implementation of new provinces and dioceses contributes to the wider issue of the motivation underlying the creation of the Tetrarchy in 293 and, therefore, Diocletian's political vision.

A *vicarius* was acting on behalf of a praetorian prefect. A praetorian prefect was an emperor's deputy. If the conjecture is right that Constantius was praetorian prefect to Maximian before 293, we have confirmation of the close working relationship between prefect and emperor, and, at the same time, a hint of what qualifications for imperial office were thought appropriate to replace heredity (Barnes 1982: 125–6, 138–9). However, recently discovered epigraphic material has challenged the assumption that the prefecture was a natural step on the career path towards imperial office; and has also weakened the claim that each Tetrarch had a praetorian prefect (Corcoran 1996, 2000[2]: 87–9, 268–70; n.b. the seductive evidence of the *Notitia Dignitatum*, II 25 **East 1, West** 1). If Corcoran's suggestion that the prefects numbered only two from 293 is right, it demands a reconsideration of imperial working practice; how, for example, would Maximian and Constantius decide to what duties and where the western praetorian prefect should be assigned? Would a *vicarius* consider himself answerable to a local Caesar or a more distant praetorian prefect?

The range of responsibilities and staff assigned to the praetorian prefects in the *Notitia Dignitatum* makes interesting comparison with what little can be reconstructed about the career paths and duties of Tetrarchic prefects. The remit of the praetorian prefect of the east in the *Notitia Dignitatum* is exclusively civilian, his staff bureaucratic (**II 25 East 2**). There is a possible Tetrarchic precedent for this, according to a recent revision of the career path of Hermogenianus (Corcoran 1996, 2000[2]: 87–9); after holding important bureaucratic positions in the east and west, this trained jurist became Diocletian's praetorian prefect sometime after 298. This provides a marked contrast with Asclepiodotus, a man it seems of distinguished military service, who led the troops in the successful campaign against Allectus in 296 whilst holding the office of praetorian prefect (**II 2 22.2**). Does this mean we can date a division of military and civil responsibilities to 297?

Probably not. The confusing image that emerges from this material calls into question the date and decisiveness of a split between military and civilian commands in late antiquity. The *Notitia Dignitatum* proves that by the reign of Theodosius the two were securely independent of each other; but although some evidence from the Tetrarchic period suggests that military and civilian offices were being separated, it is perhaps rash to attribute to Diocletian the decision to establish a dedicated civil service as a matter of policy. At the frontiers, a general (*dux* in Latin) had military responsibilities and would, no doubt, have to collaborate with civilian governors (*praesides*) (**II 25 East 1, West 1**), but surviving evidence most comfortably puts a concerted policy to separate military and civil commands to the reign of Constantine (Mann 1977). The attractions of this emerging specialisation might have been greater efficiencies in key areas of government, such as the law, taxation and defence; however, Lactantius suggests that the increase in numbers of government personnel simply increased the misery that ordinary citizens had to endure (**II 6 7.4**). A more sinister ambition has also been proposed – that by beginning to distinguish between military and civilian commands, and in particular by separating tax-raising powers from military duties, Diocletian aimed to minimise the chances of success any internal challenge to his rule might have. In the absence of any evidence that might amount to a manifesto, several hypotheses for the motivation of Diocletian's administrative changes remain open.

## 2. Provincial capitals and Rome

It has been noted above (**Introduction 2**) that the Tetrarchs were based in various provincial capitals throughout the empire (**map 1**). The motivation for this move away from the ancient capital seems to have been strategic (Millar 1977, 1992[2]: 44–53). The north Italian cities Milan, Ravenna, and Aquileia were closer to the main military areas than Rome was; in Gaul, Trier was well placed as a base from which to resist incursions from across the Rhine; Sirmium and Serdica were close to the Danube front and Thessalonika was en route to the eastern frontier; likewise Nicomedia and Antioch were important strategic locations in dealings with Persia. But if the creation of an imperial college allowed the empire to be policed by an emperor at its various critical points, the establishment of provincial capitals will also have facilitated government administration. Barnes' detailed reconstructions of Tetrarchic journeys reveals an imperial culture far removed from the sedentary lifestyle of some earlier emperors; by plotting his attested stopping-points in the year 290, for example, it can be established that Diocletian averaged ten miles each day (Barnes 1982: 47–82). Gruelling itineraries such as this would demand dedication and energy. The data on which the reconstructions depend vary in type, from details in ancient texts to coins, inscriptions and legal evidence. Regardless of the

grand constructions of imperial omnipresence found in the panegyrics
and symbolised in group statuary (**Chapter 4.1**; Rees 2002: 11–17),
these itineraries show that the emperors themselves considered it
important to maintain a real presence in the provinces.

Sometimes it is clear that military affairs dictated an emperor's
movements; at other times, travelling from town to town with his
*comitatus*, it seems a Tetrarch was on the road to supervise in person the
smooth-running of the apparatus of government. The *comitatus* was
a courtly entourage, organised on military principles but including
administrative staff as well as soldiers; it is not clear if and how the staff
accompanying a Caesar differed from those attendant on an Augustus
(Jones 1964: 51; Corcoran 1996, 2000[2]: 268–70). In panegyrics, legal
evidence and papyri, we see that anticipation of an emperor's arrival
generated a frenzy of activity; apart from the need to ensure that he and
his *comitatus* could be catered for appropriately, his stay would be an
opportunity for individuals or representatives to approach him with
specific requests, usually of a legal or financial nature. The glimpses
legal texts allow of Tetrarchic emperors as administrators in action
can be set against their military record to create an overall picture of
immensely busy men, concerning themselves with all aspects of government throughout the empire. But if some individuals or communities
could hope to benefit from the Tetrarchs' itinerant lifestyle and their
concern to prosecute their new measures with some degree of equity,
others would be far from enthusiastic. The case of Panopolis is considered below (**4**); we start with the most famous community of all.

The Tetrarchs hardly ever went to Rome. Diocletian himself perhaps
went there in 285 (Barnes 1982: 50); he certainly celebrated the twentieth anniversary of his reign there in 303, but according to Lactantius
he did not enjoy the experience and left in bad humour (**II 6 17.1–2**).
Maximian can possibly be located at Rome on four occasions, all
fleeting, as emperor (**II 2 9.27**). Constantius was never in Rome as
emperor. Galerius approached Rome once in his doomed attempt to
wrest control of the city from Maxentius (**II 6 27.2**). The lack of an
imperial presence at Rome would have made perfect strategic sense –
the frontiers were not all secure, but the ancient city nestled safely
behind the huge walls of Aurelian, completed a few years before
Diocletian's accession. But if the rationale for this new mobility of
power was strategic, there were significant political effects on Rome.

The *Verona List* does not name all sixteen provinces it promises in its
sub-title for the diocese of Italy (**II 27**). Notwithstanding this deficiency,
it is clear that Italy was included in Diocletian's programme of

provincial reorganisation; and that the new Italian provinces were subject to taxes just like the other provinces of the empire (**II 1 39.31**). From the time of Augustus, an imperial legal archive would have been kept at Rome, but under Diocletian any archive emanating from an itinerant emperor would be deposited in the nearest provincial capital, according to where the emperor was at the time (Corcoran 1996, 2000²: 29–30). Besides, now a citizen of Rome would have to wait for an imperial visit, or write, or travel to petition an emperor in person, to receive legal pronouncement. Furthermore, there seems to have been the rationale that if there were no longer any emperors resident at Rome, there was no need for the praetorian guard (the traditional imperial bodyguard) to be there either: Diocletian is said to have reduced their number a little before his retirement (**II 1 39.47**); Lactantius implies that Galerius planned the complete abolition of the guard (**II 6 26.2–3**). So in the extensive administrative changes across the empire, Rome did not just lose its emperor in person: the city lost its tax exemptions; the reassuring legal privileges that imperial presence conveyed; and its army. The support Maxentius had from the people of Rome for his coup in 306 suggests there was considerable resentment about the effects of Tetrarchic government on the capital.

The archaeological record at Rome does not suggest Tetrarchic neglect of the capital, as several prestige buildings were put up there before Maxentius' usurpation (Curran 2000): the Arch of Diocletian (known also as the *Novus Arcus*, fragments of which are now in the Boboli Gardens at Florence); the Senate House, ruined by fire in 283, and rebuilt as visible today, by Diocletian and Maximian (**II 39**); the magnificent Baths of Diocletian (begun c. 298–9, dedicated in 305; **II 20** *I.L.S.* **646**; **II 37**); and the *Decennalia* monument in the forum, originally a series of five columns topped with statues of the Tetrarchs and Jupiter, of which a single base survives (**II 43**). Aurelius Victor strikes a positive tone in noting Diocletian's building programme at Rome and elsewhere (**II 1 39.45**); but Lactantius was not persuaded, diagnosing the emperor's enthusiasm for building as a madness (**II 6 7.8–10**).

Much as Lactantius' implication that Diocletian was jealous of Rome might claim corroborating evidence in his undeniable absence from the city, the whole frame of Lactantius' argument can be challenged, not simply its particulars. Whether or not Diocletian liked the city, and would like to have spent more time there or not, is not the key point. The Tetrarchs certainly acknowledged at least some of Rome's claims to importance when commissioning buildings there. But if under

Diocletian there was an empire-wide strategic and administrative imperative which needed a harmonious imperial collective to push it through, it also needed a wider political canvas, far beyond the walls built by Aurelian. Almost *de facto* none of the Tetrarchs could live in Rome without jeopardising the harmony of the government; and besides they had to be elsewhere if they were to fulfil their essential political ambitions. The Maxentian uprising and the difference of opinion between Lactantius and Aurelius Victor suggests the Tetrarchic attitude to the ancient city was variously received and understood; and perhaps Diocletian was naïve in failing to predict this. Although the mobility of power as an aspect of political geography was an important determinant of the ideology of empire it was not one over which the wandering emperors exercised complete mastery.

### 3. Letters of the law

Not only were the Tetrarchs rarely, or in the case of Constantius never, in Rome, they were also rarely in each others' presence. Even if Barnes' tentative hypothesis that all four emperors met in northern Italy in 303 is upheld, that Tetrarchic summit seems to have been unique (Barnes 1996: 544–6). Literary texts preserve several instances where two emperors were together, but such occasions were unusual. There was no institutionalised conference on a regular basis; nor is there any evidence of imperial meetings summoned to discuss the affairs of state which strike moderns as most decisive in this period, such as the creation of the Tetrarchy in 293, the military campaigns of the 290s, radical economic and religious policies (**Chapters 3** and **5**), or the retirement of the Augusti in 305. In the last case, Lactantius writes of a conversation between Diocletian and Galerius, but it does not seem to be accorded the status of an imperial summit, rather an opportunity deliberately contrived by Galerius to speak informally with Diocletian when the other emperors were elsewhere (**II 6 18.1; Introduction 3**). The same author claims that a summit was held at Carnuntum in 308 (**II 6 29.1–2**), but this was manifestly exceptional. The question of how this college of emperors attempted to conduct the business of government without meeting to discuss it is revealing of its broader administrative procedures.

The answer seems to have lain in letters. No letters from one Tetrarch to another survive, but from incidental details in literary sources, it is apparent that letters were a standard means of overcoming the problems inherent in geographical separation (e.g. **II 4 39.7; 6 15.6,**

**18.7, 24.3**). The Roman empire had always required a very considerable communications infrastructure, including reliable scribes, couriers and roads, but with the very collegiality of Diocletian's government depending on the efficiency of the systems, the pressure must have intensified. The majority of letters referred to in the sources were perhaps unrepresentative of the sort conventionally exchanged by the emperors, more to do with matters of collegiate intrigue and fracture than routine government. Perhaps most revealing of regular administrative procedure is Lactantius' detail that Maximian and Constantius were not consulted when the decision to persecute Christians was taken by Diocletian and Galerius, but simply received letters instructing them to proceed (**II 6 15.6–7**). The text does not disclose the identity of the letters' author, but in a subsequent clause, the order [to persecute] is said to have come from Constantius' superiors. The only person to exercise seniority over the western Augustus and the senior Caesar was Diocletian (and not Galerius). This narrative suggests that decisions – even vital matters of policy – were not consensual, but that Diocletian made his mind up and communicated his ruling to his colleagues; but perhaps that the essence of the ruling was urged on the emperors in the names of them all.

Letters were also the standard means of communicating decisions to subordinates further down the chain of command; letters were sent to military commanders at the outbreak of the persecution (**II 6 10.4**); likewise the decision to end the persecution was communicated to provincial governors by letter (**II 6 48.1**); Eumenius, Professor of Rhetoric at the school known as the Maenianae at Autun, quotes in full his letter of appointment by the Caesar Constantius (*Panegyrici Latini* IX(5)14; Corcoran 1996, 2000[2]: 268–9). Presumably, official letters such as these were conveyed by the imperial post. So too would be edicts, that is, legislative pronouncements for general consumption (Corcoran 1996, 2000[2]: 170–203); the most famous examples of Tetrarchic edicts are those concerned with maximal prices (**Chapter 3**) and persecution (**Chapter 5**). An edict consisted of a text, in paper or inscribed format, for public display. A copy of an edict would be displayed prominently in the place it was issued by an emperor (such as the first persecution edict, in Nicomedia in 303 (**II 6 13.1; 8 8.5.1**); and copies would be sent, with a covering letter, for publication by relevant provincial governors, who might add their own text if appropriate (**II 22**). A procedure similar to that of the imperial edictal system but originating at a lower level of government was also in operation, as public notices from Egypt attest (**II 21 2.222–8, 229–44**).

Tetrarchic imperial edicts were issued in the names of all of the emperors (e.g. **II 19**). However, as we have seen above, there does not seem to have been in place a system by which an imperial consensus could be achieved before publication; the list of imperial names and titles at the head of an edict was perhaps more to do with the ideology of imperial harmony than the practicalities of collegiate rule (**Chapter 6**). Presumably the first persecution edict published by Diocletian in Nicomedia on 24 February 303 (**II 6 13.1**) and promulgated elsewhere in the empire soon afterwards (**II 8 8.2.4**) was in the name of all four Tetrarchs; but Constantius did not persecute, at least according to Lactantius (**II 6 15.7**) and Eusebius (**II 8 8.13.3**). Although the two are in broad agreement about Constantius, they differ in one respect which raises questions about administrative procedure. While Eusebius denies any attempt by Constantius to apply the new law, Lactantius relates that the Caesar's superficial application of the law was intended to maintain a show of imperial collegiality. It seems likely from Lactantius' account that Constantius published the edict, from Eusebius' unlikely. Either way, Constantius' reaction suggests that imperial colleagues were able to exercise considerable discretion on receipt of such orders and edicts. There was, then, a recognised command structure and communications infrastructure; but at the same time, with few checks on this system, absolute compliance could hardly be enforced. A very significant degree of collegiate goodwill would be required to maintain a united front.

Another example of Tetrarchic administration is the substantial category of responses to specific petitions, known by the generic term 'rescript' (Millar 1977, 1992[2]: 537–49). A rescript could be in the form of a separate letter or a subscript – the emperor's written response underneath the original petition. (Corcoran 1996, 2000[2]: 43–73, 95–122). Individuals could write to the emperor on their own behalf on any matter, although the postal service was not available for private use. In practice, this meant that petitioners would deliver letters themselves or arrange to have them delivered; the rescript would not be sent by the post, but was made available for collection at the point of issue. Geographical proximity to the emperor was fundamental to this process. Although with a collegiate itinerant government, the opportunities to gain access to an emperor were perhaps more frequent than ever before, it is clear that many petitioners underwent long and arduous journeys in an attempt to secure a rescript. According to surviving evidence, senators, soldiers, *decurions* (local landowners who served on city councils), women and even slaves and freedmen petitioned Tetrarchic emperors. Unsurprisingly, the subjects of these petitions vary enormously – most present specific cases of civil law relating to money, status and property (**II 30**).

An imperial response could also be sought by an official representing a wider body. Petitions of this type would normally be answered in a full and separate letter. A good example of this process of law in action is the Tetrarchs' ruling on the Manichaeans (**II 28**). This letter is a response to a petition from a proconsul of Africa; it was issued by Diocletian at Alexandria and is tentatively dated to 302. These details urge further caution about Aurelius Victor's assertion that the diocese of Africa was under Maximian's command (**II 1 39.30**). Government hierarchy and political geography did not always correspond.

The petition and response system of administration would have been time-consuming for emperors and private individuals alike. That it was exercised with energy presents Diocletian and his colleagues as keen lawmakers and judges. This is confirmed by the publication of the Gregorian and Hermogenian Codes, in c. 292 and c. 295 (1st edn) respectively. These law codes, which were to be amalgamated in the Justinianic Code of the sixth century, consisted mainly of collections of rescripts dealing with private law (**II 30**). What motivated the codification of this branch of law at the time is not clear; discovery of any information about the codes' original dissemination would be particularly welcomed. Corcoran suggests a combination of factors led to the codes' creation: a need for authoritative collections to limit legal wranglings; a need for legal manuals felt by provincial governors (possibly increasing in number by the mid-290s) to help them discharge their judicial obligations; and a general need to reduce the burden on the emperors and their secretariats (Corcoran 1996, 2000[2]: 25–42). Publication of the codes would certainly have increased public awareness of the workings of the law and the emperors' role in legal processes.

The impact of some key aspects of Tetrarchic rule upon the city of Rome was considered above; we turn now to a very different community to look at the processes of Tetrarchic law and administration.

## 4. Panopolis

Panopolis is on the Nile, some 600 kilometres south of Alexandria. Egypt, formerly one single province, was split into two in the mid-290s, known as Aegyptus and Thebais, later to be carved up again (**II 30**; Skeat 1964: xvii–xix; Barnes 1982: 211). The Thebais province was itself subdivided into Upper and Lower territories. The Lower Thebaid was

subdivided into nine administrative units called *nomes*, usually consisting of a metropolis and surrounding rural areas. This land would
be part private and part state owned; each *nome* was subdivided into
smaller administrative units, called *toparchies*. A large archive of papyri
from Panopolis, now in the Chester Beatty Library, Dublin, consists
of two rolls of official correspondence relating to the Panopolite *nome*
(II 21; Skeat 1964; Adams 2004). The first is dated to September 298,
and contains letters to superiors in the administrative hierarchy and
to local officials from the *strategos* of Panopolis. A *strategos* was the
immediate point of contact in the administrative hierarchy between the
procurator for the Egyptian province (or sub-territory) and the citizens
of the *nome*; the *strategos* was normally appointed from a different *nome*
and held his position for a period of three years. The correspondence
from this first roll is predominantly concerned with the various
provisions required for a forthcoming visit by Diocletian. The second
papyrus roll dates to February–March 300, and consists exclusively of
letters from Aurelius Isidorus, the procurator of Lower Thebais, to
Apolinarius, the Panopolite *strategos* (not necessarily the same man
as the author of the letters in the first roll); the main theme of these
letters is the payment of troops stationed in the area. Skeat concludes
that Aurelius Isidorus was probably based in Hermopolis, about 150
kilometres distant from Panopolis (Skeat 1964: xix–xx). The Panopolis
archive offers a uniquely detailed impression of the human dramas of
provincial administration under the Tetrarchy. A few observations may
suffice.

The smooth running of the operation depended upon relatively
high levels of literacy, here as elsewhere in the Tetrarchic empire. The
*strategos* had a clerk to act as scribe, not because he himself was illiterate
but to save time (e.g. II 21 1.53–9); illiterates were not excluded from
legal and administrative discourse, but had to be ratified (e.g. II 23
[In 2nd hand]). The edict of Aristius Optatus makes no provision for
illiterates and assumes that by posting written copies in every village,
everyone will be informed of the substance (II 22). To be incapable of
dealing with textual media was not to be disenfranchised completely;
but the workings of the rescript and edictal systems suggest that without
reading and writing skills, access to the law was severely circumscribed.
The Panopolis archives deal in the main with the educated sector.

The administrative and financial hierarchies, and the powers and
responsibilities exercised at each level, can be bewildering (Jones 1964:
411–27); several positions feature in the papyri. The *catholicus* was the
financial overlord of Egypt and the *procurator rei privatae* controlled the

revenue of land owned by the state in a province. The most frequently attested working relationships are those between the *strategos* and his immediate superior (the procurator of Lower Thebais); and between the *strategos* and the local senate/council of Panopolis, with its president. The local senators, men of curial class (which was inherited), were responsible for appointing men to perform tasks such as overseeing the collection of food supplies and vegetables required for the army, surveyors of transport ships (for use by the Treasury), a commissioner to repair a bakery and men to work in it to provide food for the army. The president of the local senate was directly answerable to the *strategos*. Apart from his regular dealings with the procurator, some letters attest direct communication between the *strategos* and higher levels of authority. The picture that emerges shows a bureaucracy intensely busy at a local level, but with occasional interventions from and a permanent awareness of the higher levels of provincial government (Adams 2004).

The precise dating of the letters allows a sense of the great speed with which this bureaucracy operated. For example, on 23 September 298 the *strategos* communicated in writing an order from the *procurator rei privatae* to the Panopolis council (**II 21** 1.365–8). By the time of the next letter, written later that day to the *procurator rei privatae*, the council had replied to the order in writing – this written response must have been almost instant (**II 21** 1.369–73). Before the close of the following day, not only had the *procurator rei privatae* received the letter from the *strategos*, but he had replied, and the essence of his reply had again been communicated to the council (**II 21** 1.400–4). Although it is not clear where the *procurator rei privatae* was based, the system for conveying letters was manifestly very efficient.

The whole bureaucratic machinery seems to have been intended to maximise efficiencies to ensure that the revenues from private and state land were collected and channelled in accordance with government policies. At certain levels in the system there were checks and measures in place to limit abuse and ensure a degree of accountability; the convention of appointing a *strategos* from a different *nome* would restrict the chances of collusion with the council; routinely, copies of letters were made and sent (e.g. **II 21** 1.167–79); police were available to search for people trying to evade their responsibilities (**II 21** 1.213–6); the *strategos* himself could be held personally liable for any shortfall in his *nome*'s tax revenues (**II 21** 2.32–5) or fined for negligence (**II 21** 2.61–4); dereliction of duty might also see the *strategos* and *decemprimi* (appointed to collect tax) arrested (**II 21** 2.68–71, 229–44).

However, the considerable number of restraining orders and threats of punishment in this corpus of bureaucratic documentation suggests that problems were endemic; the papyri may be evidence not of a system working well but one that is struggling. The councillors at Panopolis seem keenly aware of their constitutional responsibilities; they need to be prompted by the *strategos* to fulfil them (e.g. II 21 1.53–9) and the *strategos* feels the need to appeal against them to the procurator's higher authority (e.g. II 21 1.167–79, 1.221–4). There are what appear to be quite deliberate evasions of responsibility (e.g. II 21 1.53–9). Sometimes, the absolute, painstaking clarity of exposition of instructions seems designed to avoid wilful misinterpretation by the recipients (e.g. II 21 1.264–71, 1.353–64). Surprising levels of courtesy were maintained on paper, but at times a bureaucrat's frustration boils over (e.g. II 21 2.68–71).

There can be little doubt that corruption and extortion were common (e.g. II 21 229–44), although perhaps not to the extent Lactantius claimed (II 6 7.3–4). Lactantius might be challenged too in his assessment of the motivation for the new measures: his suggestion that there was a desire to terrorise the empire's subjects is not really borne out by the Panopolis archive. What comes through strongly here is that this government relied heavily on the willingness of its subjects to co-operate (Corcoran 1996, 2000²: 295) – a point well appreciated by some of its subjects on the ground (e.g. II 21 1.167–79; 22). If this was naïve, it was not perhaps pernicious. A charge of naïvety has been levelled against Diocletian in other respects of his government too, perhaps most prominently in economic affairs, to be considered in the next chapter.

# CHAPTER 3

# Economics

## 1. Fiscal Policy

Two aspects of the Tetrarchy's military policy (**Chapter 1**) would have had direct implications for the economy. The army had always been the most expensive burden on the state, but this pressure must have intensified when troop numbers were increased by Diocletian. Secondly, the commitment not to extend Roman rule by further foreign conquests meant that there would be no income via booty. In short, changes in the military reduced income but increased expenses.

An obvious solution to this challenge would lie in tax, and Lactantius certainly made the connection between Diocletian's bigger army and his fiscal policy (**II 6 7.2–5**). But usually, the literary sources used finances as a means of characterising their subject: Maximian is cast as a typical tyrant for his personal greed (**II 6 8.5**); Eutropius praises Constantius for his modest spending and belief that the wealth of the state was better left in the hands of private individuals than the treasury (**II 2 10.1**); when Constantine reduced the liability for the people of Trier during his visit there in 311, he was praised by an orator for his divine generosity (**II 17**). Economic policy is, of course, an important determinant of a government's popularity, but the tendency of these literary sources to collapse any distinction between financial and moral dimensions drastically underestimates the complexities of Diocletian's fiscal measures. What is lacking in these texts is the sober realisation that tax is never popular; a more realistic and reliable impression can perhaps be gained from the outraged tone of Aurelius Isidorus, the procurator of the Lower Thebaid, when he condemns and threatens those tax-collectors who, for their own profit, extorted larger payments than were due (**II 21 2.229–44**). The resentment here is not the level of the tax but the corruption in its collection. Lactantius does mention corruption amongst tax-collectors in relation to the imposition of a census, but his exaggerated description betrays a moral rather than an economic judgement (**II 6 23.1–6**).

Diocletian's innovative fiscal policy is characterised by indiction and census (Hendy 1972). (Indiction is a published schedule of budgetary requirements to be raised in a given period by tax; in effect it announces how much tax the state will demand in the period.) A system of indiction was first imposed in Egypt in 287 (Thomas 1978). (This schedule was replaced by another in 288; and revised indiction cycles began in 292 and 297. An empire-wide indiction schedule of fifteen-year cycles was introduced in 312.) It is interesting that indiction was introduced in Egypt only three years after Diocletian's accession, and many years before either the creation of the Tetrarchy or the subdivision of Egypt into two provinces. Indiction could provide at least some means of regulating tax assessment and collection; but collection procedures were subject to exploitation (especially by the *decemprimi*), and budgeting for an indiction took no account of ability to pay. For practical and theoretical reasons, then, indiction alone could result in a capricious tax-collection. An attempt to meet these problems is announced in the preamble to the edict of Aristius Optatus, the prefect of Egypt, dated to March 297 (**II 22**). According to this edict, tax liability was to be calculated for each individual according to the quantity and quality of their land and their own age. This system is understood to have been a combination of poll tax (levied on individuals categorised roughly according to their ability to work) and property tax (levied according to the land's potential fertility). It might usefully be thought of as a tax on productivity, although the ancient sources are problematic (Nixon and Rodgers 1994: 257–63).

Aristius Optatus presents the new system to the public as a change in their interests, although it is clear that the state stood to gain, as tax evasion would henceforth be more difficult. Each individual's liability could be calculated from data submitted to a census. An Egyptian example is the land declaration to the *censitor* (census-collector) by Aurelia Herois in the Arsinoite *nome* in 299, more than two years after the edict of Aristius Optatus (**II 23**); her land is described by location, type and dimensions, and a battery of witnesses confirm the process. Census procedures, and subsequent tax liability calculations, varied across the empire (Jones 1953, 1964: 61–8; Barnes 1982: 226–8; Corcoran 1996, 2000²: 346–7); and different censuses were introduced at various times in the 290s. Another census was conducted in 306, when it seems both towns and the countryside were liable to tax assessment (**II 6 23.1–6; II 17**; Nixon and Rodgers 1994: 257, 272–3); and a further census took place in 311.

Ancient responses to this fiscal policy are few and unreliable. With a census and indiction system in place, and a civil administration to oversee and enforce its application, in theory regular liabilities could be calculated, bringing a measure of order to the empire. This would no doubt have been welcomed by those who had experienced unregulated military requisitioning – that is, in effect, plundering – in previous decades; on the other hand, those who legally or otherwise had managed to avoid contributing before would hardly welcome the new system. Aurelius Victor commended the way the taxpayers' wellbeing was maintained (**II 1 39.45**); by contrast, certain fiscal innovations might have been so unpopular that they led to the usurpations by Domitius Domitianus in Egypt (Barnes 1982: 230) and Maxentius in Rome (**II 6 26.2–3**). An orator in 311 makes the point that a series of poor harvests or a drop in rural manpower could render a tax liability unattainable (**II 17 5.5–7.2**). Aurelius Isidorus does not itemise the reasons for the neglect of the irrigation systems for the fields in the Lower Thebaid, but his public notice suggests it was prevalent (**II 21 2.222–8**) – if productivity targets were perceived to be too high, or if the procedures for tax collection were felt to be capricious, it is easy to imagine taxpayers finding ways to be unco-operative. Although we may well know more about it than most people did at the time, modern understanding of the issue is tantalisingly fragmentary: the regional variety in dates and types of fiscal measures might give the impression of a cautious government working steadily towards its intended goals; or perhaps it suggests a rather arbitrary series of makeshift reactions. Whether or not there was any coherent political philosophy, or indeed government collegiality, are controversial questions.

Tax itself was by no means always paid in money. There are many sources for the *annona*, tax paid in goods in lieu of money (e.g. tax receipts in Boak and Youtie 1960). The Panopolis letters contain explicit instructions for payment in goods (e.g. **II 21 1.53–9, 167–79, 221–4**) and cash (e.g. **II 21 2.161–4**); and Aurelius Isidorus' ruling about corruption in tax collection includes the illegal practice of the substitution of cash for payment in goods (**II 21 2.229–44**). The permanent or even temporary presence of a hungry army could be a cause of grievance. Tax payment in goods could be a mixed blessing, even in a region such as Egypt's Nile valley, where significant numbers of troops were stationed and the land was fertile (**II 25 East 28**): when harvests were plentiful, resentment might be relatively minor, but in inclement or unseasonal periods, the *annona* would be unpopular. On the other hand, the attractions for the taxpayer of cash payments, such as in the case of *donatives* (**II 21 2.161–4**), would vary according to their own cash holdings, the relationship between the monetary value and the precious metal content of the coins, and the rates of pay for the army (Duncan Jones 1990: 105–17). Inflation was an economic reality known to emperors and taxpayers alike.

## 2. Mints and coins

The ability to control coin production was an essential aspect of imperial power, as the issues of usurpers such as Amandus, Carausius (**II 44**), Domitius Domitianus and Maxentius demonstrate (**Chapter 6**). It was recognised that coins had propaganda and economic value, and Diocletian seems to have been energetic and imaginative in his organisation of mints and coins. It appears that there was a need for a change. The silver content of *denarius* coins minted in the mid-third century was low, with a typical 'silver' coin actually consisting of copper with a silver wash. By itself, this development would lead to inflation, and in fact neither state nor individual wanted to accept payment in these coins, effectively rendering the new issues worthless.

Diocletian inherited an economy with high inflation and little confidence in the coins. No direct evidence for a monetary policy survives: any ambition to identify a policy and evaluate its success must depend in large part upon coin data, such as mint marks (which can establish date and place of minting), bullion content, and distribution patterns. Numismatics and archaeology are fundamental to such inquiries, as well as economic theory; and although some consensus has been reached over the broad chronological and geographical develop-ments in this aspect of Tetrarchic economics, their interpretation remains a matter of considerable controversy.

Distinctive interventions in monetary affairs began relatively soon after Diocletian's accession, and continued intermittently throughout his reign. In 286 a high-grade *aureus* (gold coin) was introduced. Its distribution seems to have been limited, perhaps because it was used primarily for military pay and moreover because pure gold pieces were unlikely to circulate far in an inflationary climate. High-grade silver coins were not produced in the time of the Dyarchy, except by the usurper Carausius (**II 44**) from his separatist regime. About the time of the creation of the Tetrarchy, perhaps in 294, the imperial mints were reformed (Sutherland 1956; *R.I.C.* 6) – the date may be of significance, as the reform may have been considered an innovation that could only be managed successfully by an increased imperial college. The reform appears to have involved an empire-wide overhaul of the system of coin production, involving both the distribution of mints and the types of denomination (Sutherland 1956; Hendy 1972). The reform saw mints in most dioceses (although the dating of the changes in provincial administration is controversial; **Chapter 2.1**); there might also be detected a gravitation towards the provincial capitals, suggesting a strategic motivation for the mints' distribution. The reform extended the high-grade bullion content to silver coins; this new *argenteus* co-existed with the silver-washed *nummus*, which was retariffed; a copper *follis* was also introduced, with the uniform legend GENIO POPULI ROMANI ('To the *genius* of the Roman people'). The long lists of subordinates and clerical staff associated with the imperial treasury in the *Notitia Dignitatum* give some indication of the logistics involved in an extensive reform (**II 25 East 13**); but the underlying ambitions remain open to speculation (Williams 1985: 117; Sutherland 1955, 1956, 1961; Sperber 1966; *R.I.C.* 6; Hendy 1972; Ermatinger 1990, 1996). With an increased number of mints and significant coin reforms, there should now have been a more dependable supply of more reliable denominations.

## 3. Market economics

A range of factors might have motivated the hoarding of coins in antiquity, but it is generally assumed that the practice reveals a certain anxiety: in the absence of safe depositaries, an individual might bury his cash holdings in anticipation of war (such as barbarian invasions), civil depredations (such as banditry or unlicensed military requisitioning), an extended absence (such as a journey), or spiralling inflation. In all such cases, it would make sense to hoard high-grade coins in particular, as they would best maintain their value while out of circulation; just as in routine cash transactions it would make sense for the purchaser to prefer to use debased currency (if they could get away with it). There are many variables here, but there might be a connection between what appears to have been the continuation of hoarding after the mint reforms of 294 and evidence for ongoing inflation (e.g. **II 6 7.6**; Ermatinger 1990).

A fragmentary inscription from Aphrodisias is the best evidence for what is known as the Currency Decree (Erim, Reynolds and Crawford 1971). It came into force in September 301. Enough of the defective text survives to establish that Diocletian sought by the force of law to retariff some coins, including the *argenteus* (at 100 *denarii*) and probably the *nummus* (at 25 *denarii*); at the same time, these new tariffs would be in immediate force for tax and commerce. The text might imply that the new values were to be applied across the empire, although no sources elsewhere confirm this (Corcoran 1996, 2000[2]: 177–8). What appears to be the decree's focus on silver coinage has been interpreted as an attempt by the government to increase the purchasing power of the high-grade coin it had introduced; by differentiating silver from other metals and between silver denominations, Diocletian was perhaps recognising the central importance of that metal to the economy, and intended to promote its use (Ermatinger 1990: 45–6). The hypothesis has met with some resistance, on the grounds that it attributes to Diocletian a command of economic theory that would have been unusual in antiquity, and which is not reflected in the preamble to the Price Edict (**see below**; Corcoran 1996, 2000[2]: 214–15). However, despite the lack of a full context for the decree, it clearly indicates Diocletian's inclination to intervene directly in market economics.

Much better attested than the Currency Decree is the Edict of Maximal Prices (**II 19**). This came into force in November–December 301. It was issued by Diocletian, at Antioch or Alexandria or between the two (Corcoran 1996, 2000[2]: 205–6). In contrast with the Currency Decree, stone fragments of the edict have been found in nearly forty different locations, allowing very full reconstruction of the text.

The edict begins with a long rhetorical preamble in which the emperors justify the introduction of the measure; it is this moralised rationale which has been cited as evidence of a weak grasp of economics. The preamble is followed by a list of itemised commodities and services, organised by categories; against each item there appears an appropriate measure or unit, and a price. This price is the maximum that can be charged (or paid) for that commodity or service; the preamble makes it explicitly clear that these prices were maximal and not absolute, so that in times of plenty a lower price could be charged. The innovative nature of this edict has been overstated at times, as there had been earlier examples of maximal prices (Ermatinger 1990: 46–7; Corcoran 1996, 2000[2]: 213–15). It is acknowledged that the sheer scale of this attempted check on market forces was unprecedented.

Another controversial issue is the relationship – if any – between the edict and the Currency Decree. The edict was published only two to three months after the decree. This proximity has been interpreted as evidence that the decree and edict were two halves of a single economic policy (Ermatinger 1990, 1996).

According to this model, the decree would raise and fix the purchasing power of silver currency (but not the other denominations which would find a 'natural' level in relation to the silver); but with a currency stabilised at a higher tariff, prices would tend to go up. To limit this, a second intervention in the form of an itemised maximal price schedule followed up the currency reform. Ermatinger concludes that Diocletian's two-pronged attack managed to restore the monetary system and halt inflation. Objections have been raised to this model: neither measure refers to the other, which might be considered odd if they were designed as a pair; and the edict's preamble in particular would be an obvious place to expound such an economic argument (Corcoran 1996, 2000$^2$: 214–15). Besides, if the government predicted that the retariffing upwards of silver coinage would precipitate inflation and so devised a price ceiling as a preventative measure, there would be no reason to wait nearly three months before publishing it. On the other hand, if the measures were completely separate, three months seems a very short period in which to establish that the currency reform had failed and a new initiative was required.

By contrast with coins, whose find-contexts are often completely unknown, reliable data are available for the edict (Corcoran 1996, 2000$^2$: 229–32). With nearly forty locations established, in terms of raw number the Prices Edict is the best surviving text in the field of classical epigraphy – this fact alone makes it an attractive subject for study. However, the distribution hardly fits with the preamble's rhetoric of universal application (**II 19 pr. 7**). All but four of these locations are in three provinces: Phrygia-Caria, Crete-Cyrene and Achaea, the first in the diocese of Asia (under Diocletian throughout his reign), the other two in Moesia (under Galerius in 301). Of the other four locations, one was Egypt (where the edict was possibly originally issued), the others Samos, Odessos and Pettorano. This distribution is provocative. The lack of evidence from the Latin west is not proof that the edict was not promulgated there – after all, many Tetrarchic edicts were published in paper form. The evidence of Lactantius is not decisive, as his biography is far from secure, and he may have known of the edict from his time in Nicomedia (**II 6 7.6–7**; Creed 1984 xxvi–vii). The hypothesis that the edict was promulgated only in a few eastern provinces, all under the control of Diocletian and Galerius, raises many questions (some of which can lead away from economics into fields such as the propaganda of government unity (**Chapter 6**)): was the edict's limited promulgation intended, and if so why?; if universal promulgation was intended and did not occur, what caused the breakdown in the administrative process?; were, for example, the economies of east and west understood as essentially discrete systems requiring different regulation?; did attitudes towards legislation vary from one emperor to another, or from one part of the empire to another?

It is not known what dictated the selection of the items on the list (Corcoran 1996, 2000[2]: 219–25). There may have been similarly long lists in circulation, perhaps for commercial or taxation purposes; perhaps the list was influenced too by the market goods available in Antioch, a provincial capital and a centre of trade. Geographical sources for some items are specified, and some herald from the west. Another broad sweep appears to be the variety of goods, from luxury to ordinary, with the meat section, for example, including both peacock and mutton suet, the wages section ranging from advocates to brickmakers (**II 19 IV, VII**). The range of goods in the edict, in origin, type and expense, might imply an attempt at comprehensive coverage of all goods involved in normal commerce – but what was normal in the east might have been exotic in the west. Another possible determining factor for the selection of items for the list is the army. The markets of a provincial capital like Antioch would conduct lots of trade with the military, and the edict's preamble mentions the crippling effects of inflation for soldiers; furthermore, the army's differentiated pay scales would accommodate a wide range of goods. Whether or not there was a dominant interest group informing the nature of the list is bound to be contentious.

Lactantius says that the law on [maximal] prices was repealed after it effectively shut the markets and encouraged further inflation (**II 6 7.6–7**). Papyri quoting the same prices for goods specified as maximal on the edict survive from ten years later – this has been interpreted variously as evidence that the edict continued in force for this period, and as merely coincidental (Ermatinger 1990: 49; Corcoran 1996, 2000[2]: 232–3). The view that the edict was only prosecuted with any determination by Diocletian might encourage the assumption that it was dropped when he retired in 305. There is some consensus that the edict did not hold for very long, although very little on how effective it was when still in force. Lactantius writes of bloody retributions, much as threatened in the preamble (**II 6 7.7**; **19 pr. 18**); doubtless this must have varied in time and place, but for practical reasons, even the most zealous of government officials would have been hard pressed to enforce the law. How could every minor transaction be policed? Perhaps in the preamble's threats to vendors and purchasers alike there can be seen some realisation from the government that the policy's success depended upon a large degree of public co-operation; perhaps too there is a naïve assumption that to criminalise a practice is to end it.

The sources for Diocletian's economy are many and varied; most, however, are fragmentary, uncontextualised, or otherwise problematic. Conjectures which identify patterns that can then be used to reconstruct economic models are bound to meet some opposition – especially any which boldly use data to infer motivation in the form of policy, or those which depend upon controversial hypotheses in the related areas of Tetrarchic administrative and constitutional history. Recent decades have brought important new sources to light, and in their wake, new and revised economic models. Most might seem suspiciously neat; on the other hand, few would deny that behind the sources lie some rational principles, no matter how elusive they are for us now, or how realistic they were then.

# CHAPTER 4

# Ceremonial

## 1. Adventus

The fourth-century literary record provides the controversial starting point for this discussion of the use made in Tetrarchic society of elaborate court ceremonial. Aurelius Victor (**II 1 39.2–4**), Eutropius (**II 2 9.26**), Ammianus Marcellinus (**II 7. 15.5.18**) and also Jerome (*Chronicon* 292–3) attribute to Diocletian the beginnings of an elaborately stylised monarchy, characterised by expensive purple dyes, fine silks and jewels, and the obligation on those approaching the emperor to worship him as a god. The later Byzantine chronicler Theophanes even claims (*Chronicon* A.M. 5793, translated by Dodgeon and Lieu 1991: 130) that Diocletian's change in appearance and bearing can be dated precisely to just after the victory over Narses – as if the confidence it inspired in him and the insight the campaign granted into Persian despotic practice captured his imagination. It is precisely because these analyses argue for a radical tendency in this, another, aspect of Diocletian's rule, that they demand close scrutiny.

The sketchbook of a Victorian Egyptologist provides curious and illuminating evidence to begin to examine the claims of the literary testimony (**II 34**). John Gardner Wilkinson was interested in the original Egyptian material which lay under Tetrarchic frescoes on the wall of the so-called imperial chamber at Luxor; his only means of access was to strip away the frescoes, but fortunately for posterity, Gardner Wilkinson made sketches, some detailed, some incomplete, before wielding his chisel (Kalavrezou-Maxeiner 1975). One unfinished scene, tentatively reconstructed by moderns, shows an orderly crowd attending on what appears to be a pair of seated emperors with their feet on a raised platform. Under Diocletian, the room at Luxor was perhaps an imperial reception chamber, with its decoration in part mirroring the room's function. Although the scene is densely populated, the dynamics of axis, direction, posture and clothing clearly indicate status and power relations. These form part of the protocols understood as court ceremonial, an almost ritualised nexus of sartorial, architectural, titular, procedural and representational elements which together articulate social order, and in particular, imperial majesty. The various components seem to have worked together to create the impression for any petitioner of Diocletian, that they were in the presence of a higher being. The date of the frescoes at the chamber is put at 296–7, which like many further examples of Tetrarchic ceremonial culture discussed below, rules out Theophanes' specific claim for Diocletian's inspiration.

But Diocletian's interest in the potential of organised display can hardly be denied – the Luxor fresco is not alone. A similar scene is described by a panegyrical orator in 291, although this time no part is played by images or decoration (II 12 11.1–4). The passage refers to a meeting between Diocletian and Maximian at Milan in the winter of 290–1, although the agenda for this first summit in two years is not revealed nor the reason for the hearing granted to the public by the emperors. However, the setting and the procedure delineate imperial majesty. Only men of certain rank are granted entry to the palace at Milan, where in an inner sanctum they make reverent obeisance to the emperors. The exclusivity of access and the quasi-religious formalities inside would clarify hierarchical niceties in a way the orator seems naturally to grasp. Nothing survives today of the Tetrarchic palace at Milan, but remains and reconstructions of contemporary palace complexes at Trier, Gamzigrad, Thessalonica, Split, Rome itself and Nicomedia provide helpful parallels (Wightman 1970; Wilkes 1986: 56–9; Srejovic 1995). Each complex is different, but it seems one constant was that, even in those possibly designed as retirement palaces, such as Split and Gamzigrad, an ornate audience chamber was required (II 35, 36, 37). Admitted through grand portals if the necessary conditions were met to the satisfaction of imperial servants, channelled through a maze of colonnaded corridors and antechambers, delegates, embassies and petitioners could be received into such a space; the way the space was organised and access to it regulated would confirm the appropriate order of things.

Surrounding the emperor would have been his most trusted advisors. In an incidental detail in his account of the first days of the persecution of Christians, Lactantius describes eunuchs as powerful support for the palace and the emperor (II 6 15.2). Eunuchs feature prominently in sources for the court ceremonial of Late Antiquity, and Diocletian in particular can perhaps be identified with the development of the phenomenon (Hopkins 1978: 172–96; Garnsey and Humfress 2001: 33–4). Court eunuchs were of servile or barbarian origin, and so for physiological and social reasons could not hope to become emperor themselves; they could, however, amass for themselves considerable influence by their proximity to the emperor and the confidence he put in them. As a buffer between the emperor and his public, eunuchs were perfectly placed to control approaches to him, to advise him, manipulate opinion and further particular causes. As the powerful lowborn usually are in essentially aristocratic societies, court eunuchs of Late Antiquity were much resented by the wider public; the extent of this resentment is no doubt a useful index of the sway they could garner in the context of imperial ceremonial. The artistic, architectural and literary sources permit a vivid reconstruction of the deliberately intimidating nature of an approach to the emperor.

Also closely choreographed was an imperial visit to the people. The ceremonial occasion of *adventus* ('arrival') into cities is particularly prominent in our sources, although *consecratio* ('deification') and accession feature too (MacCormack 1981: 17–33, 106–15, 168–77). *Adventus* evolved into a highly stylised eye-catching theatre, with all ranks of society fulfilling their appropriate role in the display. As we have seen (**Chapter 2.2**), Tetrarchic government was essentially itinerant, so throughout the empire the ceremony of *adventus* would be enacted regularly. Every imperial journey through towns and cities would provide several opportunities for the ceremonial of *adventus*. It seems that good notice was given of an imperial visit – the letters from Panopolis demonstrate how the billeting arrangements for the imperial *comitatus* required considerable attention (**II 21 1.53–9, 167–79, 221–4, 249–51, 332–7**). On the day itself, a delegation would meet the emperor outside the city walls to offer welcome; this would be followed by a procession into the city, the streets lined with crowds to celebrate the emperor's arrival, no doubt cheering and clapping (**II 17 8.1–4;** see also Ammianus Marcellinus 16.10.1–3). The ordinary citizens of Milan would also see Diocletian and Maximian as they left their meeting, an episode the panegyrist relates charged with enthusiasm (**II 12 11.1–4**).

The Arras Medallion, a magnificent gold piece perhaps minted for distribution amongst the military elite only, offers another grand perspective of the ceremony of *adventus* (**II 45**). The medallion dates to 296 or 297 and commemorates in a triumphalist tone the reconquest of Britain by Constantius' army. The highly economical scene is set at a time after the military victory; Constantius on horseback approaches the city of London; the personification of the city greets him from a kneeling position; the legend REDDITOR LUCIS AETERNAE ('Restorer of the Everlasting Light') casts Constantius as a saviour. The salutary qualities of his reign are here condensed into the representation of a single ceremony.

The Arras Medallion would no doubt have enjoyed official approval. On the ground however, the obligations incumbent on towns on the occasions of *adventus* were met with varying levels of enthusiasm – some towns would be genuinely pleased to receive an emperor, others much less so. The formulaic language and exasperated tone of the Panopolis *strategos* in anticipation of Diocletian's arrival there in 298 (e.g. **II 21** 1.53–9) is perhaps a more realistic example of the usual response than the panegyrical orators' elevated descriptions; but this discrepancy reminds us of the gap between reality and appearance which was so fundamental to preserving order.

The tension between realism and idealism can also be seen in monumental statuary. The most famous statue groups of the Tetrarchs are the porphyry groups now in St Marks, Venice and the Vatican Library (**II 46, 47**). Porphyry was a prestige stone, the preserve of elites such as the imperial family. The Venice group shows four emperors together, in two pairs. They are identically dressed in Pannonian hat, uniform and military tunic. Each emperor grips his eagle-headed sword-handle with his left hand, and with his right he embraces his colleague. The details of dress (and face) are at odds with the lack of concern for anatomical proportion, as each emperor stands uncomfortably, the thin legs seeming too weak to support the outsized right hands. Discussion of the political interpretation of the porphyry groups appears below (**Chapter 6.1**); at this point, the groups' symbolic claims for the emperors' physical togetherness should be noted, since as was discussed above (**Chapter 2.2**) the emperors were rarely in the same place at the same time (if indeed ever). Yet these intimidating statue groups suggest their capacity to overcome the natural limits of time and space. The order which controlled Tetrarchic practice did not extend merely to earthly power.

A similar example in relief sculpture is the scene of the enthroned emperors on the Arch of Galerius in Thessalonica (**II 40**). The relief is quite badly eroded, making positive identification of individual characters impossible. Two emperors are seen seated together, flanked by the other two. The two emperors on the outside raise kneeling personifications of submissive provinces. The enthroned emperors sit above busts representing, it has been argued, sky and earth. Other deities fill the scene, with personifications of earth and sea reclining at the sides (Pond Rothman 1975, 1977; MacCormack 1981: 176–7). Whether or not specific identifications are upheld, the scene clearly projects the cosmic nature of Tetrarchic rule, imperial influence reaching far beyond the mundane concerns of government.

Rhetoric could convey this message too. In the panegyric of 291, the emperors' descent into Milan from the Alps is described in terms and tone deliberately recalling a divine epiphany, culminating in the equation of the emperors with their heavenly patrons Jupiter and Hercules (**II 12 10.5**). Long gone is Augustus' Republican charade of 'first among equals'; to be with a Tetrarch is to be in the presence of a higher being. If the panegyrical orators sometimes seem reluctant baldly to identify their emperors as gods, in their armoury of exaggerated conceits they are very comfortable to imply such status (Rodgers 1986). For example, the duties of imperial office grandly catalogued by an orator in 289 hardly locate Maximian in the human realm, although he is not quite called divine (**II 11 3.3–4**). In 297, another orator favourably compared the accession of the Caesars Constantius and Galerius on 1 March (293) with the blessings of the earth's creation, traditionally put at the same spring date in Roman mythology (**II 13 2.2–3.1**). The same orator then goes on to select a range of fundamental 'quaternities' (groups of four) as parallel examples of divine approval of systems such as the Tetrarchy (**4.2**). These coincidences of canonical time and order urge appreciation of the pre-ordained, cosmic essence of the government. These emperors are generally not called gods, but they are clearly elevated above the concerns of ordinary mortals.

But if Julio-Claudian practice was definitively eschewed and Narses and his harem are ruled out as a source of inspiration for Tetrarchic ceremonial, the origins must be sought elsewhere. To a certain extent, ceremonial depends upon repeated patterns, to establish normative codes of behaviour and representation. The fraught decades before Diocletian's accession, with their violent cycles of military appointments, assassinations and civil wars hardly permitted repetition of this sort, but the reign of Aurelian in particular (270–5) has been identified as an important precursor. Although in origins a soldier, Aurelian associated himself as closely as possible with the cult of *Sol Invictus* ('The Victorious Sun-god'); by claiming a divine agency on media such as his coinage, Aurelian's was an important new direction in the 'imperial cult' (Watson 1999: 183–202). The effect seems not to have been to present Aurelian as a deranged megalomaniac in the fashion of Domitian, but more subtly to shift appreciation of the emperor's power base away from the military towards the gods. Divine approval had been a mainstay of imperial legitimacy since Augustus, but in the tempestuous 270s Aurelian handled the phenomenon in this original way; he gave the impression not so much of promoting himself (as divinely favoured) as promoting his office (as divinely appointed). Perhaps here can be found the inspiration for the Tetrarchs' self-definition.

In fact Aurelian's innovations did not serve him particularly well, as he was killed after only five years as emperor. Diocletian's longer reign suggests that, with luck, ceremonial could become a self-fulfilling prophecy: the longer an emperor reigned the more repeated occasions and anniversary celebrations would be clocked up, each a specific display in itself and cumulatively a confirmation of divine approval. Perhaps it is the case, then, that Aurelius Victor, Eutropius, Ammianus and Jerome were wrong to assume elaborate ceremonial began with Diocletian, when instead his policy was a rigorous and concerted continuation of a practice he would have seen in operation ten years before he came to office. The historians' mistake is understandable – the duration of Diocletian's reign would have enabled him to develop and consolidate practices which, half a century later, might appear to have been innovative at the time.

## 2. Panegyrics

The *Panegyrici Latini* is a collection of twelve speeches addressed to emperors; eleven are from Late Antiquity, all delivered in Gaul, with Trier a particular focus, or by a Gallic orator; nine of them date to the period between Diocletian's accession and 321. The rationale for the collection is not clear, although it is widely accepted that the collection was put together in Late Antiquity, perhaps by the author of the latest speech, addressed to the emperor Theodosius (Nixon and Rodgers 1994: 3–8). The speeches are not preserved in the manuscripts in chronological order. The manuscripts provide little information beyond the raw texts, so many speeches are anonymous; but individually they reveal information about their authors and circumstances of delivery. Although flattering of their addressees, they were not written by government employees or lackeys, but by distinguished orators with significant political independence (Nixon 1983). This fact would seem to rule out any characterisation of panegyrics as government propaganda; a sensible orator would be alert to the main themes of current propaganda and would be wise to reflect them in his speech insofar as they chimed with his own agenda and that of the people he represented (Rees 2002).

An imperial *adventus* would provide a regular context for delivery of a panegyric. Capital city basilicas such as Constantine's at Trier (**II 41**) or Maxentius' at Rome (**II 42**) were no doubt grander than the reception chambers smaller towns had for such formalities, but they indicate clearly how architectural space could be used to determine and confirm social order (Wilkes 1986; Ward-Perkins 1981; Sear 1982). Members of the imperial bodyguard would have attended in number; the emperor's advisors and associated staff might be present too, swelling the crowd of those locals distinguished enough to gain entry (**II 12 11.1–4; 17 2.1**). The emperor would take his place at the apse (the semicircular recess at the end of a building), and the rhetoric of welcome could begin. This would be an intimidating experience for an orator, even for those of considerable experience (**II 17 9.3**). The surviving speeches tend to be quite short, and in fact include occasional references to the pressure of time on the orators; perhaps the emperor would be addressed by several orators on one day. One speech even preserves the curious detail that the emperor stood to be addressed (**II 13 4.4**, but see also Nixon and Rodgers 1994: 114); if this really were the norm, the orators would have had an extra incentive not to be long-winded.

Although it seems the orators whose work survives were talented and experienced men, some even teachers of rhetoric, the survival of a treatise recommending how to address a speech to an emperor suggests that some men charged with the responsibility needed guidance. Menander Rhetor's *basilikos logos*, a Greek text dated to the Diocletianic era, advises that a panegyrical speech be structured around the emperor's biography and his examples of the four virtues of courage, justice, temperance and wisdom (Russell and Wilson 1981; Russell 1998). The survival of this contemporary treatise (albeit in Greek, not Latin) allows for a careful comparison between theory and practice in political oratory; and the *basilikos logos* can be a useful tool in classifying all the surviving speeches as 'all the same' or distinctive (Smith 1997: 195–201; Rees 2002: 23–6). The content of the speeches, characterised by formalised rhetoric, elevated expressions and exaggerated praise, is not to modern taste; but considered together with their performance context, in them can be identified a form of ritualised celebration of imperial government, where the orator celebrates the emperors' right to rule and publicises the loyalty to them of the community he represents.

Occasions other than the *adventus* of an emperor could also be marked by a panegyric. The evidence of the *Panegyrici Latini* yields a range of other reasons for delivery of a celebratory speech at a civic gathering: imperial victories, anniversaries of accession to the throne, imperial weddings, the emperor's birthday, the birthday of the city, or of Rome (Nixon and Rodgers 1994: 4–5). On the whole surviving evidence comes from Gaul, but it is clear that speeches were addressed across the empire. Unless the revelation contained in a speech addressed to Constantine in 321 that that emperor was not actually present at the time is extraordinary (*Panegyrici Latini* IV(10)3.1), it seems likely that on certain days of the year, communities would gather throughout the empire, and the celebrations might include a panegyric, whether or not an emperor was present. This image of the civic calendar at the time of the Tetrarchy marks a significant change from the early Roman *fasti* which were dominated by ancient religious festivals, often closely associated with the countryside. Now it seems the various rites of the imperial cult regulated the civic calendar (Salzman 1990).

The repeated rhythms of civic life, both enacting and giving literal voice to the community's loyalty to the government, constituted powerful ceremonial. Hard evidence for the dating of this emerging culture is difficult to find (and of course it would itself be subject to change the following century when Christian festivals could first feature in civic calendars), but it seems probable that it was an evolving process rather than a decisive changeover. But the remarks of Aurelius Victor, Eutropius and Jerome are suggestive (**above, 1**). Despite the range of occasions on which surviving panegyrics were delivered, the treatise of Menander Rhetor provides only a single model; separate texts provide advice about birthday addresses and other occasions, but they are not specifically imperial. This disparity between Menander and the speeches might be accounted for by geography alone, with practice in the Latin west differing from that of the Greek east, but the survival of one speech delivered in Latin in Constantinople in 362 (*Panegyrici Latini* II(11)) is difficult to accommodate in this scheme. Alternatively, perhaps the *basilikos logos* predates the surviving corpus of speeches, and soon after the treatise, there developed a culture of civic display, enshrined in regular ceremonial activity, which served to affirm and heighten the profile of the emperors' presence and influence in all matters. Against those attributing primacy to Diocletian in ceremonial affairs, such a culture would more likely be a codification of elements of existing practice than a radical change. But, certainly if the reconstruction is right that, for example, on 21 April each year, throughout cities and towns of the empire, communities would gather to hear a local orator give praise to the emperors for Rome's wellbeing on this the ancient city's birthday, it can be seen that Tetrarchic ceremonial could be an almost irresistible means of cementing the prevailing political order.

### 3. Names

We have seen how in particular visual and rhetorical material contributed to a deeply-held sense of the emperors' superiority; and that if Diocletian and his colleagues were not as radical as later writers saw them, they did at least add considerable impetus to the development of court ceremonial. A further area to be considered in this regard is names. The *Notitia Dignitatum* and the papyri from Panopolis provide excellent evidence that inflation in titles was fully established throughout the machinery of imperial government (**II 21, 25**). Titles such as 'right honourable', 'illustrious', 'most eminent', 'your clemency' and 'most perfect' reveal not so much a culture of obsequiousness as an ingrained appreciation of a hierarchy which advertised and maintained the appropriate social classes. Titles denoted relative authority, as much in government administration as in the army.

This reflects the practice in the imperial college itself, with two Augusti and two Caesars. The inscription from the Baths of Diocletian at Rome (**II 20** *I.L.S.* **646**) has the further rank of senior Augustus. This was the position to which Diocletian and Maximian retired. It is unclear what authority it brought them – although some deference was paid to Diocletian when at Carnuntum in 308 as a senior Augustus, the appearance of Diocletian and Maximian on the inscription before the Augusti and Caesars essentially seems honorific. Contemporary writers seem to have had a clear idea of a hierarchy within the college of four. Eusebius was able to identify the emperors without their names but by reference to their rank alone (**II 8 8 Appendix**). Lactantius rather casually observes that when they were Augusti, Constantius was superior to Galerius, although it is not clear what qualified Constantius for this status (**II 6 20.1**). It certainly did not reflect any divine hierarchy some have seen as a fundamental principle in the adoption, years earlier, of imperial *signa*.

From the beginning of his reign, dedications of Diocletian's coinage were predominantly to Jupiter; from 285 Hercules appeared regularly too, and on occasion the two together (*R.I.C.* 5.2). From his accession in 285, Maximian minted coins dedicated to Hercules, Jupiter and the two together. Aurelian's close association with the cult of *Sol Invictus* would have stood as a recent precedent. However, sometime before 289, the

Dyarchs launched a new step in the imperial cult when they each took on a *signum*, Diocletian calling himself 'Jovius' and Maximian 'Herculius'. When the Tetrarchy came into being in 293, each new Caesar took on his Augustus' *signum* too, with Constantius becoming 'Herculius' and Galerius 'Jovius'. Adoption of a *signum* was popular practice at the time, at many levels of society, but the emperors were unusual in taking theophoric names – that is, names which conveyed association with gods. The related questions of the date of adoption of the *signa*, the motivation for their adoption, and their significance, have been much discussed (Rees 2004). While only thirty years later Lactantius sneered that the names had been forgotten, utterly destroyed by God (II 6 52.3), much later in the fourth century historians could use the *signa* alone to identify the emperors, confident that their readers would be able to follow (II 1 39.19, 25, 30, 33; 29.22, 27; 4 39.6). They clearly had some currency.

Perhaps the *signa* were adopted to emphasise the legitimacy of the Dyarchs' right to rule precisely at the time when Carausius challenged it by proclaiming himself emperor. Another possibility is that the Dyarchs took the *signa* in 286 when Maximian was promoted to the rank of Augustus. The fundamental function of the *signa* was clearly to claim for the emperors some divine agency, relating Diocletian and Maximian to Jupiter and Hercules respectively. This agency was perhaps akin to coin legends denoting an emperor as COMES ('companion') of a god. While avoiding outright claims to divine status (which might offend public sensibility), such designations certainly elevated the emperors above the normal herd. One intended function of the imperial *signa* might have been to delineate the relationship between Diocletian and Maximian; as Hercules' father, Jupiter enjoyed clear superiority. But if this was the original intention, it had been superseded by 305 when, it seems, Constantius Herculius was senior to Galerius Jovius.

Modern understanding of the *signa* is limited by the fact that coins, papyri and legal sources do not mention them at all. A few medallions, inscriptions and panegyrics are the only contemporary evidence. The inscriptions seem to be dedications to the emperors by local benefactors and reveal little of the way the *signa* were understood; addressing speeches to Maximian and Constantius, the panegyrical orators of Trier use the *signum* Herculius variously as a starting-point for consideration of their addressees' origins, virtues and status. While this reveals the orators' dexterity and hints further at their independence from the steely hand of imperial control over the content of their speeches, again we learn nothing about the emperors' motivation for using the names.

The medallions, though few in number, are perhaps most revealing in this regard (Rees 2004). Medallions are usually thought to have been distributed among high ranking officers. The appearance of the *signa* on medallions might suggest a military origin for them – and that Jovius and Herculius, terms used to name some Tetrarchic units (**II 25 East 5; Chapter 1**), were nicknames or tags which grew out of their soldiers' devotion to Diocletian and Maximian. Whatever the origins and inspiration, the *signa* seem not to have been widespread in other media, a fact which might suggest they were intended only to appeal to a particular interest group.

It now seems likely that Aurelius Victor, Eutropius, Ammianus Marcellinus and Jerome were not right in claiming that Diocletian was the first emperor to employ aspects of royal ceremonial; yet perhaps we could concede that Diocletian and Tetrarchic aristocratic society generally were clearly preoccupied to an extent not seen to such effect before with protocols of appearance, deportment, dress, titles and terminology. This culture probably represented a codification of practice rather than a revolution; but the extent to which it had new momentum under Diocletian, and the degree to which it was to inform other levels of society, seem to have been new. This all contributed to a sense of order, with individuals clearly defined in relation to each other and to other ranks, and as Diocletian's reign continued, making him the longest serving emperor for many decades, repetition of ceremonial features and occasions established patterns and rhythms which had their own capacity to authorise.

# CHAPTER 5

# Religion

## 1. Sacrifice

The previous chapter saw how from Antiquity on, the impetus Diocletian gave to ceremonial, which served in part to articulate difference in status, be it in levels of human society or in immortal and human realms, has been much discussed. Some of the evidence, such as the adoption of theophoric *signa* or the confident implications of divine status implied in the scene of the emperors enthroned on the Arch of Galerius (**II 40**) can support the claim that in religious affairs the Tetrarchs were progressive. At the same time, although epithets denoting divinity such as sacred (*sacer* in Latin) were used of emperors and even their administrative offices (e.g. **II 11 1.1; 12 11.1; 25 East 13**), the emperors seem to have been reluctant plainly to proclaim themselves divine. An attempt to characterise Tetrarchic attitudes towards religion needs to be far from one-dimensional; some further factors are raised here.

The surviving base of the *Decennalia* monument at Rome has several scenes which, it has been suggested, were repeated on the other bases. One of the best preserved reliefs shows a procession leading to the traditional *suovetaurilia* (**II 43a**) – the expensive, elaborate and public sacrifice of a pig, sheep and bull. Another shows a togate figure – presumably the emperor – performing sacrifice to the gods by pouring a wine libation onto a fire, surrounded by approving deities, such as Mars and winged Victory (**II 43b**). This constellation encapsulates a great deal about Tetrarchic religion: in performing sacrifice, the emperor demonstrates his belief in the ancestral gods of Rome; as he does so he is crowned by the winged Victory, thus forging a link between the emperor's religious attitude and the state's success; and although sacrifice was a means of communication from the human to the divine realm, the fact that the emperor is attended by gods as he pours the wine makes equivocal his own status. That the emperor should be seen in the traditional dress of the Roman aristocracy performing this sacrifice in the heart of the ancient city is clear indication of the potential propaganda value of religion.

The conjecture that the surviving reliefs featured also on the other *decennalia* bases is particularly attractive in light of the high frequency of representations from elsewhere of the Tetrarchs performing sacrifice. The sacrifice scene from the Arch of Galerius, with (in this case) emperors and altar, surrounded by divine attendants, is strikingly similar to the *decennalia* relief (Pond Rothman 1977). The simplicity of a sacrifice scene, with little more than an altar or tripod required, made it very suitable for the iconic representation needed in the restricted canvas of coin imagery. In addition to the common legend types such as CONSERVATOR JUPITER ('Jupiter fellow-saviour') or HERCULES INVICTUS ('Unconquered Hercules'), the emperors at sacrifice was a common religious type in Tetrarchic coins. Inherent in these very frequent Tetrarchic images of imperial sacrifice is the traditional Roman virtue of *pietas* – a quality with many applications, but which always involved a sense of religious devotion. The adjective *pius* was a standard epithet in imperial titles (e.g. **II 20** *I.L.S.* **613, 620, 640; 19 pr. 1–2**), and the introductory remarks in the Price Edict preamble further confirm the emperors' religious disposition. No less than earlier emperors, the Tetrarchs were concerned to convey strong impressions of their religious decorum and of the favour they enjoyed from the gods. Jupiter and Hercules were particular favourites, but not to the exclusion of other gods from the traditional pantheon.

## 2. The Manichaeans

Because sacrifice was the quintessential ritual in Roman pagan religion, performance of sacrifice was to become the hallmark of religious affiliation in the Tetrarchs' clash with the Christians. Although the so-called 'Great' Persecution was a defining episode in the histories of the church and of the Roman empire, modern analyses have tended to emphasise important continuities, especially from the mid-third century (**see below, 3**). Another well-known text relating to Tetrarchic religion which forms a vital part of the context for the 'Great' Persecution is the letter on the Manichaeans (**II 28**). The letter is now usually put at 31 March 302, although 297, which was for a long time the preferred date, 287 and 307 remain unlikely possibilities (Barnes 1982: 55; Corcoran 1996, 2000[2]: 135–6). If the current orthodoxy is upheld, this letter on the Manichaeans can be seen as an immediate and aggressive precedent for the 'Great' Persecution which began in February 303. This text is a legal rescript, outlawing the Manichaean belief in the Roman empire; it is directed initially at that faith's leaders, although provision is made for their followers too.

The focus of this faith was the third-century Parthian Mani; his was a dualistic doctrine, articulated around conflicts between light and darkness. It was not the essence of the faith to which the emperors objected in their rescript to Julianus, it was the novelty of Manichaeism and its association with Persia that were intolerable. This was an aggressively Roman religious ideology, promulgated in a period when relations between Rome and Persia were very hostile. Although it was a rescript dealing with what seems to have been an issue only in Africa, one way in which it represents an interesting precedent for the 'Great' Persecution is in its attempt to legislate against religious conviction. Details are not clear from the rescript, but given the broad ideological antipathy to Manichaeism, it appears that an ordinary follower of Mani in Africa would have to abandon all aspects of their faith or face punishment; how this was to be tested in law and how effectively the law could be applied are matters for speculation. Sources for the 'Great' Persecution are more forthcoming.

## 3. The 'Great' Persecution I 303–5

Lactantius identifies sacrifice as the litmus test (**II 6** 10.1–4). The martyr acts of St Crispina and Julius the Veteran each present a dialogue in which the inquisitor is concerned simply with the defendant's refusal to perform sacrifice to the gods for the wellbeing of the emperors (**II 31** 1; **33** 1–2). In his earnest attempts to dissuade Julius from his determined course, the sympathetic prefect Maximus seems almost to belittle any claims for profound significance associated with the sprinkling of some incense on the altar, although it is of course a mark of Julius' great distinction that he upholds his Christian principles, and refuses to submit (**33** 2). Perhaps then there is an important difference between the Tetrarchic actions against the Manichaeans and the Christians; both were legal actions, but while the former criminalised a complete lifestyle attitude, the latter was (at least at certain stages of the persecution) specifically concerned with the act of sacrifice. A follower of Mani would fall foul of the law even if they sacrificed incense; a Christian making pagan sacrifice would compromise their standing in the church community, but they would satisfy the state.

Refusal to sacrifice had been criminalised before, in Diocletian's lifetime. Some intermittent and localised pogroms had broken out in the earlier empire, but a universal action against Christians was not undertaken until the mid-third century (Frend 1984; Leadbetter 1996; Beard, North and Price 1998). Recent analyses of Decius (emperor 249–51) have concluded that his intention was not to crush Christianity, but to appease the gods through the traditional means of sacrifice at a time when the empire was stricken in various ways. Those who performed sacrifice before a magistrate received a certificate to prove it, and were free to go. Valerian, another emperor (253–60) whose propaganda emphasised his role as a restorer of traditions, launched a broader attack against the Christians: his act to outlaw Christian assembly and his call to Christians to return to traditional religion suggest that Christianity was now understood by the state as 'un-Roman'. Apparently Aurelian too was planning a renewed assault against Christians when he died (Lactantius *On the Deaths* 6.1–2). With their different emphases, the actions against Christians by Decius and Valerian stood as important, recent precedents for the 'Great' Persecution.

Apart from the issue of precedence, the question of motivation is interesting, especially in the context of Diocletian's long reign. There is no date given for Lactantius' dramatic account of the unsatisfactory outcome of the *haruspices*' rites which led to Diocletian's order that all active soldiers perform sacrifice (**II 6 10.1–4**). The suggestion of 299 or 300 makes for an interesting evolution in Diocletian's policy (Creed 1984: 91). This date falls after some martyr acts for Diocletian's reign: for instance, for his Christian faith, Maximilian preferred death to recruitment in the army in 295; Marcellus renounced his military service in favour of Christ, and was executed in 298 (Musirillo 1972: 244–59). These men were not victims of persecution edicts but of military regulations, but their examples of insurrection might have triggered Diocletian's anxiety about the presence of Christians in the army.

Eusebius states that the persecution began in the army (**II 8 8.1.8**). His *History of the Church* and the *Martyrs of Palestine* are important sources for the 'Great' Persecution; and perhaps equally importantly, the *History of the Church* represents a major milestone in ecclesiastical historiography. Eusebius was probably born in Caesarea in Palestine, about 260. He became bishop of his home city about 313. One of the most productive early Church fathers, his literary output (in Greek) was enormous. His *History of the Church* (also known as the *Ecclesiastical History*) begins with Christ and closes with the monarchy of Constantine. The circumstances of its composition have been much debated. There is a consensus that the work was published in several editions over a number of years, although the details are contested; one theory is for the publication of Books 1–7 before the outbreak of the 'Great' Persecution, and of Books 8–10 in 313–14 (Barnes 1980). A rival theory argues for initial publication of all the books together, in approximately 312 (Louth 1990). The controversy about the dates of publication is intriguing because they affect appreciation of Eusebius' motivations. According to Barnes' model, for example, Eusebius conceived of his work before the outbreak of the 'Great' Persecution, and Books 8–10 were added later; the *History* then appears a rather unbalanced, inorganic work. According to Louth's model, the 'Great' Persecution is a defining episode in the history of the church, which by design interrupts the apostolic and episcopal successions of Books 2–7, just as the persecution interrupted the peaceful progress of the church. There are acknowledged inconsistencies in style across the work, with Books 2–7 distinctly annalistic and archival in character, and Books 8–10 more elaborate and ornamental. Whether these differences can be traced to the dates of composition, or whether they reflect a fundamental change in Eusebius' source material – and perhaps his reliability – are difficult questions.

While they have much in common, Eusebius and Lactantius can be sharply differentiated. Eusebius identifies the cause of the 'Great' Persecution as the Christians themselves, who had become idle and deserving of punishment (**II 8** 8.1.7). Without absolving the persecuting emperors at all, the persecution is thus introduced as the salutary workings of a Christian theodicy. Lactantius' work too is underpinned by a Christian theodicy, but to it are attributed the deaths the persecuting emperors met, but not the origins of the persecution. Very few scholars would now accept the elements of divine causation or agency in these works, but Lactantius in particular has proved very durable. His account of the inspiration for Diocletian's first edict against the Christians, long time accepted by scholars, has only recently been treated with circumspection (**II 6** 10.6–8; Davies 1989). Rejecting as unlikely Lactantius' claim that Diocletian was persuaded to persecute simply by the force of Galerius' pathological fanaticism, Davies proposed a scheme which takes account of a wider perspective and puts Diocletian back in the centre ground: the popularity of Christianity was growing in the late third century, but perhaps levels were not intolerable to Diocletian until fifteen years or more after his accession; Diocletian did not have first hand experience of the strength of Christianity in its heartland – the diocese of the East – until he was there from 296 to 301; and until the Persian war was over, Diocletian needed as many men as possible in the army, so the faith of any one soldier was not a priority until 298. This rational scheme does not account for the delay from the late 290s to the beginning of the persecution in 303, but it does move away from themes of divine and biographical causation which characterise the narrative texts.

The first edict of persecution was drawn up on 23 February 303 (**II 6 12.1**). It was published (in paper form) the following day in Nicomedia, and elsewhere in the weeks and months that followed (**II 6 13.1; 8 8.2.4**; Corcoran 1996, 2000[2]: 179–81). The text does not survive, but from the narrative accounts it is reasonably secure that it ordered the razing of churches, the burning of Christian scripture (cf **II 32 and above 2**), the loss of judicial rights for defiant Christians, the loss of relevant rights for Christians in high office, and the enslavement of any defiant Christians serving in the imperial household (Keresztes 1983: 382). It seems likely that pagan sacrifice was used to establish an individual's faith in the relevant rulings, but the broader ambition of the measures – apparently, to dismantle the workings of the church – make this edict reminiscent of Valerian's assault on Christianity.

The Martyr Act of Felix, bishop of Tibiuca in Africa, provides an example of this legislation in action (**II 32**). The consular years give the dramatic date of 303; the date of publication of the edict in Tibiuca is given as 5 June. In the Act, Felix refuses to surrender the Christian scripture in his possession; he is given opportunity to rethink his position, and the presiding magistrate Magnilianus finally passes the bishop's case to the proconsul Anullinus, who quickly orders the execution of Felix. The reliability of the Martyr Acts is of consistent and central concern, but if this text is taken at face value, it reveals some interesting insights: it took three months for the edict to reach Tibiuca (Corcoran 1996, 2000[2]: 179); with a marked distinction between the powers available to the magistrate Magnilianus and the proconsul Anullinus, different levels of jurisdiction were in place at this stage in the persecution; and by the terms of the edict the magistrate was authorised to *confiscate* the scriptures by force, but a main theme of the dialogue is the bishop's refusal to *surrender* them. This last point turned the process of law into a collision of wills. One is left wondering if this was how Diocletian meant it to be, or whether perhaps local and petty tensions between civic and religious leaders were inflated into clashes of ideologies.

As with the repeated scenes of pagan sacrifice in Tetrarchic monumental sculpture and coinage (**see above, 1**), Christian Martyr Acts have readily identifiable characteristics. Although each Act is distinctive in some of its details, there are regular patterns in scenario, dialogue and speech, plot and resolution, and in characterisation – each martyr is strong, calm and determined, and shows no fear in the face of death. This repetitiousness is an important literary strategy because out of disparate and appalling material it generates a strong sense of a triumphant Christian collectivity. In this respect the Christian written record of the persecution served absolutely to nullify the edicts' ambition to break the church. In a Martyr Act, each death becomes not just an addition to a catalogue of imperial injustice, but a reflection of Christ's grace on the cross, and therefore provides further inspiration to the Christian reader.

A second edict was announced later in 303 (**II 8 8.2.5, 6.8–9**) which ordered the imprisonment of clergy (Keresztes 1983: 382, 386–7; Corcoran 1996, 2000[2]: 181). This intensification of the campaign against the Christians occurred a few months after the initial edict; this short time lag invites our attention. There is credible evidence that the first edict was applied with some success (if unevenly) (Keresztes 1983: 386–7); the publication of a second edict, however, suggests either that Diocletian was not aware that the terms of the first edict were being applied, or, more credibly, that although he knew the edict was being applied, he felt it was not achieving all his wishes as quickly as he wanted. The short time lag also suggests that the imperial administration was functioning very efficiently (**see above, Chapters 2.3 and 3.3**).

Lactantius makes no specific reference to the edict, although he mentions the arrest of clergy, but adds that violence was perpetrated against all Christians without discrimination (**II 6 15.2–5**). This might urge caution about his reliability. We can probably assume that clergy could apostatise (by performing sacrifice) to avoid imprisonment in the application of the second edict, and that Diocletian's intention was to break the Christian community either by removing its leaders or leaving them unworthy of their position in the eyes of their congregations.

According to Eusebius, the second edict served only to fill the prisons (**II 8 8.6.9**). Exaggeration aside, it is possible that the second edict was perceived to have failed in its ambition, because a third edict appears to have been quick to follow. Eusebius writes of what is assumed to be a third edict, commanding that all imprisoned clergy be forced to sacrifice, and that on doing so, they be freed (**II 8 8.2.5, 6.10**). There is some confusion about this edict – which does not survive – in relation to the announcement of an amnesty for prisoners generally, on the occasion of Diocletian's *vicennalia* on 20 November 303. It would be a surprising turn for government policy if an amnesty edict freed clergy against whom a third and more drastic persecution edict had just allowed violence to be used (Keresztes 1983: 382–3); but the conditional nature of the clergy's release (that is, on the proviso that they sacrificed) has been understood to indicate a partial extension of the amnesty to the imprisoned clergy (Corcoran 1996, 2000[2]: 181–2). Diocletian would stand to benefit from the good publicity of ordering an act of great clemency in the amnesty and/or the release of clergy; at the same time he may have hoped to weaken the bonds holding the Christian community by making it known that the released clergy had apostatised.

In early 304 the fourth Persecution Edict was published, ordering the whole community to sacrifice (Corcoran 1996, 2000[2]: 182). There is no record of certificates being issued, as they had been under Decius (**see above**); instead, the sources seem to imply that performance of sacrifice before official witnesses was adequate, although it is not known how this process was conducted. The edict might represent a considered move away from the attempt to break down church leadership towards a general assault on Christians; this would be a significant change in strategy. The date and extent of its application are not clear, opening up a controversy about the main instigator of the edict – was it Diocletian, or Galerius? According to Lactantius, Diocletian himself was ill for much of 304 (**II 6 17.2–9**). It has been claimed that the earliest attestation for the edict's application in areas directly subject to Diocletian's control dates to 305, and that by contrast, Galerius and Maximian were busy applying the edict from as early as February 304 (Keresztes 1983: 383–4). These details could be used to confirm Lactantius' impression of Galerius as the most zealous persecutor of Christians and a bully of Diocletian; in this interpretation can be identified early signs of collegiate dysfunctionalism, which would readily lead to collapse in the system over the next few years. On the other hand, a rigid territoriality in Tetrarchic authority seems not to have been exercised at this stage, and nothing in the sources suggests that Galerius was overreaching his powers as Caesar (**see above, Chapter 2.1**). It remains quite possible that the fourth edict was sponsored by Diocletian, and that despite his poor health, he and Galerius were co-operating well in 304.

The first edict had denied access to judicial procedure to all Christians; this would not have affected all Christians, as some no doubt had no reason to enter into legal process. Thus the fourth edict would have been the first to bring the force of law into direct conflict with all ordinary Christians – until this point, the main objects of the persecution had been Christians in the army, and the texts, fabric and leaders of the church, but now it seems entire communities, one by one, were required to perform sacrifice before magistrates or other office holders. Lactantius does not reflect this progression at all clearly: his narrative hardly distinguishes between the imprisonment of clergy (demanded by the second edict) and the drive for mass sacrifice (demanded by the fourth edict) (**II 6 15.1–5**). With graphic detail Lactantius collapses the course and diversity of the persecution, as suggested in the reconstruction of the four edicts, into one dramatic impression of universal suffering. Martyr Acts of lay Christians provide an interesting point of comparison. The Act of St Crispina is dated specifically to December 304 – that is, after the publication of the fourth edict (**II 31**). Crispina is up before the same African proconsul Anullinus who, seventeen months earlier, had condemned the bishop Felix for refusing to obey the first edict (**II 32**; Barnes 1982: 181); this progression indicates that in Africa at least, the letter of the prevailing edict was being applied at the appropriate time, and that universal, indiscriminate persecution did not occur until the fourth edict. The Act of Julius the Veteran can be used in a similar way as a contrast to the elaborate pages of Lactantius (**II 33**).

The years 303–5 are seen as the first stage of the 'Great' Persecution; in 305 Diocletian and Maximian retired, and the internal politics of the imperial college were to change, as new priorities took over. Continuities have been identified between the third-century persecutions and the Tetrarchic measures (Leadbetter 1996); from the policies of Decius who had sought to appease the pagan gods by enforcing universal sacrifice and of Valerian who had viewed Christianity as essentially unRoman, Diocletian seems to have taken examples for his own attacks on the church. In this sense, the first stage of the 'Great' Persecution need not be thought of as radical.

The pronouncement of four separate edicts against Christianity in the year from February 303 can be interpreted as evidence that the persecution was not going well – that each increasingly severe edict proves the failure of its predecessor. The reason for the serial failure of these measures is open to speculation. Implicit in the Christian projects of Eusebius and Lactantius, and perhaps too in the anonymous Martyr Acts, is the idea that the steadfast resolve of the Christian community and its preference for death over apostasy wore down and ultimately defeated the emperors. This construction emphasises Christian triumph. There is no suggestion in these texts that the state administrative machinery was not working well, but in reality there might have been problems. The rapid succession of edicts might suggest that communication, including promulgation, was efficient, and that the government was immediately alert to the effects of its legislation; but there is also evidence that application of the legislation was patchy. As with the Prices Edict, the inconsistency in the application of Persecution Edicts can be thought to reveal a lack of harmony amongst the emperors (**Chapters 3.3 and 6.1**); but it might be thought better to reflect the very inconsistent distribution of Christians across the empire, with particularly high concentrations, it seems, in the Oriens and Asia dioceses. Another relevant factor is the issue of enforcement; the Christian texts lionise the dignity of the martyrs who refused to duck the challenge the edicts posed to their principles, but it is probably reasonable to assume that Christian communities found ways and means of helping individuals to evade the law without compromising their faith.

## 4. The 'Great' Persecution II 306–13

There is no evidence to connect the apparent failure of the first four edicts of persecution with the decision of the *Augusti* to retire in May 305. The 'Second' Tetrarchy would have plenty to occupy them in the first instance, and there is no record of further legislation until 306. Eusebius says that in 305 the new Caesar Maximinus Daia enforced the persecution in the east, but whether persecution continued elsewhere in the first six months of the 'Second' Tetrarchy is not clear (Eusebius, *Martyrs of Palestine* 4.1). Eusebius also says that in 306 Maximinus Daia issued edicts ordering that individuals be summoned by their registered name to perform sacrifice (*Martyrs of Palestine* 4.8). This is said to have occurred in Caesarea, Eusebius' home town. A recent interpretation sees this simply as Maximinus Daia's means of enforcing the fourth edict, and thus casts Maximinus as collegiate, if zealous, at this point of the 'Second' Tetrarchy (Corcoran 1996, 2000[2]: 182). An alternative hypothesis, that Maximinus went far beyond the terms of the fourth edict in insisting on the use of registers of names (presumably recently compiled in the census of the same year), figures him more aggressive and independent of his imperial colleagues (Keresztes 1983: 384).

Unmistakably independent is the edict that Lactantius tells us another new emperor pronounced in 306 – on his father's death, Constantine's first act was to restore legal status to Christianity (**II 6**

**24.9**). The truth of this claim has been doubted by some (Creed 1984: 105–6). It certainly fits very comfortably the image Constantine's defenders wished to promote of the early career of the man who was to become the first Christian emperor (Chadwick 1967, Frend 1984); and even if accurate, the claim probably overstates the need for such an edict in Britain, where according to Lactantius' own testimony, Constantine's father Constantius had not been enforcing the Persecution Edicts with any enthusiasm anyway (**II 6 15.7**). But religion aside, in the two proposed edicts of 306 – those of Maximinus Daia and Constantine – there might be traced some early signs of the Tetrarchy's fragmentation. Another contemporary challenge was Maxentius' usurpation in Rome (**Chapter 6**); Eusebius records that Maxentius revoked the Persecution Edicts in Rome, although only to improve his own reputation (**II 8 8.14.1**; Corcoran 1996, 2000²: 185). Eusebius can hardly be relied on here – he could not have known Maxentius' motivation, but at the same time he would not want to present a positive picture of the man Constantine was to confront in 312 – but his claim is a reminder of the contribution religious policy could make to government popularity in the period.

There was one further edict of persecution, issued by Maximinus Daia, in 309 (Eusebius, *Martyrs of Palestine* 9.2; Keresztes 1983: 384; Corcoran 1996, 2000²: 185–6). The command for universal sacrifice was restated, pagan temples were to be reconstructed and pagan high priests appointed. This edict seems to have been an attempt to breathe new life into a policy that was flagging; it also appears to have been issued only in the Oriens diocese. Maximinus Daia was still a Caesar at this stage, to be hailed Augustus in 310 (Barnes 1982: 6); while this helps to establish that Tetrarchic Caesars as well as Augusti had constitutional power to issue edicts, his unilateral edict might also mark a further breakdown in the collegiality of the 'Second' Tetrarchy (Corcoran 1996, 2000²: 270–1).

Just before his death in spring 311, Galerius, then the senior Augustus, published an Edict of toleration (Keresztes 1983: 392–3). This edict was published on 30 April, and its text is preserved in Latin by Lactantius and in a Greek translation by Eusebius (**II 6 34.1–5**; *History of the Church* 8.17.2–11). Both writers claim that Galerius was driven by his worsening physical condition to confess the Christian God (**II 6 33.11**; **8 8.17.1**); while this claim helps to construct the emperor's illness as Christian retribution (a unifying theme of Lactantius' work), there is no evidence of a Christian confession in the text of the edict. In any period, reversal of a government policy requires careful rhetoric; Galerius' edict is notable for its emphasis on imperial clemency, not

contrition, and a rather grudging tone towards Christians. Nor is there
any corroboration of the texts' claim that publication of the edict was
a deliberate death-bed act. Eusebius' translation preserves the full
imperial titles for Galerius, Maximinus Daia, Licinius and Constantine,
a claim for collegiality which events elsewhere show to be empty, but
which might suggest that the motivations for the edict were political
and not personal. Persecution had begun over eight years earlier and its
failure to break the church would have been conspicuous; meantime,
although Maximian was dead, the Tetrarchy had constitutional problems of its own, and Maxentius still ruled in Rome; Galerius had
travelled considerably since 303 and would have been aware of some of
the regional variety in the effects of the persecution – perhaps he even
knew of its revocation in the west under Constantine and Maxentius.
Galerius might have seen that the persecution which had hoped to
crush Christianity was in the end exacerbating other problems in the
empire and the government.

The publication of the edict was not the end of the persecution;
Galerius himself died, and no evidence suggests Licinius or Constantine
defied its terms, but following a period of grudging deference to the
edict, Maximinus Daia apparently resumed his persecution six months
after the publication of the Toleration edict in April 311 (Eusebius
*History of the Church* 9.1.1–6; Corcoran 1996, 2000²: 148–9; II 8 9.2.1).
There are some discrepancies about this stage of the persecution
between the accounts of Eusebius and Lactantius, for example, on the
use of capital punishment, although it can probably be assumed it was
brutal (II 6 36.6–7; 8 9.6.1–7.15). Characteristically, Eusebius cites at
length documentary evidence in the form of a rescript (of 312), which
can be tested against surviving inscriptions (Mitchell 1988); if this
process recommends Eusebius' reliability, it can be checked by his claim
that the measure was published in every province (II 8 9.7.15; Corcoran
1996, 2000²: 149–51). Eusebius seems guilty either of clumsiness or
wilful exaggeration, for although the territory subject to Maximinus
Daia's control had increased on Galerius' death in 311 to include the
dioceses of Asia and Pontica, there is no evidence to suggest that his
legislation had any force elsewhere (II 6 36.1). This new measure reflects
a confident and assertive emperor – even if he contrived the rescript, at
this stage he appears to have been more concerned to be seen to be
responsive to his subjects than to be part of a unified imperial college
(II 8 9.2.2.–4.2).

Eusebius preserves a further twist in Maximinus Daia's dealings with
Christians. In May 313, after crushing defeat in battle with Licinius,

Maximinus Daia issued an edict of toleration, presumably in Cappadocia (II **6 46.11–47.5; 8 9.10.7–11**; Mitchell 1988; Corcoran 1996, 2000²: 189). The edict is headed only in Maximinus Daia's name; it commands toleration of Christians, including permission to practise their faith and build churches, and the restoration of confiscated property. The emperor claims in the edict that he had in the previous year sent letters to his provincial governors ordering toleration of Christians, but because that order had in some instances been ignored, it needed to be restated in this unequivocal form.

Eusebius' citation of documentary evidence is generally held to be reliable, so it should not lightly be dismissed as fictional; but this is an odd text indeed. Eusebius goes on to express outrage at such a *volte face*, and pronounces Maximinus Daia utterly deserving of the fatal illness he says was god-sent to kill him. The sequence has much in common with the accounts of Galerius' recantation and death, a fact which suggests the workings of a literary typology and a sacrifice of historical accuracy. In support of Eusebius, it can be observed that progress of Christian justice in his narrative would be smoother without the edict, and that therefore its inclusion demonstrates his scrupulous concern for accuracy. Certainly, Lactantius makes no reference to an edict of toleration from Maximinus Daia, although he presents the emperor's agonising death as a punishment for his sins against the Christians (II **6 49.7–50.1**). In the edict, Maximinus Daia makes no apology for the persecution, and the fact that he blames others for the harm caused in his name suggests a political rather than a religious motivation for the edict. In the spring of 313 Constantine and Licinius were in league with each other and at war with Maximinus Daia (e.g. II **6 45.1–46.11**). Respectful references to Diocletian and Maximian in the edict might present Maximinus Daia as dutiful and collegiate, but the edict is in his own name only and makes no conciliatory reference to the other current emperors. If the edict's ambition in part was to secure for Maximinus Daia the loyalty of the eastern Christians in anticipation of further battles with Licinius, overall it suggests a determined monarchical programme.

Before Licinius pursued Maximinus Daia into the east (where the latter was to die), he published the 'Edict of Milan', on 13 June 313 (Corcoran 1996, 2000²: 158–60). The text is preserved in Latin (II **6 48.2–12**) and in a Greek translation by Eusebius (*History of the Church* 10.5.2–14). The edict was in fact a letter, issued at Nicomedia, where Maximinus Daia had been only a month earlier (II **6 47.5**). The edict is issued in the names of Licinius and Constantine, and takes its name from the conference between the two at Milan earlier that year, at which much was discussed, including religious affairs (**II 6 48.2**). According to the edict, privileges and property were to be restored to Christians; and religions including Christianity were now to be tolerated unequivocally. The edict thus grants considerably more concessions than Galerius' Toleration Edict two years earlier and that of Maximinus Daia a month previously (about which Licinius and Constantine could have known nothing when at Milan, and possibly still knew nothing in June) (**see above**). Rather than Christian triumphalism, there is, however, an even-handedness in the Edict of Milan, which might reflect a compromised collegiality between its signatories. Neither emperor admits to being Christian, although a diplomatic concern not to inflame resolute pagan subjects might account for this.

Within ten years of Diocletian's retirement, the Tetrarchic experiment was over, Christianity had been legalised, and Christian writers felt safe to sneer at his memory (e.g. **II 6 52.3**). The 'Great' Persecution tends to loom large in modern images of the Tetrarchy and Constantine. It may be that this gets things out of proportion. Although their silences might be explained away by generic arguments, there is no mention of the persecution in Aurelius Victor or Eutropius or the contemporary panegyrics from Gaul. Historians must rely for the main part on literary sources whose selection and organisation of material were aimed to further a Christian agenda. Christian interpretations and those of secular scholarship have different perspectives: the former attribute the failure of the 'Great' Persecution to the resilience of the Christian community and the workings of Christian justice in the universe; but divine causation, be it pagan or Christian, has not been recognised in mainstream academic argument for many decades, so secular historians tend to identify flaws in administrative procedure, mechanisms for enforcement, and lack of harmony in the imperial colleges as fatal to the persecution's chances of success. Although it is recognised that in some areas and for some time persecution was vicious and real, the regular apparatus of modern classical scholarship has been applied to these texts to test some of their central claims – such as the scale of the persecution (e.g. Ste Croix 1954).

What is not controversial is that by means such as legislation and political art, Diocletian sought to intervene directly in religious affairs, and that distinction between religion and politics is sometimes very difficult. Whether Diocletian was manipulating ceremonial to present himself as quasi-divine, picturing the Tetrarchy as traditional pagans at sacrifice, or promoting the image of himself and Maximian (and in time their Caesars too) as agents of Jupiter and Hercules, or persecuting Manichaeans and Christians, it is orthodox to see in him a far-reaching ambition to affect not just how people behaved but how and what they believed. This hardly makes him radical in a Roman imperial context, but the variety and extent of his interventions in religious affairs argue strongly for his unusual energy and imagination.

# CHAPTER 6

# Unity, Succession and Legitimacy

## 1. Unity

Traditionally, Roman imperial government was monarchical and not collegiate. Typically too the monarchy was patriarchal and dynastic, with sons (natural or adopted) inheriting power from their fathers. And so, periods of Roman imperial history tend to be seen in terms of ruling families or 'houses', such as the Julio-Claudians, Flavians, and Severans. When there had been instances of power-sharing, the same familial relationships had provided the vital element of unity; a late third century example, which Diocletian knew well, was the short reign of Carus (282–3), who appointed his sons Carinus and Numerian fellow emperors. Although short-lived, this was a familial, collegiate government. Whatever ambitions Diocletian entertained for his collegiate governments of two, then four emperors, the unity of the college would be central to his chances of realising them – if each emperor were systematically to act independently, the empire would no doubt descend again into civil war.

Diocletian had no son, but it would perhaps be rash to assume that this motivated his decision to appoint unrelated men as emperors – he could have adopted a son if he had wished. Whatever motives underlay his decision to create a college of emperors which was not related by blood, its unity would have to be real and visible for it to work. For the Tetrarchs in 293, common origin in the Balkan provinces and successful military careers were no doubt vital qualifications for imperial office; but collegiate unity it seems was also strengthened by marriages, with the Augusti fathers-in-law to the Caesars (**see above; Introduction 2**). Thus it seems collegiate unity was forged in a variety of ways. It also had to be projected to the people and here was a challenge, because the Tetrarchs rarely met up with each other (**Chapter 2**). For the government's chances of survival, wide perception of collegiate unity would be essential, and propaganda was the key.

Inscriptions provide good examples of the imperial college's determination to present a unified front. Edicts and dedications routinely include elaborate naming formulae for the entire college, regardless of the original location (and, in certain cases, instigator) (**II 19; 20** *I.L.S.* **620, 640, 646**; Eusebius *History of the Church* 8.17.3–5; Barnes 1982: 17–29). Furthermore imperial titulature such as that preserved at the beginning of the Edict of Prices, demonstrates that it was customary for a victory title secured by any Tetrarchic emperor to be extended to all of his imperial colleagues – and so, for example, Constantius who spent his entire reign in the west, shared the victory title *Persicus maximus* and in turn, Galerius who had personally led a successful campaign against the Persians and had not ventured into the west, had amongst his titles *Brittanicus maximus* (**II 19**; Barnes 1982: 27). If the principle is accepted that announcement of every colleague's name and reciprocity in victory titles are marks of collegiality, all imperial edicts and inscriptions can be seen as potential indicators of their author's political aspirations.

Another propaganda medium which can be analysed in a similar manner is coins. A few medallions from the Dyarchic years feature both Diocletian and Maximian, a clear statement of collegiate unity (e.g. Williams 1985: 114; Rees 2002: 59). Large medallions with their high grade metal can accommodate images of two men on one piece, but for smaller coins it was a little more complicated; Carausius' coin showing himself and the two Dyarchs in profile seems to have been a uniquely ambitious issue (**II 44**). Instead, the unity of the central emperors tended to be advertised on coins by the convention of reciprocal minting: there were several mints across the empire (**Chapter 3.2**), and by issuing coins in the names of all members of the college and not just the 'local' emperor, a mint could promote the government's unity. For example, in the late 280s in Gaul, a Roman citizen might have had an opportunity or occasion to see Maximian, but Diocletian was elsewhere; but by issuing coins in the name of Diocletian as well as others for Maximian, the mint at Lyons would help to remind the ordinary citizen of the united imperial college (*R.I.C.* 5.2). This reciprocity was a regular means of promoting unity in the time of the Tetrarchy too (*R.I.C.* 6); if this practice is seen as a normative expression of Tetrarchic unity, again deviation from it by particular mints at certain times could be seen as advertising contrasting ambitions in the name of the issuing emperor.

The idea of collegiate unity was also promoted in relief and free-standing sculpture. Despite the fact that all the statues and all but one of the bases have been lost, the *Decennalia* monument is a good example: the appearance of the columns and statues in the background of the *adlocutio* scene on the frieze on the Arch of Constantine at Rome gives the clear impression that the monument celebrated the whole college. The ideology of unity in four (or five, with the occasional addition of Jupiter, as at Rome) was clearly prevalent, with remains of similar configurations identified at Luxor, Split and Ephesus (Kalavrezou-Maxeiner 1975: 244–8; Rees 1993).

It has also been argued that in their iconography, the propagandistic media of coins and sculpture promoted the ideology of collegiate unity. According to this interpretation, similarities between coin and sculptural images of different emperors are a mark of political *concordia* (Sutherland 1963; L'Orange 1965: 46–52; Rees 1993). The claim is perhaps at its most compelling in the case of the porphyry groups now in the Vatican Library and Venice. There are two identical Vatican groups (**II 47**); each depicts two emperors standing shoulder to shoulder, each man in his left hand holding an orb (representing universal dominion), and embracing his colleague with his right. Natural likeness has been sacrificed – individual emperors are indistinguishable and in each pair one emperor's right arm is disproportionate, exaggerating the embrace. The Venice group is broadly comparable (**II 46; Chapter 4.1**). It comprises one group, with two pairs of Tetrarchs; right hands again embrace, and the left hands grip eagle-headed sword handles. One figure in each pair has thin stubble – usually thought to identify them as the Augusti. Otherwise, as with the Vatican groups, the emperors are indistɪ ̄guishable. Through this *similitudo*, the interpretation has it, collegiate unity is emphasised. This interpretative model of *concordia* through *similitudo* can then be extended to the porphyry busts which survive by themselves and without a context, such as those at Massachusetts (**II 48**) and Cairo (**II 49**), or the bust recently discovered at Gamzigrad (**II 50**). The assumption underlying this interpretation of the individual busts is that they were originally part of a group of four or, if not, that the iconographic features they share with each other, with coins and with the complete groups, were so similar that in their original contexts they would have put their viewers in mind of the college and its unity.

With the exception of the Gamzigrad bust, almost nothing is known about the original contexts for the various porphyry statuary; nor is their dating very secure, relying as it does on a typology of coin images for guidance (usually resulting in the convenient attribution of 'c. 300'). These vagaries do not rule out the hypothesis that unity was promoted through *similitudo*, but they can accommodate alternative interpretations. One such denies that *similitudo* was ever a particular ambition of most Tetrarchic sculpture and coinage, and that when a collective aspect can be identified, it is better accounted for as the result of processes of production and distribution, and not of Tetrarchic policy (Smith 1997: 180–1). In effect, arguing that surviving porphyry sculpture is unrepresentative of the emperors' ambitions, this approach says that images which do not so readily fit the model of *concordia* through *similitudo* have been unduly marginalised.

Although the propagandistic element of panegyrics is difficult to determine (**Chapter 4.2**), the surviving texts certainly engaged with contemporary imperial ideologies (Rees 2002: 190–1). Imperial unity is a good case in point, since it dominates significant sections of the surviving speeches. In the earliest speech, unity between Maximian and Diocletian is figured in various ways: they are cast as brothers, although not by blood but virtues (**II 11 9.3**); as having *similitudo* ('similarity'), not in their looks but in their characters (**9.5**); as harmonious and unanimous, and as ruling together with a metaphorical *dextrarum iunctio* ('handclasp') (**11.1**; Rees 2002: 55–63). These claims for fraternity and *concordia* ('harmony') are the earliest in surviving Dyarchic evidence. No Dyarchic (or Tetrarchic coins) feature the theme of fraternity, although Carausius claimed a brotherhood with Diocletian and Maximian on a coin usually dated to 291 (**II 44**), the dedication inscription for the Baths of Diocletian in 305–6 speaks of Diocletian and Maximian as brothers (**II 20 *I.L.S.* 646**), and later Lactantius referred to them similarly (**II 6 8.1**). In later, Tetrarchic coins, *concordia* was to become a very common legend, but had not appeared yet in 289 (*R.I.C.* 5.2, 6). One conclusion that might be drawn from the original ways in which the panegyric of 289 expresses collegiate unity, is that the orator enjoyed liberty to find his own colourful expressions; alternatively, it might have been the case that government officials in Trier had encouraged him to give rhetorical expression to propagandistic themes that were already being considered.

Fraternity and *concordia* are also prominent figures of Dyarchic unity in the speech of 291 (**II 12**; Rees 2002: 73–91). So too is the presentation of the Dyarchs' meeting in Milan almost as a lovers' tryst (**II 12 12.3–5**). In the earliest Tetrarchic speech to survive, the number four is granted cardinal significance as the orator expounds the quaternary nature of the cosmos' most fundamental systems and organising principles; but later in the same speech, Galerius is conspicuously absent from a list of the emperors (**II 13 4.2, 21.1**; Rees 2002: 110–14, 120). In the speech of 307, delivered on the occasion of Constantine's marriage with

Maximian's daughter Fausta, the orator faced particularly delicate challenges: of his two addressees, Maximian had returned to power at the invitation of Maxentius his usurping son, and Constantine, proclaimed emperor by the soldiers on the death of his father the previous year, had yet to achieve much worthy of flattering oratory (II 15; Nixon 1993, Rees 2002: 164–84). Unity is expressed through the addressees' new relationship as in-laws – marking a decisive break with the metaphors for unity in surviving Tetrarchic and Dyarchic speeches. The absence of images of unity in the speeches addressed to Constantine in 310 and 311 mark another important stage in his move away from a collegiate government (II 16; 17; Warmington 1974, Rodgers 1989).

Images of government unity in propaganda and contemporary oratory are one thing; of course the reality could be quite another, and some are inclined to assume that the relentless advertisement of government unity in propaganda actually signals the presence of friction (e.g. Nixon and Rodgers 1994: 43–4). Gauging the reality of the imperial college's unity is a multifarious exercise. Lactantius writes of the unity between Diocletian and Maximian, but his presentation of Constantius as non-persecuting and Galerius when Caesar as impatient for higher office suggests this harmony did not extend to the Tetrarchic college in full (II 6 8.1, 8.7, 9.8, 18.6). Aurelius Victor asserts that Diocletian kept secrets from his imperial colleagues through fear that full disclosure would disrupt collegiate harmony (II 1 39.46). Other details can be adduced: for example, from historiography, such as the occasion of Galerius' walk beside Diocletian's carriage (see Chapter 1.1) or the young Constantine's captivity in the court of the eastern emperors (II 5 2.2); from documentary sources, such as the apparent variability in the distribution of the Price Edict (Chapter 3.3), the application of the Persecution Edicts (Chapter 5.3–4), or reconstructions of consular lists (Barnes 1982: 91–5; Cullhed 1994: 34–5); from coin legends and types, such as those minted by Maximinus Daia (*R.I.C.* 6). In evidence like this, greater or lesser tensions might be seen to have existed, running counter to any claims for collegiate unity.

## 2. Succession

The importance of collegiate unity is well highlighted in consideration of the mechanics of succession – a vital, but potentially fraught process since the first imperial succession when Tiberius followed Augustus. Although some ancient testimony records that Galerius did not become

Caesar until May, it is now generally accepted that Constantius and Galerius were appointed Caesar at the same time, 1 March 293 (Barnes 1982: 62; Nixon and Rodgers 1994: 112). Through marriage alliances the Caesars were also sons-in-law to the Augusti, but these were emphatically not dynastic appointments; how widely anticipated this step was, or whether or not it was considered a precedent to rule out the possibility of dynastic appointments in future are moot points. Maxentius was perhaps only 10 years old in 293, but traditionally the attractions of dynastic succession had been able to prevail over any anxieties about the immaturity of an emperor's son (Barnes 1982: 34; Williams 1985: 68). An orator in 289 spoke of the boy Maxentius' qualities, but falls far short of predicting that he would assume imperial office (**II 11 14.1**; Nixon and Rodgers 1994: 75). Our evidence really cannot support definitive conclusions about plans Diocletian might have had in 293 for his eventual succession; neither do we know if Maximian was willingly party to such plans, nor indeed if there were any plans at this stage (Nixon and Rodgers 1994: 50–1). What the silence of the evidence currently available does suggest is that whether Diocletian was devising a master-plan for his own succession or improvising desperately, he was little inclined to reveal his hand. Perhaps the Roman public knew as little as we do.

Although no emperor's son came to the throne in 293, the marriages of Constantius (to Maximian's (step-)daughter Theodora) and of Galerius (to Diocletian's daughter Valeria), even though insecurely dated, indicate that family ties were still considered an important bond in the imperial college (Barnes 1982: 37–8). The later marriages of Constantine (in 307, to Fausta, Maximian's daughter by Eutropia) and Licinius (in 313, to Constantine's sister Constantia) confirm the political role that marriage could play, albeit not in these cases within a Tetrarchic college (**II 15; 6 45.1**). The orator's claim in 307 that Constantine had been engaged to Fausta from childhood is now exposed as false, but it was clearly a lie worth propagating at the time (Rees 2002: 168–71). The lack of detailed evidence for the marriage of Maxentius to Galerius' daughter Valeria Maximilla frustrates attempts to establish what that alliance might have promised, to Maxentius in particular (**II 6 18.9**); it must have taken place between Maxentius' majority (late 290s) and 304, but which ruling emperors, if any, gave it their blessing is unknown (Cullhed 1994: 16; Leadbetter 1998b: 76). If Maxentius ever enjoyed Galerius' favour, he had certainly lost it by 306 (**see Introduction 3**). His marriage to Valeria Maximilla might suggest that Maxentius was being groomed – or was grooming himself – to succeed. Marriage was clearly a means of cementing a political axis, and following the example of the alliances within the first Tetrarchy, it might have been felt by some to secure and indicate a promise of succession.

According to Lactantius in a passage discussed above, Diocletian had intended dynastic succession in 305, with the appointment of Maxentius and Constantine, but was bullied out of this by Galerius (**II 6 18.2–15; Introduction 3**). This intention can be squared with the fact that Maxentius was passed over for office in 293: at that point Diocletian might have considered the military situation too tense to appoint a young boy Caesar, but have been minded to let Maxentius take office in time. It is perhaps less easy to accommodate the virtual house-arrest the *Anonymous Valesianus* says Constantine experienced under Diocletian and Galerius, unless we assume that in fact Constantine was being trained for office by Diocletian rather than kept from it (**II 5 2.2; 1 40.2**). The problem with highly speculative reconstructions such as this is that they tend to beg more questions than they answer – for example, would Constantius, Maximian and even Constantine himself have been aware of this intention? Was Galerius in any communications loop? Was Maxentius being trained for office in a similar fashion?

Whatever the answers to questions such as these, and whatever the truth of Lactantius' image of Galerius as a man who bullied Diocletian, the fact is that the successions in 305 were not dynastic. In Lactantius' account of that tense meeting, Galerius calls Maximinus Daia his relative (*affinis*); it is likely Galerius was his uncle and that they were related by marriage (**II 18.14**; Barnes 1999). Interestingly, in nominating Maximinus Daia, Galerius overlooked his son Candidianus – why, it is not clear. Perhaps Galerius considered him too young. Conversely, dynasticism was clearly the dominant factor in the proclamation of Constantine by Constantius' troops in July 306; and later in the same year, loyalty to the memory of the retired Maximian is said to have persuaded Severus' troops to abandon their new emperor in favour of Maxentius (**II 2 10.2; 6 26.6–7**). As one might expect, Constantine's panegyrical orators were to cite dynasticism as a means of validating his reign; his relationship with Constantius features several times (e.g. **II 15 14.3**; *Panegyrici Latini* XII(9)4.2–3, IV(10)14.5–6). By contrast, in a speech after Constantine's victory in the battle of the Milvian Bridge in 312, the panegyrical orator voices doubts that Maximian was in fact Maxentius' father (*Panegyrici Latini* XII(9) 3.4, 4.3; **II 4 40.13**; Barnes 1982: 35), a claim whose force relies upon the acceptance of dynastic succession as a sound principle. Most remarkably, a very grand dynastic claim is made in the speech of 310 – that Constantine was descended from the emperor Claudius Gothicus (268–70) (**II 16 2.1–2**; Warmington 1974; Nixon and Rodgers 1994: 219–20). The truth of the claim aside, the speech unequivocally cites birth as the essential qualification for imperial office (**II 16 3.1**). Succession was once again dynastic, and would in essence remain so throughout the fourth century and beyond.

Another short-lived constitutional innovation of Diocletian's was the retirement of the Augusti in 305. He is praised for it in some sources (e.g. **II 1 39.48; 2 9.28**). An orator in 307 speaks of the retirement as a plan agreed by the Augusti (**II 15 9.2**); later, another orator commends Diocletian's commitment to the plan (**II 16 15.4**). Of course, these orators had the benefit of at least a little hindsight, to which they could add their tireless agility in adapting the exemplification of their addressee's greatness to the shifting landscape of contemporary politics. But if their claims are to be treated with suspicion, they need not necessarily be swept aside by Lactantius' alternative version of events in March 305 (**II 6 18.2–3**). Lactantius too had reasons for characterising the emperors in certain ways (Nixon and Rodgers 1994: 188–90). The fact is we have no evidence for a plan to retire that can be securely dated to before 305. Eutropius says that Diocletian retired to Split, and the epitomator includes an image of the retired emperor tending his vegetables there, but both texts were written much later and neither can be adduced as evidence that the retirement was long planned (**II 2 9.27–8; 4 39.5–6**). The palace at Split is thought to have been designed for a retired emperor, and no doubt it took several years to build, but there is no clear evidence for when construction began or finished – it might have been an ongoing process after 305 (Wilkes 1986: 8–10). Similarly the palace complex at Gamzigrad might be thought to have been intended for Galerius' retirement – and yet, he died still in office despite extremely poor health.

If we are to accept the orators' claims that Diocletian and Maximian had planned their retirement, we might assume, in the absence of any evidence anticipating such an unprecedented step, that the decision was kept secret until May 305. This would make particularly good sense if the Augusti were intending to make further non-dynastic appointments as they had in 293, since announcement of the intention would no doubt have precipitated a period of frenzied lobbying and posturing amongst would-be Caesars, as well as dangerous discontent between Maxentius and Constantine. Civil war would have been very likely. But would loyalty to the college have extended so far that Maximian and Constantius, if party to discussions, kept the succession plan secret from their sons who were to be disappointed? On the other hand, the three sources who record that Maximian retired against his own wishes might be thought to confirm that the plan to retire was Diocletian's alone (whether or not it was forced upon him by an aggressive Galerius) and that Diocletian had a hold over Maximian (**II 1 39.48; 2 9.27; 6 26.7**); within eighteen months of his retirement Maximian was back as Augustus, invited by his son, but by this time perhaps, Diocletian was no longer able or maybe willing to influence his former colleague. But the sketchy evidence for a conference at Carnuntum in November 308, attended by Galerius, Licinius, Maximian and Diocletian (who was consul that year despite his retirement three years previously) suggests that Maximian could now once more be cowed by Diocletian (**II 6 29.2**; Creed 1984: 109).

Much as it is absolutely clear that they did retire, it should be obvious from these scenarios that reliable evidence relating to wider issues associated with the retirement of Diocletian and Maximian is minimal. Any modern attempt to construct a plausible narrative for the relevant events and motivations is bound to include hypotheses which cannot be substantiated. Surer footing can probably be found on the question of the *effects* of the retirement of the Augusti. Most significantly, as a precedent it failed to impress any later emperor. Perhaps also of significance were the proclamations of Constantine and Maxentius as emperors in 306, of Domitius Alexander in 308, and of Maximian himself in 308. As a constitutional experiment, it flopped; and if it was designed as an attempt to prevent crises of succession, it was a disaster.

The patchy evidence for the processes of retirement and succession is unusually tolerant of a wide range of interpretations. On a positive side, to have been able to push through such a scheme without open dissent, when in all probability he faced considerable opposition, Diocletian might appear shrewd and immensely persuasive. But from a most unsympathetic angle, if Diocletian's ambition was to introduce non-dynastic succession at the unpublicised time of an emperor's retirement, it can be viewed as an incitement to all and sundry to proclaim themselves emperor whenever they wanted.

## 3. Legitimacy

To succeed, any man who proclaimed himself emperor would have to convince others of his legitimacy. The history of the Roman empire demonstrates that imperial legitimacy was not a stable concept. From the time of Augustus, imperial power had been conferred by a variety of means, including the senate's approval, dynastic succession, and heredity through adoption. Diocletian, possibly of servile origins, himself came to power in 284 through none of these means, but followed the principle example of the previous few decades when he became emperor by nomination by the army (**II 2 9.19; 4 39.1**); by the time he retired in 305 he was clearly recognised as a legitimate emperor although he eschewed (or renounced) dynastic succession, be it natural or through adoption, and appears not to have courted the senate. There were many means by which Diocletian's legitimacy would have been impressed on the empire: these include his success in battles, his self-presentation through ceremonial, and his reputation as a judge and administrator (**Chapters 1–4**). All these factors could be interpreted as signs of the favour of the gods, a useful claim in an attempt to assert legitimacy. Another notable advantage for Diocletian would have been the length of his reign – the longer he ruled and the stronger his grip became on the reins of command, the more his power will have seemed natural and appropriate. It is important to note that the way imperial status was conferred on Maximian in 285, Constantius and Galerius in 293, and Severus and Maximinus Daia in 305 was by nomination by Diocletian. That is, Diocletian had the power to make emperors, a powerful indication of his legitimacy and theirs. But there were others claiming themselves emperors in these years, all recognised to an extent, but not by Diocletian (Barnes 1982: 10–16). Questions of status and legitimacy were more complicated after 305, with the proclamation of Constantine, Maxentius and Maximian (and others e.g. **II 4 40.1–2**). How men tried to claim imperial power, especially in relation to the Dyarchic and Tetrarchic governments, and how their claims were received and why, are questions which do not always yield clear answers but do shed light on the nature of imperial government in these decades.

Literary sources for the reign of Carausius (c. 286–93) and that of his assassin and successor Allectus (293–6) are very meagre (e.g. **II 1 39.20–1, 39–42; 2 9.21–2**): a surviving panegyric includes a narrative of the reconquest of Britain in 296 (**II 13**; Eichholz 1953). From the areas under the control of Carausius and Allectus themselves there is little; some archaeology from the Saxon Shore can be dated to Carausius' reign (**Chapter 1.4**), and some scraps of epigraphy survive, but the most revealing medium is coinage (Casey 1994: 12). Between them, these sources allow a tentative reconstruction of Carausius' attempts to assert his legitimacy and the reaction of the Dyarchs Diocletian and Maximian.

Carausius had been an officer charged to clear the English Channel of pirates, and when he seized power in Britain and northern Gaul he took very considerable resources with him. The Dyarchy had existed for only one or two years, and although Maximian had already crushed one rebellion in Gaul in that time, perhaps Carausius felt that as a successful and powerful military commander, his claims to legitimate rule were as valid as those of Diocletian and Maximian. The Dyarchs' response was to prepare a fleet and attack, but the expedition failed (Nixon and Rodgers 1994: 106–8); a treaty was signed, and Carausius advertised the peace on a coin dated to 290–2 (**II 44**). The obverse shows three emperors in profile, with the legend CARAUSIUS ET FRATRES SUI ('Carausius and his brothers'); the reverse legend reads PAX AUGGG ('The peace of the Augusti') with the triple termination G indicating that there were three Augusti. Not only is this coin promoting the idea of a 'Tryarchy', it is also borrowing the fraternity imagery which was used in contemporary Dyarchic panegyrics (**see above, 1**). Another Carausian coin legend AUGUSTIS CUM DIOCLETIANO ('To the Augusti with Diocletian') indicates his recognition of the seniority of Diocletian (Rees 2002: 33).

But if a peace was concluded, the Dyarchs seem not to have intended to observe it for long; no evidence suggests that Carausius' assertion of a united government of three emperors was reciprocated, and the panegyrics to Maximian in 289 and 291 make no attempt to accommodate Carausius (**II 11, 12**; Rees 2002: 91–2). It has also been suggested that the expansion of the central imperial college into Tetrarchy in 293 was motivated in part by the desire to crush Carausius/Allectus (Casey 1994: 110); the defeat of Allectus was celebrated with the assumption by all four Tetrarchs of the victory title *Brittanicus maximus* and the issue of triumphal medallions (e.g. **II 19, 45**).

Carausius had in many ways behaved like a Roman emperor: he had led an army, minted coins, constructed buildings, and proclaimed himself consul (Casey 1994: 58); further, he had been sensitive to the collegiality of the government. But despite these features, and the fact that his army would offer stubborn resistance, Carausius had not been able to persuade Diocletian and Maximian to acknowledge his legitimacy. Although he was a successful soldier, he did not share the Dyarchs' Balkan origins; Diocletian and Maximian had not witnessed him at close quarters, as praetorian prefect and/or son-in-law, unlike the situation with Constantius and Galerius. Perhaps they felt that after his initial coup, he could never really be trusted; or that recognition of his legitimacy would encourage others to seek imperial office by force. We do not know that Carausius would not have been a sound and loyal member of the imperial college if he had been given the chance; the fact that he was not given the chance might reveal more about Diocletian than it does about him.

The other man whose claims to imperial legitimacy were not accepted despite a tenacious hold on a fair degree of power was Maxentius. If he based any hopes for appointment as emperor on his father Maximian's position, they were disappointed twice, in 293 and 305. He took power in Rome in October 306, a few months after Constantine had been proclaimed emperor by Constantius' troops. The sources for his reign include literary accounts, coins and archaeology (e.g. II 1 40.5–24; 2 10.2–4; 4 40.2–7; 6 26.2–44.9; 42). Some sources suggest that his coup at Rome was fuelled by local discontent with new taxes; it is also quite possible that he was inspired by Constantine's recent rise to power.

The position Maxentius claimed for himself was *princeps*, an ancient title and not one used by the Tetrarchy; this situation might have been intended as a temporary one until Galerius conferred the title of Augustus or Caesar on him, as he had done for Constantine; or it might have been a deliberately aggressive anti-Tetrarchic statement by Maxentius (Cullhed 1994: 33). Some of his coins gave prominence to traditional Roman icons and themes, such as the wolf suckling Romulus and Remus; in the heart of the city Maxentius built a large basilica and an elaborate temple to Venus and Roma (**II 42**). Propaganda moves such as these suggest that Maxentius was keen to appeal to the city of Rome and its traditions – a policy which might not have been thought to chime with Tetrarchic practice (**Chapter 2.2**). Furthermore, he invited his father out of retirement to join him in office; in doing so he was claiming the right to make emperors himself, regardless it seems of the Tetrarchs. Maxentius did not ignore the other emperors, but he seems to have been selective: he minted coins from Rome in his own name, and also to Maximian, Constantine and Maximinus Daia, but not to Severus, whom he soon faced in battle, Galerius who ordered Severus to attack, or Licinius (*R.I.C.* 6). Galerius, however, was one of the entries in the consular list at Rome in 307, a fact which might be best explained as a conciliatory gesture initiated by Maximian, by then at Rome with his son (Cullhed 1994: 34–8).

It seems likely from the changing picture of Maxentius' propaganda and diplomacy that he was not simply seeking to join the imperial college as Carausius appears to have been. Many of his measures can be seen as unTetrarchic; but at the same time he seems not to have been determinedly uncollegiate. His claims to legitimacy appear to have been based on a combination of dynastic succession from Maximian, the approval of the people, senate and praetorian guard at Rome, and good relations with some of the other emperors, some of the time. He had resources to hand, and was able to mint money. He was the son of one emperor (Maximian), the son-in-law of another (Galerius) and from September 307 the brother-in-law to a third (Constantine), and he enjoyed the support and considerable defensive security of the ancient capital; but he fell out with all of these emperors and foolishly came outside the city walls for his final showdown with Constantine in 312. Perhaps Maxentius was guilty of a series of poor decisions; but maybe it was unfortunate for him that these other emperors were not on the best of terms themselves, and as their relationships changed, so inevitably did his standing.

Constantine's career provides notable contrast. In certain ways, his prospects after the creation of the 'Second' Tetrarchy in 305 were poorer than Maxentius', or Carausius' in 287: Constantine had not been appointed emperor, he was being watched with suspicion, and he had no army or money at his disposal. Within eight years he and his colleague Licinius ruled the empire; later he was sole emperor. Sources generally agree that a dramatic series of events saw Constantine proclaimed emperor after Constantius' death in York in July 306 (e.g. II 1 40.4; 2 10.2; 5 2.4; 6 24.3–25.5); there is also a consensus that he was proclaimed Augustus by Constantius' troops, but accepted the position of Caesar which Galerius offered him within a reconstituted 'Second' Tetrarchy (Barnes 1982: 5). This is usually interpreted as an early mark of Constantine's sensible diplomacy rather than sincere abasement. Certainly Constantine's coinage as Caesar in 306–7 makes interesting comparison with his later issues: in legend and type, a Tetrarchic character has been identified in his earlier issues, to be replaced in time with a very different message (Sutherland 1956; *R.I.C.* 6; Bruun 1976).

But as well as conforming to Galerius' will to have him take his allotted place in a Tetrarchic college, Constantine did not reject other alliances which could be of use to him, such as marriage to Maximian's daughter Fausta (II 15; Warmington 1974; Rodgers 1989). Even if he entered into a period of cold war with Galerius, he was to develop a good working relationship with Licinius, Galerius' appointee after Severus' death. Perhaps Constantine benefited from some good fortune where Maxentius was unlucky; or perhaps he had a rare capacity to judge when a particular diplomatic position could be of use to him, and a ruthless streak when he felt that usefulness was past. Certainly he seems to have been prepared to adopt a more conciliatory tone at times than Maxentius was, and to have been able to persuade others of the strength of his position. Constantine's successful rise from a position of relative weakness demonstrates that imperial legitimacy was a mercurial quality, the product of the practical ability to command and implement the traditional resources and machinery of government (such as mints, armies and administration) and success in persuading others that this was appropriate (through propaganda and diplomacy). Thus legitimacy was not so much a statement of facts as an argument.

# Conclusion

## 1. Diocletian

Despite the very considerable range of evidence relating to him, his government and society, Diocletian remains enigmatic. In the extremes of the panegyrical oratory and Christian polemic of antiquity, evaluations of his government were closely – even causally – linked to consideration of Diocletian's character, but modern analysis tends to stop far short of such an explicitly moralising conception of leadership. Besides, given that imperial rescripts and edicts were penned by others in the emperor's name, and that we do not know enough about the means of production of media such as coins and sculpture to be sure of an emperor's level of input, it can be difficult to see the man through the sources. We do not even know when he was born or when or how he died. Perhaps it is because Diocletian is at once elusive and captivating that the only modern biography of him is a fictional poem (Higham 1995). This cannot be attributed solely to the relative dip in the popularity of the biographic form in academic ancient history today – rather, there are too many gaps in what can be known about Diocletian's motivation, policies and ambitions to allow a continuous narrative of his personal and political life to be written which is anything other than highly speculative. On the question of his death, for example, there are variant accounts: Lactantius claims Diocletian starved himself for grief that his reign had not been appreciated (**II 6 42.1–3**); the anonymous epitomator speaks of suicide by poison, prompted by fear of Constantine and Licinius (**II 4 39.7**); Eusebius writes of a fatal condition (**II 8 8.Appendix 3**); Aurelius Victor makes no mention of Diocletian's end at all; and Eutropius gives no details, but speaks of his death and deification in terms which suggest neither suicide nor illness (**II 2 9.28**). There can be no compromise between the various sources, and the reliability of each can be challenged on some ground or another (Barnes 1982: 31–2); but in particular, if either of the accounts of his

86

suicide were to be favoured, there would be significant implications for appreciation of wider politics.

And so it is for much of the evidence relating to Diocletian: exegesis of specific details is immediately controversial and vulnerable. What can be said with confidence is that details of Diocletian's private life were little known even in his own lifetime. Certainly, few will now feel as free as Gibbon did in the eighteenth century to pen a detailed character profile of Diocletian:

His abilities were useful rather than splendid – a vigorous mind improved by the experience and study of mankind; dexterity and application in business; a judicious mixture of liberality and economy, of mildness and rigour; profound dissimulation under the disguise of military frankness; steadiness to pursue his ends; flexibility to vary his means; and, above all, the great art of submitting his own passions, as well as those of others, to the interest of his ambition, and of colouring his ambition with the most specious pretences of justice and public utility. (**Chapter 13**)

It is noteworthy that this portrait is consciously shot through with paradoxes, as if seeking to balance some polarised sources, but who is more revealed, Diocletian or Gibbon?

## 2. Government

An alternative approach to the biographic method, which also attempts to encapsulate Diocletian's achievement, is one which compares the Roman empire as Diocletian inherited it in 284 with the legacy that he left for his successors. Conspicuous in this model is the characterisation of the mid-third century as a time of crisis, particularly in constitutional, military and economic affairs (Jones 1964: 35; Alföldy 1974); against this is set the raft of initiatives under Diocletian, especially of course in the same areas of the constitution, defence and the economy. Positive language dominates, as policies are cast as 'reforms', changes as 'recovery'. Examples of this exercise in large-scale historical comparison tend to present Diocletian's government as successful – its economic measures well-intended if misplaced, the persecution of Christians a regrettable aberration, but the consolidation of the frontiers, the reorganisation of administrative machinery and the introduction of rational fiscal policy responsible for a welcome stability which would long outlive the Tetrarchs themselves (e.g. *C.A.H.* xii; Williams 1985). If this interpretation shares much of the tone (if little of the detail) of original Dyarchic and Tetrarchic panegyric, it stands in obvious contrast to the contemporary viewpoints of Lactantius and Eusebius, who present the Tetrarchic period as a time of escalating misery, out of which the Christian Constantine could emerge triumphant.

However, if the model of a third-century crisis is challenged, then some of the force of the characterisation of Diocletian as the empire's saviour figure can be diluted. There were clearly some endemic problems in leadership, with a proliferation of emperors, but greater attention to regional variety in economic patterns, for example, suggests that the impression some sources give of an empire-wide crisis is exaggerated (Cameron 1993: 3–12; Rathbone 1996). At the same time, there has been an increasing tendency to see in Diocletian's empire something of its predecessors; aspects of Tetrarchic government culture and policy, such as court ceremonial, collegiate rule, the use of military personnel, the itinerant emperor away from Rome and the persecution of Christians might all be seen to have had major precedents in the third century. Perhaps these features were treated with new urgency and determination under Diocletian – comparison of their extent across different reigns is likely to be difficult, given how short-lived most emperors were in the third century, but the argument is taking shape in tandem with a re-evaluation of that period, that many Tetrarchic measures are better explained as a codification or intensification of recent or existing practice than as innovation. As such, although Diocletian's empire is regularly termed 'new', it might seem little to represent a radical break with the past.

In many ways, the fifty or so years from Diocletian's accession to Constantine's death can also be seen as a continuity. Sources such as the *Notitia Dignitatum* and archaeology do not always allow precise distinction between the Diocletianic and Constantinian periods, but in fundamental aspects of administration, military and economics, the measures across these decades now seen more a unity than was ever acknowledged by Christian sources, keen to differentiate the persecutor of the church from its champion, or Constantine's panegyrical orators, determinedly celebrating his legitimacy in a way which sets him apart from the Tetrarchs (Jones 1964; Barnes 1982; Corcoran 1996, 2000[2]). In this sense, the decisiveness, extent and date of Constantine's break with the Tetrarchy remain open questions.

Looking beyond his understandably wretched reputation with Christian sources, it is remarkable how enduring many of Diocletian's reforms were, as sources such as the Justinianic Code (**II 30**), the *Verona List* (**II 27**) and the *Notitia Dignitatum* (**II 25**) testify. But his experimentation in government failed – no matter the date at which the

'Second' Tetrarchy is deemed to have dissolved, there can be little doubt that that form of government hardly survived one generation. Certain aspects of unity and succession can be posited as likely reasons for this (**Chapter 6**); what unity there was in the 'First' Tetrarchy might well not have survived the peculiar process of succession in 305. The Roman world was not ready – nor ever would be – for a decisive break with the tradition of dynastic succession. Was Diocletian bullied by Galerius out of an intention to appoint emperors' sons as new emperors? If that was not his intention, was he culpably unrealistic in thinking a new system of succession would work?

Related to the failure of the experiment in Tetrarchic government is the question of how it ever managed to survive as long as it did. There are several testimonies and hypotheses that suggest that the imperial college was far from united. How collegiate can the government have been if Maximian insisted on being promoted to the rank of Augustus, if there was no enthusiasm in the college for the Edict of Maximal Prices, if Constantius ignored the order to punish Christians, if Galerius forced Diocletian to retire? Was the force of Diocletian's personality the glue which held the 'First' Tetrarchy together? Or was the Tetrarchy actually a very fragile alliance whose *concordia* was a myth carved in porphyry?

At times, the neatness and harmony of this government of four have been urged by scholars; welcoming the implications of propaganda such as the Venice porphyry and other media such as panegyrical oratory, this school proposes a Tetrarchic *system* of power-sharing, delegation and succession, and identifies in Diocletian a calculating and visionary leader. More recently, alternative readings have emerged which generally ignore any ideological boasts and focus instead on the practical machinery and effects of Tetrarchic government: here, in regional varieties and problems and contradictions in source material, there can be found details which might suggest a powerful tendency in the government to improvise and compromise. According to this view, the whole concept of a *system* is better replaced by a vision of a make-shift alliance of affiliated emperors, each able and willing to negotiate in certain areas, but in others sometimes determinedly individualistic.

## 3. Society

Details of defining influences, lasting legacies and government ideologies will continue to be debated, no doubt, but given the unusual range of sources for Diocletian's reign, it is tempting to try to create a composite image of life at the time. Inevitably, such a snapshot is contrived, perhaps even to the point of artificiality, so it will not meet with universal agreement.

Under Diocletian, there was now a conspicuously bigger army; most importantly, barbarian invasions were stopped and frontiers were pacified (**Chapter 1**). Civil uprisings were crushed ruthlessly and as quickly as possible, indicating further the government's desire to maintain the empire's integrity (**Chapters 1 and 6**). In addition to the peace it brought or imposed, in terms of recruitment, *annona* and cash taxation demands, and no doubt occasional billeting, this increased army would have had a distinct impact on Tetrarchic society (**Chapters 1 and 3**). At the same time, the beginnings of a move towards a separation of military and civilian command structures might have reduced the incidence of ruthless requisitioning under the guise of tax collection (**Chapters 2 and 3**).

There was an increase in bureaucracy and bureaucrats, with the central and local governments gathering more information about the empire's resources and issuing demands accordingly (**Chapters 2 and 3**). For the middle classes and above, social status and hierarchies were very clearly defined in several ways (**Chapters 2 and 4**). Law was the primary vehicle for religious, economic and fiscal policies; legal redress was available too (**Chapters 2, 3 and 5**). Evasion of responsibilities and lack of compliance were possible and rife, and no doubt too some people were the unlucky victims of over-zealous officials (**Chapters 2, 3 and 5**).

The Tetrarchy seems to have been a government of high profile and enormous ambition. It was by design an interventionist regime, prominent in its influence on local government administration; in taxation and legislation; in propaganda; in monetary policy; in defence; in its provincial capitals; even in the culture of the itinerant emperor. It did not achieve all of its goals, and in this respect, might be considered somewhat unrealistic or even naïve – but what government ever has realised all of its ambitions? Of course, for the citizen body, there was considerable variety across the empire, and even from one individual to another; to have been a committed Christian of low birth in the Oriens diocese under Maximinus Daia would have been a very different experience from that of a loyal military veteran in Gaul, or a scribe in Panopolis, and so on, but the large number of changes and policies under Diocletian will have impacted on a very significant percentage of the empire's population. Whether or not it was for their own good, or even if they liked it, are questions that cannot be considered here.

# Part II

# Documents

*Part II consists of source material of various types. To facilitate cross referencing from Part I, each source has been numbered. A little information about each source is given and, where appropriate, an explanation of the specific reference system is provided.*

## 1. Sextus Aurelius Victor: *Book of the Caesars* (c. 361)
Translated from Latin. This selection begins
at Chapter 39 (**I Introduction 1**)

[39.1] But after the murder of the emperor Numerian was betrayed by the smell of his rotting body, at a council of generals and tribunes the commander of the household troops, Valerius Diocletian, was elected for his wisdom. He was a great man, but with the following habits: [2] he was the first to want a robe woven with gold, and sandals with plenty of silk, purple and jewels; [3] although this exceeded humility and revealed a swollen and extravagant mind, it was nothing compared to the rest, [4] for he was the first of all emperors after Caligula and Domitian to allow himself to be called 'master' in public, to be worshipped and addressed as a god. ... [8] But these faults in Valerius [Diocletian] were covered over by other good qualities: in this very matter – that he allowed himself to be called 'master' – he behaved as a parent; and it is reasonably clear that this wise man wanted to demonstrate that severity of circumstance rather than of titles caused harm. ... [11] But when Carinus reached Moesia, immediately he met Diocletian in battle at the River Margus; while he eagerly pursued the defeated, he was killed by his own men because with uncontrollable lust he used to seduce the wives of many of them. ... [13] Therefore in his first address to the army, as he looked to the sun with his sword drawn and swore that he had known nothing of the plot against Numerian and that he had not wanted power, Valerius [Diocletian] stabbed Aper as he stood next to him. [14] The rest were pardoned and nearly all the enemy were kept on, in particular on account of his services an outstanding man called Aristobulus, the praetorian prefect. ...

[17] After the death of Carinus, Diocletian discovered that in Gaul Helianus and Amandus had roused a force of peasants and bandits (known to the inhabitants as Bagaudae), and with much of the countryside ravaged, had taken hold of many cities; Diocletian immediately appointed his trusted friend Maximian emperor, a good soldier and talented, although he was semi-civilised. [18] Later he took the name Herculius from the cult of the god, as Valerius [Diocletian] took the name Jovius; from here the name was even given to the auxiliary units

93

which were pre-eminent in the army. [19] [Maximian] Herculius set out to Gaul where he routed or captured the enemy and had calmed everything in no time. [20] For his very resolute actions in this battle, Carausius a Menapian citizen, stood out; for this, and at the same time because he was held to be an experienced helmsman (he had plied this trade as a youth), they appointed him to prepare a fleet and drive out the Germans who were terrorising the seas. [21] Carausius was lifted by this, and when he was crushing many barbarians but failing to hand over all the booty to the treasury, through fear of [Maximian] Herculius, by whom he discovered his own assassination had been ordered, he weakened the empire's resources and took over Britain.

[22] At the same time, the Persians were causing serious trouble in the east, Julianus and the Quinquegentiani peoples in Africa. [23] A man called Achilleus had yet assumed the insignia of absolute control in Egyptian Alexandria. [24] For these reasons, Diocletian and Maximian appointed as Caesars Julius Constantius and Galerius Maximian (whose surname was Armentarius). Marriage alliances were made [25]: with their former wives divorced, Constantius married the daughter-in-law of [Maximian] Herculius; Galerius married Diocletian's daughter. ... [26] In fact all these men came from Illyricum; although they knew too little refinement, however, because they were sufficiently versed in the miseries of the countryside and military service, they were the best men for the state. ... [28] The harmony of these men made it absolutely clear that character and good military experience, such as had been set as a precedent for them by Aurelian and Probus, is almost enough for virtue. [29] Finally, they used to admire [Diocletian] Valerius like a father or a mighty god; from the foundation of the city up to our own times, the crimes of relatives have revealed the extent and nature of this issue. [30] And because the mass of wars which I mentioned above was pressing more urgently, the empire was divided into four, and all of Gaul beyond the Alps was entrusted to Constantius, Africa and Italy to [Maximian] Herculius, the coast of Illyricum right up to the straits of the Black Sea to Galerius, and the rest to [Diocletian] Valerius.

[31] From this then, the great evil of taxation was imposed upon part of Italy. For although all Italy used to pay the same reasonable tribute to support the army and emperor, who were always or generally there, a new law for payments was passed. ... [33] Meanwhile [Diocletian] Jovius set out for Alexandria entrusting his own territory to the Caesar [Galerius] Maximian so that he could cross the frontier and advance into Mesopotamia to ward off the Persian incursions. [34] At first Galerius was seriously troubled by the Persians; he quickly assembled an

army from veterans and recruits and rushed towards the enemy through Armenia, which is almost the sole, or the easier route to victory. [35] There he finally brought king Narses under his sway, together with his children and wives and the royal court. [36] Such was the victory that unless [Diocletian] Valerius, by whose nod everything was controlled, had not refused (it is unclear why), the Roman *fasces* would be carried in a new province. [37] However, some territories of reasonable use to us were acquired. ... [38] But negotiations in Egypt easily overcame Achilleus and he paid the penalty. [39] Matters were completed in a similar way in Africa, and only Carausius' control over the island [of Britain] was conceded, after he was thought to be better suited to govern the inhabitants and defend them against hostile peoples. [40] In fact, six years later, a man called Allectus overcame him in a plot; [41] with Carausius' permission he was in charge of the treasury, but in fear for his life because of his offences, he had seized power by a crime. [42] He exercised this power briefly, until he was destroyed by Constantius who sent his praetorian prefect Asclepiodotus in advance, with some of the fleet and legions. [43] And meanwhile the Marcomanni were slaughtered and all the Carpi people were transferred to our lands – some of them had been there since Aurelius' time. [44] With no less enthusiasm, the most equitable laws bound the administration of peace and the pernicious position of *frumentarius* was abolished. ... [45] At the same time, the cities' corn-supply and the taxpayers' wellbeing were maintained with care and attention, and with the promotion of more respectable men and, by contrast, the punishment of criminals, eagerness for virtuousness was growing. The oldest cults were practised most chastely and, in an amazing way, the hilltops of Rome and other cities, especially Carthage, Milan and Nicomedia, were ornamented with novel and beautiful buildings. [46] However, despite these achievements, the emperors were not faultless. Indeed, [Maximian] Herculius' lust was such that he could not even keep his sick mind from the bodies of hostages; through fear of discord, [Diocletian] Valerius certainly had too little honest faith in his allies, because he thought the harmony of the partnership could be unsettled by disclosures. [47] For this reason too, Rome's forces were truncated, as it were, by a reduction in the number of praetorian cohorts and citizens bearing arms; indeed, many maintain that for this reason he resigned his rule. [48] For Diocletian investigated future events, and when he discovered that civil disaster was fated and a certain fracture, as it were, of the Roman state was looming, he celebrated the twentieth anniversary of his reign in decent health, and gave up his control of the state, when he had talked round to his opinion [Maximian] Herculius, who was most reluctant and had been in office for one year fewer. And although regard for truth is corrupted amongst the variety of opinions, however it seems to me that he moved down to ordinary life because in his excellent nature he spurned ambition.

[40.1] And so, when Constantius and [Galerius] Armentarius succeeded them, Severus and Maximinus, Illyrican natives, were appointed Caesars; Severus to Italy and Maximinus to the territories which [Diocletian] Jovius had held. [2] Constantine, whose able and ambitious mind was agitated from childhood on with a desire to rule, could not bear this; for under the pretext of a religious scruple, Galerius was holding him as a hostage. Having contrived an escape, Constantine reached Britain after he had killed the post-horses he had used on his journey, to frustrate his pursuers. [3] At that same time and place, his father Constantius was near his life's end. [4] On his death, with all those present urging him, Constantine assumed power. [5] Meanwhile at Rome, the crowd and the praetorian units proclaimed Maxentius emperor, although his father [Maximian] Herculius hesitated for a long time. [6] When [Galerius] Armentarius heard this, he quickly ordered the Caesar Severus, who happened to be near the city, to attack the enemy. [7] As he drew up around the walls, Severus was deserted by his men, who were seduced by the lure of Maxentius' rewards, and he fled to Ravenna where he died in a siege. [8] Galerius was more fierce at this, and having consulted [Diocletian] Jovius in a meeting, he appointed as Augustus, Licinius, a friend of long standing. Galerius left Licinius to protect Illyricum and Thrace, and hurried to Rome. [9] When he was detained there by the siege, the loyalty of his troops was tested by the same method as their predecessors, and fearing that he would be deserted, he departed Italy; he died from an infected wound a little later, after he had made land in Pannonia useful to the state by felling huge forests and channelling Lake Pelso into the Danube; [10] for this reason, he named the province Valeria after his wife. [11] His reign lasted five years, Constantius' one, although each of them of course as Caesar had exercised power for thirteen years. [12] Their natural abilities were so amazing that they would certainly have been thought outstanding if they came from educated minds without offensive taste. [13] Therefore we know that learning, elegance and charm are especially necessary in emperors, since without them they may be despised as if unrefined or even uncouth. ... [16] When Constantine learned that Rome and Italy were being ruined and the armies with two emperors had been driven out or bought off, he settled peace throughout Gaul and made for

Maxentius. [17] At that time, Alexander, the deputy-prefect at Carthage, had usurped power stupidly, since he was frail in age and more foolish than his Pannonian peasant parents and had armed barely half of the troops he had recruited in a rush. [18] Finally the tyrant [Maxentius] sent the praetorian prefect Rufius Volusianus and some generals with very few cohorts and they destroyed Alexander in a light battle. [19] At his defeat, wild, inhuman and more foul for his great lust, Maxentius had given the order to devastate, pillage and burn Carthage, the glory of the earth, together with the more beautiful parts of Africa. [20] Still an unwarlike coward, he was so shamefully prone to idleness that when war was raging through Italy and his own men were routed at Verona, he behaved no less lazily than usual, and was unmoved by his father's death. [21] For [Maximian] Herculius was headstrong by nature, and at the same time through fear of his son's laziness, had unwisely sought to regain power. [22] Finally he had met a deserved end when in an organised plot he made a violent attempt on his son-in-law Constantine while pretending to offer help. [23] But Maxentius, who was getting more violent by the day, finally came out very reluctantly from Rome about nine miles to the Saxa Rubra; with his frontline slaughtered he took himself back to Rome in flight. As he crossed the Tiber he was cut off by the very ambush he had set for his enemy on the Milvian Bridge; it was the sixth year of his tyranny. [24] It was incredible how joyously and delightedly the senate and people exulted in his death; he had beset them so much that once he had assented to the praetorians' slaughter of the people, and in a most terrible decree he was the first to force the senators and farmers to contribute money for his own indulgence, pretending it was a tax. [25] With the contempt of these people, the praetorian legions and auxiliary units, more suited to factions than to the city of Rome, were completely abolished, together with the use of weapons and military uniforms. [26] Furthermore, the senate dedicated to the deserving Flavius [Constantine] all the magnificent buildings which Maxentius had constructed, the temple of the city and the basilica.

[41.1] While this occurred in Italy, after two years as Augustus in the east, Maximinus, routed and forced to flee by Licinius, died at Tarsus. [2] And so, control over the Roman world lay with two men [Constantine and Licinius].

## 2. Eutropius: *Breviarium* (c. 369)
The original, written in ten books, is in Latin
(I Introduction 1)

[9.19] Carus Augustus had been lost to a lightning strike, and Numerian Caesar to a plot. As the soldiers returned victorious from Persia, they made Diocletian emperor, a man originating from such an obscure birth in Dalmatia that most people think he was the son of a scribe, and some the freedman of the senator Anullinus. [20] At the first gathering of the troops, Diocletian swore that Numerian had not been killed by any treachery of his; and in full view of the troops, Diocletian plunged his sword through Aper, who had committed the ambush. Later, in a great battle at Margus, he defeated Carinus who was despised by everyone, betrayed by his own army (even though it was superior in number), and was in fact deserted between Viminacium and Mt Aureus. Thus Diocletian took control of the empire.

When peasants in Gaul had staged an uprising, given the name Bagaudae to their faction, and claimed Amandus and Aelianus as their leaders, Diocletian appointed Maximian Herculius Caesar and sent him to crush them. Maximian tamed the peasants in light engagements, and re-established peace in Gaul.

[21] At this time, Carausius, of very low birth, had gained an outstanding reputation in a vigorous military career. He had received orders at Boulogne to clear the stretch of sea off Belgica and Armorica of dangerous Franks and Saxons. When he had taken frequent barbarian prisoners but returned the booty intact neither to the provincials nor to the emperors, it was suspected he was admitting barbarians by design so that he could catch them as they crossed with their booty and take the chance to enrich himself. Maximian ordered his execution, but Carausius assumed the purple and took over Britain. [22] And so, the whole world was in crisis: Carausius was rebelling in Britain and Achilleus in Egypt; the Quinquegentiani were attacking Africa, and Narses was making war in the east. Diocletian promoted Maximian Herculius to Augustus from Caesar, and appointed as Caesars Constantius and Maximian [Galerius]. Constantius is said to have been the grandson of Claudius II by his daughter; Maximian Galerius was born near Serdica in Dacia. In order to be bound by marriage, the two were forced to divorce their wives, and Constantius married Theodora, the step-daughter of [Maximian] Herculius, who gave birth to six children, the brothers of Constantine; Galerius married Valeria, the daughter of Diocletian. War was tried in vain against

Carausius, who was a very experienced soldier, and finally a peace was concluded. After seven years, Carausius' ally Allectus killed him and himself held Britain for three years. With the praetorian prefect Asclepiodotus in command, Allectus was crushed and Britain was recovered after ten years.

[23] At the same time, Constantius fought with success in Gaul. On one day near Langres, he had bad and good luck: for a sudden barbarian attack forced a retreat into the city with such urgency that the gates were shut and he was lifted onto the wall by ropes; but when his army advanced, he killed nearly sixty thousand Alamanni in barely five hours. Maximian Augustus ended the war in Africa by overcoming the Quinquegentiani and reducing them to peace. Diocletian set siege to Achilleus in Alexandria, and after about eight months he defeated and killed him. He exploited his victory harshly; he disfigured all of Egypt with severe proscriptions and slaughter. However, on that occasion, he organised many sensible regulations which survive to our own day.

[24] Galerius Maximian was unsuccessful in his first battle with Narses, between Callinicum and Carrhae, although more for lack of counsel than for cowardice, since he committed to battle against a very large enemy when his own force was quite small. Defeated he set off to join Diocletian. When he met him en route he is said to have been received with such insolence by Diocletian that he ran beside Diocletian's chariot for several miles in his purple. [25] Soon, however, when he had gathered troops throughout Illyricum and Moesia, Galerius fought again with Narses the grandfather of Hormisdas and Sapor, in Greater Armenia; he had great success, with more planning, and courage at the same time, since with one or two cavalrymen he even undertook the responsibility of scouting. When Narses had been driven back, Galerius seized his camp, captured his wives, sisters and children, besides countless of the Persian nobility and a very rich store of Persian treasure; he forced Narses himself back into the furthest wildernesses of his kingdom. And so, Galerius went back in triumph to Diocletian who was at that time waiting in Mesopotamia with reinforcements, and he was received with great honour. Then together and separately they fought wars against the Carpi and Bastarnae, when the Sarmatians were subdued and beaten, and they settled countless numbers of prisoners from these nations inside the Roman frontiers.

[26] Diocletian was cunning by nature, shrewd as well, and of a very subtle brain. He was willing to account for his own severity with the unpopularity of others. However, he was a most hardworking and able emperor. He was the first to introduce to the Roman empire the

apparatus of regal custom rather than Roman liberty, and he demanded
that he be worshipped, where all previous emperors had been greeted.
He ornamented his clothes and shoes with jewellery, where before the
badge of imperial office was only the purple robe and everything else
was ordinary.

[27] On the other hand, [Maximian] Herculius was openly wild and
uncivilised in character – even the horror of his expression revealed his
fierceness. Indulging his own nature, he followed Diocletian in all his
more savage measures. But when Diocletian was weakened by age
and considered himself unsuitable to manage the empire, he persuaded
[Maximian] Herculius that they should retire to private life and hand
over the responsibility of protecting the state to stronger and younger
men; his colleague obeyed reluctantly. Nevertheless, after they had
celebrated at Rome a famous triumph over many nations, with an
distinguished procession of booty, and the wives, sisters and children of
Narses led in front of the chariot, both men exchanged the insignia
of imperial office for private dress on the same day – Diocletian at
Nicomedia, [Maximian] Herculius at Milan. They retired, one to Split,
the other to Lucania.

[28] After his retirement, Diocletian grew old amid notable peace in
his villa, not far from Split. He had shown extraordinary virtue, since he
alone of all emperors since the foundation of the empire had returned
of his own accord from such high office to private life and civilian
status. Therefore, his enrolment amongst the gods after his death in
private life is a unique achievement in the history of mankind.

[10.1] Therefore, when Diocletian and Maximian had retired from
administrating the state, Constantius and Galerius became the Augusti,
and the Roman world was split between them so that Constantius
received the Gallic provinces, Italy and Africa, Galerius Illyricum, Asia
and the east, and two men were appointed Caesar. But Constantius was
content with the position of Augustus and declined the responsibility
of administrating Italy and Africa; an outstanding man, exceptional in
humility, he was concerned for the wealth of provincials and private
people, not thinking only of the treasury's interests; he used to say that
the state's money was better held by private individuals than within one
vault. However, his habits were so moderate that if he had to entertain
his many friends with dinner on a public holiday, his dining room
would be laid with the silverware of private citizens he had borrowed by
going from door to door. Not only was this man sociable, he was even
venerated by the Gauls in particular because in his reign they had
avoided the suspect prudence of Diocletian and the bloodthirsty rash-

ness of Maximian. Constantius died at York in Britain in the thirteenth year of his reign and he was enrolled among the gods.

[2] Galerius was an honest man by nature and outstanding in military affairs. When he realised that Constantius had allowed him to administrate Italy as well, he appointed two Caesars: he put Maximinus in charge of the east, and Severus Italy. Himself he stayed in Illyricum. But when Constantius died, Constantine his son from a rather insignificant marriage was made emperor in Britain and he succeeded his father as a most popular leader. Meanwhile in Rome the praetorians incited an uprising and proclaimed as Augustus Maxentius, the son of [Maximian] Herculius, who was spending some time in a public villa near Rome. This announcement inspired [Maximian] Herculius to hope to resume the high office he had resigned against his will; he rushed to Rome from Lucania, a place in the most idyllic countryside he had chosen to grow old in after retirement. He even wrote to Diocletian, encouraging him to take up again the power he had resigned; the letter had no effect on him. The Caesar Severus was sent to Rome with an army by Galerius to counter the uprising by the praetorians and Maxentius; as he besieged the city he was deserted by his treacherous troops, and Maxentius increased his wealth and confirmed his rule. Severus fled and was killed at Ravenna.

[3] However, after this, at an assembly of the troops, [Maximian] Herculius tried to strip his son Maxentius of the purple, but he brought upon himself the resistance and protests of the soldiers. From Rome he set out for Gaul with the deception planned that he had been expelled by his son, so that he could ally with Constantine by making him his son-in-law, but intending to kill him if the opportunity arose. After Constantine had slaughtered the Franks and Alamanni and thrown their captive kings to the beasts in the magnificent spectacle of games he had prepared, he ruled in the Gallic provinces with the huge support of the soldiers and provincials. Therefore, when his plot had been unveiled by his daughter Fausta, who had informed her husband of the deception, [Maximian] Herculius fled and was overcome at Marseilles from where he was planning to sail to his son; the man was punished with a most deserved death, inclined as he was to every viciousness and savagery, untrustworthy, inept, completely without humility.

[4] Meanwhile, Licinius was made emperor by Galerius; born in Dacia and known to Galerius through long acquaintance and in the war which he had waged against Narses, he was energetic in his tasks and acceptable in his duties. The death of Galerius followed quickly; thus at that stage the state was held by four new emperors, Constantine and

Maxentius the sons of Augusti, Licinius and Maximinus, new men. But in the fifth year of his reign, Constantine launched a civil war against Maxentius, scattered his forces in many engagements, and finally at the Milvian Bridge at Rome defeated him as he raged with all kinds of ruin against the nobility. Constantine took over Italy. A little later in the east as well, having devised an uprising against Licinius, Maximinus anticipated his own imminent death by an accidental death at Tarsus.

### 3. Festus: *Breviarium* (c. 370)
from the Latin original (**I Introduction 1**)

[25] Under the emperor Diocletian, a famous victory over the Persians was celebrated. At the first engagement, when with a small force Caesar Galerius had clashed fiercely against a countless multitude and was forced back, he withdrew and was received with such indignation by Diocletian that he ran in his imperial robes in front of Diocletian's carriage for several miles. When he had undergone this, with his army restored with frontier troops from Dacia, in order to seek again a military result, together with two cavalrymen the emperor himself reconnoitred the enemy in Greater Armenia; with 25,000 troops he suddenly overcame the enemy camp, attacked innumerable Persian units and cut them utterly to pieces. Narses the Persian king fled; his wife and daughters were captured and treated with utmost dignity. For this respect shown them, the Persians confessed the Romans were superior not only in arms but also in custom. They returned Mesopotamia with the lands across the Tigris. Peace was concluded and remained in force until the politics of our own lifetime.

### 4. Anonymous *Epitome about the Caesars* (late fourth century)
from the Latin original (**I Introduction 1**)

[39.1] Diocletian of Dalmatia, a freedman of the senator Anulinus, ruled for twenty-five years. His mother and hometown likewise were called Dioclea, from which name he was called Diocles until he took power; when he took control of the Roman world, he converted the Greek name to the Roman fashion. [2] He made Maximian Augustus; he appointed as Caesars Constantius and Galerius Maximianus, surnamed Armentarius, giving Theodora, the step-daughter of Maximian Herculius, in marriage to Constantius, when his first wife had been divorced. [3] In this period, having been made emperors Carausius in Gaul, Achilleus at Egypt, and Julian in Italy met various ends; [4] with a dagger through his ribs, Julian flung himself onto a fire. [5] In fact, of his own accord, Diocletian resigned the imperial *fasces* at Nicomedia and grew old on his own estate. [6] When [Maximian] Herculius and Galerius asked him to take up power again, cursing it like some plague, he replied in this way: 'If only you could come and see the vegetables I have planted with my own hands at Split, certainly you would conclude that that should never be attempted.' [7] He lived for sixty-eight years, of which nearly nine were spent after holding office. It is sufficiently clear that he took his own life, through fear. For in old age, Constantine and Licinius invited him to a wedding; when he made his apologies, saying that he was not well enough to attend, he received threatening letters, accusing him of having shown favour to Maxentius and favouring Maximinus still; suspecting a shameful death, he is said to have drunk poison.

[40.1] In the course of these days, the Caesars Constantius (the father of Constantine) and [Galerius] Armentarius were pronounced Augusti, and appointed Caesars were Severus in Italy, and Maximinus, Galerius' nephew, in the east; and at the same time, Constantine was made Caesar. [2] Maxentius was made emperor in the villa six miles from Rome, on the Lavicanus road, then Licinius was made Augustus, and in similar fashion Alexander was made emperor at Carthage; in the same way, Valens was made emperor. Their deaths were as follows.

[3] The Caesar Severus was killed by [Maximian] Herculius at the Three Tabernae at Rome, and his body was carried to the tomb of Gallienus, which is nine miles from the city on the Appian Way. [4] Galerius Maximian died of genital decay. [5] [Maximian] Herculius was besieged by Constantine at Marseilles, and when he was captured was punished with the lowest form of death, hanging. [6] Alexander was strangled by Constantine's army. [7] Maxentius joined in battle with Constantine a little beyond the Milvian bridge; as he was hurrying onto the pontoon bridge from the side, he slipped from his horse and sank into the deep; swallowed in the mud by the weight of his breastplate, his body was recovered with difficulty. [8] Maximinus died a simple death at Tarsus. [9] Licinius punished Valens with death.

[10] Their characters were of the following type: Aurelius Maximian, with the surname Herculius, was wild by nature, ablaze with lust, stupid in his judgements, and of a barbarous, Pannonian origin. Even today the place is not far from Sirmium, with a palace built there, where his parents used to ply their trade. [11] He died in his sixties, having been emperor for twenty years. [12] By his Syrian wife Eutropia, he fathered Maxentius and Fausta, the wife of Constantine; he had given his

daughter-in-law Theodora in marriage to Constantine's father Constantius. [13] It is said Maximian was not Maxentius' father but that by womanly skill Eutropia managed to control the mind of her husband as he had wrestled from childhood with the most pleasing prospect of becoming a father. [14] This Maxentius was dear to no-one, not even his father or father-in-law Galerius. [15] But although Galerius had an uncivilised and barbarous sense of justice, he was praiseworthy enough, fine in figure, outstanding and successful in war, born of country people, a cattle stockman, whence his surname Armentarius ['Cowherd']. [16] Born in Dacia Ripensis, there he was buried; he had called the place Romulianum after the name of his mother Romula. [17] Insolently he dared to insist that his mother had conceived him after joining with a serpent, like Olympias, the mother of Alexander the Great. [18] Galerius Maximinus, nephew of [Galerius] Armentarius was in fact called by the name Daca before his rule; he was Caesar for four years, then Augustus in the east for three. He was a herdsman by origin and way of life, yet valued all wise men and letters; of quiet nature, he was rather keen on wine. [19] Drunk on wine, his mind addled, he used to give some harsh orders; but if he regretted the act, he decided to postpone the orders until sober the next morning. [20] Alexander was Phrygian by birth, shy in nature and unequal to the task because of the deficiencies of old age. ...

[41.1] When they were all dead, control of the empire came to Constantine and Licinius.

## 5. *Anonymous Valesianus I* (c. 390)
### From the Latin original (I Introduction 1)

[2.2] [Constantine was kept] hostage by Diocletian and Galerius, and fought under them bravely in Asia; after Diocletian and [Maximian] Herculius resigned power, Constantius asked Galerius to return his son; but Galerius exposed him to many dangers first ... [2.4] Then Galerius sent Constantine to his father. ... After a victory against the Picts, his father Constantius died at York, and Constantine was made Caesar with the consent of all the troops.

[3.5] Meanwhile, two others were appointed Caesar, Severus and Maximinus; Maximinus was granted rule over the Orient; Galerius kept Illyricum, Thrace and Bithynia for himself; Severus took charge of Italy and whatever [Maximian] Herculius had controlled.

## 6. Lactantius: *On the Deaths of the Persecutors* (c. 315)
From the Latin original (**I Introduction 1**)

[1.1] Dearest Donatus, the Lord had heard the prayers you poured out in His sight hour on hour, and the entreaties of our brothers who by glorious confession secured for themselves the eternal crown as their faith deserved. [2] Look, with all its enemies removed and tranquillity restored across the world, the church, recently downtrodden, is rising again. ... [7] I resolved to testify to the deaths of the persecutors so that all who were far distant or all future generations should know how far God on high has shown His excellence and majesty in crushing and destroying those hostile to His name.

[7.1] When Diocletian, who invented crimes and plotted evils, destroyed everything, he could not even keep his hands from God. [2] He turned the world upside down with his greed and cowardice. For he appointed three men to share in his reign, divided the world into quarters, and multiplied the armies – this when each of his colleagues strove to have a far larger number of troops than previous emperors had had, even though they had governed the state by themselves. [3] Those receiving money began to outnumber those contributing to such an extent that when farmers' resources had been eaten up by the size of cash levies, farmland was abandoned and cultivated fields degenerated into woodland. [4] And, so that terror should fill everything, the provinces too were cut up into fragments, many governors and more officials encumbered individual regions and almost every city, and likewise, there were many accountants, directors and deputy prefects; the conduct of all of these was very rarely civil, but condemnations and proscriptions were common, and they exacted countless tax payments, I won't say frequently but always, and during these exactions the injustices were intolerable. [5] And how could the measures for raising troops be endured? Insatiably greedy, Diocletian would never allow his treasures to be diminished, but he always accumulated extraordinary wealth and funds for distribution so that he could keep intact and untouched what he had hidden away. [6] Because his various iniquities were causing huge inflation, he tried to decree a law about the price of market goods; [7] then, much blood was spilled for small and cheap items, and amid the fear, nothing was put up for sale at all, and inflation flared up even worse until after many deaths, the law had to be repealed. [8] To this can be added Diocletian's limitless passion for building – and in the provinces there was no less an exaction to raise workmen, craftsmen, wagons and everything required for building construction.

[9] Here there were basilicas, there a circus, here a mint, there an arms factory, here a house for his wife, there one for his daughter. Suddenly a great section of the city was destroyed; with their wives and children, everyone became refugees as if the city had been captured by the enemy. [10] And when the construction was over – and the provinces ruined – he would say: 'They have not been built properly; they are to be done differently.' They had to be demolished and altered, perhaps even to be knocked down again. Diocletian was always mad like this, eager to make Nicomedia equal Rome.

[11] I pass over the fact that many people died for their possessions or wealth; for in the normal practice of wrongdoings, this was usual and almost lawful. [12] But this habit of Diocletian's was outstanding – whenever he saw a well-cultivated field or an embellished building, false allegations and the death penalty were immediately prepared for the owner, as if he could not steal without bloodshed.

[8.1] What of his brother Maximian who was known as Herculius? He was not unlike Diocletian; for they could not join together in so loyal a friendship unless they were of one mind, the same inclinations, and identical opinions. [2] Their only difference was that Diocletian was more greedy but more timid, Maximian less greedy but more determined, not to do good, but evil. [3] For when he held Italy – the very seat of empire – and controlled very wealthy provinces like Africa or Spain, Maximian was not very concerned to safeguard the riches of which there was an abundance. [4] When there was a need, very wealthy senators were available to be accused on suborned charges of aspiring to power – the lights of the senate were continually snuffed out. [5] Maximian's exchequer flowed most bloody with evilly gained wealth. In this diseased man there was a lust not only to debauch males, a hateful and detestable practice, but even to violate the daughters of leading citizens. [6] For wherever he travelled, maiden daughters were immediately torn away from the embrace of their parents. He gauged his personal happiness by and reckoned the wellbeing of his rule depended on his refusal of nothing to his lust and evil desire.

[7] I pass over Constantius, who was unlike the rest and deserved to control the world alone.

[9.1] The second Maximian, [Galerius], whom Diocletian had received as son-in-law, was worse not only than the two men our times have known, but even than all the evil men who have ever lived. [2] In this beast was a natural barbarity, a wildness alien to Roman blood; it is not surprising, since his mother had crossed the Danube and fled into New Dacia when the Carpi were attacking. [3] His body was consistent with his habits – tall in stature, with his mass of flesh spread and swollen to a frightful size. In words, and actions and appearance, he was a source of terror and fright to everyone. Even his father-in-law [Diocletian] feared him most acutely. ... [5] The Persian king Narses was very eager to occupy the [Roman] east, urged on by his own family's example (that of his grandfather Sapor)... [6] Then Diocletian ... did not dare to meet Narses, but sent Galerius through Armenia while he stayed in the east and awaited the outcome. [7] ... Galerius overcame the Persians easily, and after the flight of the king Narses, he returned with great booty and profit, making himself arrogant and Diocletian timorous. [8] Elevated to such a height of conceit after this victory, he then resented the title of Caesar. [9] From then on he began to behave most insolently – he wanted to appear and to be called the son of Mars, as if a second Romulus, preferring to defame his mother as adulterous to be seen to be born of the gods. ... [11] Diocles – for that was his name before he came to power – ruined the state with such policies and colleagues, and he deserved everything for his crimes. However, he ruled with the greatest success as long as he did not defile his hands with the blood of the innocent.

[10.1] Once when he was involved in the east, he was sacrificing cattle and searching in their innards for portents. [2] At that moment, some of his attendants present at the sacrifice who had knowledge of the Lord put the immortal sign on their foreheads; the demons were put to flight by this action, and the rites were disturbed. The *haruspices* were anxious and they did not see the usual signs in the entrails, and so, as if they had not made offerings, they sacrificed more times. [3] Again and again the sacrificial victims yielded no sign, until Tagis the chief *haruspex* said, either out of suspicion or insight, that the rites were not responding because profane men were present at the religious ceremony. [4] Wild with anger at this, Diocletian ordered that not only those attending the rites make sacrifice, but even everyone in the palace, and that if they refused they be flogged as punishment; and he instructed that letters be sent to commanders and soldiers be forced to [make] the unspeakable sacrifices, and that any who disobeyed be discharged from service. [5] His fury and anger reached this point, and he did nothing more against the law and religion of God.

[6] Then, after a significant interval, Diocletian went to winter in Bithynia, and the Caesar [Galerius] came there too, aflame with wickedness, to incite the useless old man, who had already made a start, to persecute the Christians. ... [11.3] For a long time the old man resisted Galerius' fury, making it clear how ruinous it would be to

disturb the world's peace, to spill lots of blood; it was the Christians' practice, he said, to die willingly; it would be sufficient to prohibit palace staff and soldiers from that religion. [4] But he could not divert that hasty man's madness. ... [8] And so Diocletian was dissuaded from his policy and, since he could not fight against his friends, the Caesar and Apollo, he tried to preserve moderation, so that although the Caesar wanted those who refused to sacrifice to be burnt alive, Diocletian ordered the affair be conducted without bloodshed. [12.1] An appropriate and promising day was needed to carry the matter out, and most suitably the *Terminalia* festival of 23 February was chosen – so that this religion could be terminated, as it were. ... [2] When it was still twilight that day [in 303], the prefect came to the church with generals, tribunes and accountants, and beat the doors down; they looked for the image of God, burnt the scriptures they found, granted booty to everyone, caused plunder, fear, panic. ... [5] In a few hours that highest building was levelled to the ground. [13.1] The next day an edict was posted warning that people of that religion would be stripped of all rank and status, that they would be subjected to torture, no matter their class or position, that every legal action against them would be valid, that they themselves would have no access to the law for cases of wrongdoing, adultery or theft, finally that they would have no liberty or legal voice. ...

[14.1] But Galerius was not content with the rulings of the edict; he prepared to beleaguer Diocletian by other means. [2] To force him to a policy of the cruellest persecution, he had attendants secretly start a fire in the palace, and when part of it had burnt down, the Christians were denounced as public enemies. ... [15.1] So he [Diocletian] now began to rage not just against his household staff but against everyone, and first of all he forced his daughter Valeria and his wife Prisca to be tainted by making sacrifice. [2] Eunuchs, onetime so powerful, the support for the palace and the emperor himself, were killed; priests and deacons were seized and condemned without proof or confession, then led away with all their dependants. [3] People of both sexes and every age were taken for burning, not individually since they were so great in number, but in groups they were surrounded by flames; with millstones tied to their necks, household staff were drowned in the sea. [4] The persecution fell no less violently on the rest of the population. For judges were sent to all temples and tried to force everyone to sacrifice. [5] The prisons were full, unknown forms of torture were invented, and to prevent justice being dispensed rashly against anyone, altars were put up in council chambers and law-courts so that litigants could sacrifice first and thus plead their case. ... [6] Orders to do the same thing had even been sent by letter to Maximian and Constantius – their opinion had not been consulted in this most serious issue. Indeed throughout Italy, the old man Maximian happily obeyed – a man not much given to mercy. [7] So that he should not seem to disagree with his superiors' orders, Constantius allowed the churches – that is, the walls which can be rebuilt – to be pulled down, but the temple of God, which is inside mankind, he preserved intact. [16.1] Thus the whole world was under attack, and except for Gaul, the three most vicious beasts raged from east to west. ...

[17.1] When good fortune had deserted him, Diocletian proceeded at once to Rome in order to celebrate there his *vicennalia*. ... [2] When this had been celebrated, he could not bear the independence of the Roman people, and just before 1 January when his ninth consulship was due to be conferred on him, he rushed from the city, impatient and weak in mind. ... [3] Having left when winter was raging he was lashed by cold and rainstorms, and caught a light but lasting illness; he was troubled for the whole journey, and was carried for most of it on a litter. [4] He spent the summer on a tour of the banks of the Danube and came to Nicomedia when his illness was now getting worse. Although he saw he was being ground down, a full year after his *vicennalia* he was carried out to dedicate the circus he had had built. ... [9] [By 1 March] he had recovered his spirit although incompletely, for he was demented, so that at certain times he was mad, at others he regained his senses.

[18.1] A few days later the Caesar [Galerius] arrived, not to congratulate his father but to force him to resign his imperial power. He had recently clashed with Maximian and had terrified him by adding the fear of civil war. [2] Initially Galerius approached Diocletian gently and amicably, saying that he was now an old man, less able, and not fit to govern the state; he said he should rest after his exertions. ... [3] Diocletian said that it would be improper to come down to the shadows of lowly status from the great brilliance of lofty office, and that it would be more dangerous because during such a long reign he had earned the hatred of many people. ... [4] But he said if Galerius wanted to secure the title of emperor, there was no reason why they should not all be pronounced Augusti. [5] But Galerius, who had by now set his hopes on the whole world, saw little or nothing coming his way beyond a name; he replied that Diocletian's arrangement should be preserved for ever, so that there would be two senior emperors in the state who held supreme authority, and two juniors to help them; he said harmony could easily be maintained between two equals, but not between four.

[6] If Diocletian did not want to step aside, Galerius said he would look to his own interests, so he should not be the junior and subordinate emperor any longer; it was now fifteen years since he had been sent to Illyricum – that is, to the banks of the Danube – to wrestle with barbarian tribes, while the other emperors ruled amid luxury in easier and calmer lands. [7] Having heard this, the feeble old man who had already learned in a letter from Maximian everything Galerius had said and that he was increasing his army, tearfully replied: 'If this is what you want, let it be.'

[8] It remained to elect the Caesars with the common agreement of all the emperors.

'What need is there for agreement, when those two must consent to whatever we do?' Galerius asked.

'Quite right,' Diocletian said, 'for we must appoint their sons.'

[9] (Maximian's son Maxentius was Galerius' son-in-law, a danger-ous and evil-minded man, so proud and insolent that he would not worship his father or father-in-law, and for that reason was hated by both of them. [10] Constantius' son was Constantine, a most virtuous young man, entirely worthy of high position; for his distinguished and handsome bearing, his military vigour, his sound morals and unusual affability soldiers loved him and civilians wished for him; he was present at that very time, having been appointed tribune of the first rank by Diocletian).

[11] 'What must we do?' Diocletian asked.

Galerius said: 'Maxentius is not worthy of it. What will he do when appointed emperor if he despised me when he was a private citizen?'

'But Constantine is popular and will rule in such a way that he will be considered better and more compassionate than his father,' said Diocletian.

'If that happens, I will not be able to do what I want,' said Galerius. 'Men should be appointed who will be under my authority, who will fear me and do nothing except at my bidding.'

[12] 'Who then?'

'Severus,' said Galerius.

'That dancing boozy drunkard who keeps night as day and day as night!'

'He is deserving,' said Galerius, 'because he led his troops loyally. I have sent him to be invested by Maximian.'

[13] 'So be it,' said Diocletian. 'Who will be your other Caesar?'

'This man,' he said, pointing out a semi-barbaric young man called Daia. ...

[14] 'Who is this man you offer me?'

'My relation,' Galerius said.

Diocletian groaned: 'You are not giving me men fit to care for the state.'

'I have tested them,' said Galerius.

[15] Diocletian said: 'It is for you to look to – you are going to take control of the empire. I have laboured enough and taken care that the state should be safe when in my power. If anything adverse happens, it will not be my fault.' ...

[20.1] When the old men had been driven out and Galerius had what he wanted, he thought he was the sole master of the whole world. For although Constantius had to be called the senior emperor, Galerius hated him for his mild nature and troubled health. [2] Galerius hoped he would die soon, or if not, that he could be removed from power easily, if unwillingly. [3] For what could Constantius do, if he were forced by the other three to resign his power? Galerius had Licinius with him, an old messmate and friend from their first military service, whose advice he used in all decisions; but he did not want to make him Caesar, so that he need not name him his son, and so that later, in place of Constantius, he could appoint him Augustus and brother – [4] then indeed he could hold principal position himself, rage against the world according to his own whim and celebrate his *vicennalia*, and then he could lay down power, replaced by his own son [Candidianus] as Caesar (at that time he was nine years old). In this way, with Licinius and Severus holding the highest authority, and Maximinus Daia and Candidianus the secondary position of Caesar, he would live a secure and peaceful old age surrounded by an impregnable wall. ...

[23.1] A cause of public calamity and general mourning was a census imposed at the same time on provinces and cities. ... [2] Fields were measured sod by sod, vines and trees were counted, animals of all kinds were registered, the population was noted. ... [6] There was no trust in the same officials, but one group was sent in after another, as if they would find more; tax was always doubled, not because they found anything, but because they added to it as they wished, in case they appeared to have been sent in for nothing. ...

[24.3] When Constantius was seriously ill, he had written to Galerius asking him to send him his son Constantine to see. ... [4] Galerius was very unwilling. ... [8] Travelling at unbelievable speed, [Constantine] he reached his father as he lay dying; Constantius commended him to his troops and handed over to him imperial power. Thus Constantius died peacefully in his bed, as he had wished. [9] When he had assumed power, as Augustus Constantine did nothing before restoring Christians to their faith and their god. Restoration of the sacred religion was the first measure he sanctioned. ... [25.4] Galerius' plans had been disturbed, and he could not announce a second Augustus outside the existing number as he had wished. [5] However, he contrived to pronounce as Augustus Severus who was older, and to order Constantine to be known not as emperor, as he had been made, but Caesar together with Maximinus [Daia]. ...

[26.2] When Galerius had decided to devour the world by instituting the census, he leapt to such a point of insanity that he was unwilling even to let the people of Rome be immune from this slavery. Officials were appointed to be sent to Rome to register the people. [3] About the same time, he had withdrawn the praetorian guard. And so, the few soldiers who had been left in the camp at Rome took the opportunity, and with the agreement of the people, who had been roused, they killed some magistrates and invested Maxentius with the purple. ... [5] Galerius summoned Severus, encouraged him to recover his power, and sent him with Maximian's army to storm Maximian's son – he sent him to Rome where those soldiers had very often been welcomed with the finest niceties, and who not only wanted the city to be safe, but even to live there themselves. [6] ... Although by the claims of heredity, Maxentius could win over his father's troops to his side, he felt it might happen that in fear of this his father-in-law Galerius would leave Severus in Illyricum and come himself to attack with his own army. He planned how far he could defend himself against the impending danger. [7] To his father Maximian, who had been living in Campania after he had resigned his power, he sent the purple and nominated him Augustus for the second time. Maximian, who had resigned reluctantly, was eager for rebellion and gladly accepted the offer. [8] Meanwhile Severus advanced and marched under arms to the city walls. Immediately his men threw away their standards and left – they defected to the man they had come to fight. [9] What but escape remained for the deserted Severus? At the arrival of Maximian, who had resumed his power and come to attack him, Severus fled to Ravenna and shut himself in with a few soldiers. [10] When he saw he was going to be handed over to Maximian, he gave himself and his purple cloak up to the man from whom he had received it. [11] By this deed he gained nothing but a decent death – for he was forced to cut his wrists and die gently.

[27.1] ... Maximian fortified the city and carefully equipped it against enemy attempts, then left for Gaul to win Constantine over to his side by giving him his younger daughter in marriage. [2] Meanwhile Galerius gathered his army and invaded Italy; he approached the city, intending to destroy the senate and butcher the people, but he found everything barred and defended. There was no hope of storming, attack was difficult, and he had too few forces to lay siege, for he had never seen Rome and assumed it was not much bigger than those cities he knew. [3] Then, hating the crime that a father-in-law should attack a son-in-law and that Roman soldiers should attack Rome, some of the legions transferred their standards and left Galerius' command. [4] Other troops were already wavering when in fear of an end like Severus', with broken pride and spirit gone, Galerius fell at his soldiers' feet and begged them not to hand him over to the enemy, until he won their minds with huge promises, then turned his standards and took flight in anxiety, since he could easily be crushed if anyone followed with a few troops. ... [8] Galerius had once taken the name of emperor; now he professed himself an enemy of the term 'Roman' and he wanted to change the title of the empire from 'Roman' to 'Dacian'. ...

[28.2] The old man Maximian took it badly that he could not act as he pleased, and in childish jealousy he envied his son. His plan therefore was to expel the young man ... this seemed easy because he had with him the troops who had abandoned Severus. [3] He summoned the people and troops as if to hold a meeting about the state's present ills. When he had said much about this, he pointed to his son and said he was the author of these ills, the cause of the problems the state was enduring; Maximian ripped the purple from his shoulders. [4] Stripped in this way, Maxentius left the platform and was welcomed by his soldiers, whose angry shouting disturbed the faithless old man Maximian, and drove him from the city of Rome like another Tarquin the Proud.

[29.1] Maximian returned to Gaul and spent some time there before going to see his son's enemy Galerius as if to talk with him about settling the constitution, but in fact to take the opportunity granted by the reconciliation to kill him and take over his realm, having been denied his own. [2] When Maximian arrived, Diocletian was there, just summoned by his son-in-law to do in his presence what he had not done previously – grant power to Licinius as a replacement in Severus' place. This happened with both men present, and thus there were six [emperors] at one time. [3] This frustrated the old man's plans, and Maximian devised a third struggle. He returned to Gaul full of evil and criminal intent to trap the emperor Constantine, his own son-in-law and the son of his son-in-law in an evil plot; to enable the deception, he laid aside the imperial garb. ... [30.5] Reproached for his disloyalty and crime, finally Maximian was granted the freedom to choose how to die. ... [6] Thus that 'greatest' emperor of the Roman name, who after a long interlude [in Roman affairs] had with great glory celebrated the acclamation of a twenty year reign, ended his detestable life in a foul and ignominious death, his proud neck crushed and broken.

[31.1] In vengeance for His faith and people, God turned His eyes from Maximian to Galerius, the author of the unspeakable persecution, so that He could show in him the power of His majesty. [2] By now Galerius was considering his *vicennalia* celebrations; for a long time he had been afflicting the provinces by imposing taxes of gold and silver; now to meet his promises, his axe fell for a second time, in the name of his *vicennalia*. ...

[32.1] Maximinus Daia was angry when Licinius was pronounced emperor, and was not content himself to be called 'Caesar' and be third in the chain of command. [2] Galerius sent him several envoys, begging him to obey and preserve the arrangement, to yield to his [greater] age and defer to his grey hair. [3] But Maximinus Daia raised his horns more boldly and fought back with claims of priority – he said he ought to be given seniority because he had taken the purple earlier. He held Galerius' prayers and commands in contempt. [4] The beast [Galerius] grieved and moaned that he had appointed as Caesar such a low-born man so that he would be obedient – but the faithless man had forgotten this great kindness and was resisting his will and prayers. [5] Overcome by [Maximinus Daia's] stubbornness, Galerius abolished the title 'Caesar' and called himself and Licinius 'Augusti' and Maximinus Daia and Constantine 'sons of the Augusti'. Maximinus soon wrote announcing that in a recent military assembly he had been proclaimed Augustus by the army. Galerius received this in sadness and misery and ordered that all four men be called emperor. [33.1] In the eighteenth year of his reign, God struck Galerius with an incurable illness. A malignant ulcer arose in the lower part of his genitals and spread more widely. ... [11] Finally he was tamed by these ills and was forced to confess God. In the intervals between the pain renewing its urgency, he shouted that he would restore the temple of God and compensate for his crime. On the point of death, he issued an edict as follows:

[34.1] 'Amongst the other affairs we are always arranging for the state's advantage and expedience, previously we had wanted to make everything accord with the old laws and public discipline of the Romans and to see to it that even the Christians, who had abandoned their parents' way of life, should return to sound sense, [2] since somehow such an inclination had overcome the Christians and such stupidity held them that they would not follow those ancient traditions which their own ancestors had perhaps established, but according to their own judgement and pleasure, they made laws for themselves to follow and in diverse places gathered together various people. [3] Finally, when we published such a command that they should return to the traditions of old, many of them were subjected to danger and many were struck down. [4] But since very many persisted in their purpose and we saw that they were not offering due worship and observance to the gods or recognising the god of the Christians, we gave thought to our most gentle clemency and everlasting custom by which we are used to granting indulgent pardon to all men, and came to the belief that to these people too our very prompt indulgence should be extended so that immediately they can become Christians and construct their meeting places as long as they do nothing contrary to good order. [5] In another letter to magistrates we are about to indicate what conditions they ought to observe. According to this indulgence of ours, they ought to pray to their god for our wellbeing, the state's and their own so the state be safe on all sides and that they can live at peace in their homes.'

[35.1] This edict was published at Nicomedia on 30 May 311. ... [3] A few days later, Galerius commended his wife and son to Licinius' legal authority; with his limbs dissolving throughout his body, he was consumed by horrific decay.

[36.1] Hearing this news, Maximinus Daia arranged transport from the east and rushed to occupy Galerius' provinces and while Licinius delayed, to claim everything up to the straits of Chalcedon for himself. He entered Bithynia and to everyone's great delight scrapped the census to win himself immediate favour. ... [3] He cancelled the pardon granted to the Christians in the communal decree. ... [6] He was preparing to do what he had been doing for a long time in the east. Although for the sake of appearance he professed leniency and forbade the killing of God's servants, he ordered them to be crippled. [7] And so, confessors had their eyes gouged out, their hands amputated, their feet lopped off, their noses and ears cut away.

[42.1] ... Constantine ordered that the statues of the old man Maximian be torn down, and any pictures where he had been portrayed be removed. And since the two old men had generally been portrayed together, pictures of both of them were taken down together. [2] Thus Diocletian saw happening in his lifetime what had never befallen any emperor, and with a twofold grief decided he must die. His spirit wavering in sorrow, he would toss himself here and there, taking no sleep or food; there were sighs and groans, frequent tears, his body endlessly turning now on his bed, now on the floor. [3] So the emperor who had been so blessed for twenty years was cast down by God to a lowly life, trampled with wounds and drawn to a hatred of life; in the end he was killed by hunger and anguish. ...

[43.2] Maximinus Daia heard that Constantine's sister had been betrothed to Licinius; he thought that this relationship united the two emperors against him; secretly he sent envoys to Rome to ask Maxentius for an alliance and friendship. He even wrote on familiar terms. His envoys were received generously; the friendship began and images of the two men were placed together. [4] Maxentius embraced his help happily as if divine; for he had already declared war on Constantine, intent on avenging his father's death. [5] From this grew the suspicion that that ruinous old man had fabricated the disagreement with his son to make his way clear to strike down the other emperors, and with them all removed, to claim authority over the whole world for himself and his son. [6] But this was false; his plan had been to get rid of his son and the others, then restore himself and Diocletian to rule.

[44.1] Civil war had begun between Maxentius and Constantine. Although Maxentius stayed within Rome (because an oracle had revealed that he would die if he went beyond the city gates) he conducted the war through suitable generals. [2] Maxentius had the bigger forces because he had recovered his father's army from Severus and had recently brought his own back from the Moors and Gaetuli. [3] Fighting began, and Maxentius' forces had the upper hand until Constantine renewed his spirit and ... moved all his forces nearer to Rome and made his base around the Milvian Bridge. ... [5] Constantine received warning in a dream to mark the heavenly sign of God on his shields and thus join battle. He did as was ordered. ... [6] Equipped with this sign, his army took up their weapons. The enemy came forward without their emperor and crossed the bridge. The battle lines clashed, their front ranks equal; each side fought with utmost vigour. ... [9] Maxentius came to the front line; the bridge was cut down behind him; at this sight the fighting became worse and the hand of God overhung the battle-line. Maxentius' army was terrified and he himself turned in hurried flight to the bridge which had been collapsed; oppressed by the fleeing crowd, he was thrown down into the Tiber. [10] This most bitter war was over and Constantine was received as emperor to the great joy of the senate and people of Rome; he learnt of the treachery of Maximinus Daia when he discovered letters and found statues and portraits. [11] Because of his virtue, the senate decreed

Constantine the title of 'senior emperor' – which Maximinus Daia was claiming for himself. When news of the victorious liberation of the city reached Daia, he received it as if he had himself been defeated; [12] when he learned of the senate's decree, he blazed with such grief that he openly admitted his hostility and directed insults mixed with jokes against the 'greatest' emperor.

[45.1] With matters arranged in the city, the next winter Constantine went to Milan; Licinius met him there to receive his bride. ...

[46.11] Licinius and Maximinus Daia proceeded to talks. Maximinus Daia could not be brought to peace, for he hated Licinius and thought he would be deserted by his troops; ... he had planned to acquire Licinius' army without a battle and with his army doubled immediately to proceed against Constantine.

[47.1] The armies drew nearer, trumpets blasted and the standards advanced. Licinius' army launched an assault and broke through the enemy. ... [4] Maximinus Daia saw the business going contrary to his expectations. He threw aside his purple, escaped in the garb of a slave and crossed the straits. ... [5] On 1 May he came to Nicomedia [where] he took his children, wife and a few friends from the palace and made for the east, [6] but he halted in Cappodocia and gathered together some troops from the fugitives and eastern forces. He resumed the purple. ... [48.1] Licinius entered Nicomedia and gave thanks to God, with whose help he had been victorious, and on 13 June [313] he ordered the letter sent to the governor about the restoration of the church to be displayed in public:

[2] 'When I, Constantine Augustus, and I, Licinius Augustus, met at Milan and discussed everything relating to the public's advantage and security, respect for the divine featured among the other matters we thought would benefit the majority or we believed required priority in our administration; so that we granted to Christians and to all men the liberty to practise whatever religion they want, so that whatever divinity is in the heavens can be placated and propitious towards us and all those drawn up under our authority. [3] And so with sound and very proper reasoning, we believe we must embark upon this plan of thinking that no-one at all should be denied the opportunity to devote his mind to the observances of the Christians or whatever religion he feels most suits him, so that the highest divinity, whose faith we practise with free minds, can show us accustomed favour and kindness in all matters. [4] Therefore, governor, you should know that we want absolutely all those conditions about the name of the Christians previously communicated to your office by letter to be set aside, and each of those who

are inclined to observe the Christian faith to hasten to do so freely and openly without difficulty or interference. [5] We believed this had to be brought to your attention most fully so that you know we have granted to the Christians free and unconditional opportunity to practise their faith. [6] When you see we have granted this to the Christians, according to the peace of our times, you understand that similarly open and free licence in faith and observance is given to others, so that in practising what each man wants, he may have free opportunity. ...

[7] 'In addition, we have decided it must be decreed about the Christian community as follows: if from our treasury or any other source, anyone has in the past bought land in which Christians had previously been accustomed to gather and concerning which fixed laws had been established in letters sent to your office, that land must be restored to the Christians without payment or any negotiation about price, with all hindrance and equivocation put aside; [8] if any land was received as a gift, likewise it must be returned to the Christians even more quickly; if those who bought land or received it as a gift seek some compensation from our benevolence, they should appeal to the deputy to consult our clemency on their behalf. Without delay through your intervention, all these lands should be handed back to the body of Christians immediately. [9] And because these same Christians are known to have owned not only those places where they used to gather, but other property too which belongs by right to their body – that is, to the church, not to individuals – according to the law we have set out above, you will order all this to be returned without equivocation or argument to the Christians – that is to their body and assemblies – with the principle given above preserved, that those who return the property without payment may hope for compensation from our benevolence. [10] In all these matters, you must offer to the aforementioned body of Christians your most effective support so that our command is fulfilled more quickly so that in this matter too, thought be given to the state's peace through our clemency. [11] Thus it will happen that as we have explained above, the divine favour towards us which we have experienced in the most important matters will endure for all time, with our flourishing successes and the public wellbeing. [12] So that everyone can be aware of the form of this decree and of our benevolence, it will be proper for you to publish this document everywhere, together with your own proclamation, and to bring it to the attention of everyone, so that the decree of our benevolence cannot be hidden.'

[13] ... Thus from the overthrow of the church until its restoration it was ten years and about four months. ...

[49.7] As he groaned as if he were being burnt, Maximinus Daia breathed out his harmful spirit in a detestable manner of death. [50.1] In this way, God crushed all the persecutors of His name. ... [52.3] Where are those magnificent and widely known names of the Jovii and Herculii, which were first insolently adopted by Diocletian and Maximian and then flourished when transferred to their successors? Certainly, the Lord has destroyed them and erased them from the earth. [4] Therefore, let us celebrate the triumph of God in exultation, let us throng the Lord's victory with praises, let us celebrate with prayer by day and night, let us celebrate so that He may confirm for eternity the peace which was granted His people after ten years.

### 7. Ammianus Marcellinus: *History* (c. 395)
From the Latin original (**I Introduction 1**)

[14.11.10] [Constantius II said that] their Caesars had obeyed Diocletian and his colleague [Maximian] as if their attendants, not resident in one place but hurrying here and there; and in Syria the purple-robed Galerius had walked in front of the carriage of his angry Augustus for nearly a mile.

[15.5.18] For Diocletian was the first to introduce the foreign and royal manner of adoration, when previously we have read that emperors were greeted like higher officials.

[23.5.2] Diocletian encircled Cercusium, formerly small and vulnerable, with walls and high towers when he was organising the inner lines of defence on the actual frontiers with the barbarians, so that the Persians would not overrun Syria, as had happened a few years previously, to the provinces' great loss.

### 8. Eusebius: *History of the Church* (c. 324)
From the Greek original (**I Introduction 1**)
This selection is taken from books 8 and 9

[8.1.7] But when because of abundant freedom, we [Christians] fell into laxity and idleness and envied and reviled each other, and were almost, as it were, taking up arms against one another, rulers assailing rulers with words like spears, and people forming parties against people, and monstrous hypocrisy and dissimulation rising to the greatest height of wickedness, as the crowds still continued to gather, with forbearance, as is its pleasure, the divine judgement gently and moderately harassed the episcopacy. [1.8] This persecution began with the brethren in the army. ...

[2.4] It was in the nineteenth year of the reign of Diocletian, in the month Dystrus, which the Romans call March, when the feast of the Saviour's passion was near at hand, that royal edicts were published everywhere, commanding that the churches be razed to the ground and the Scriptures be destroyed by fire, and ordering that those who held places of honour be degraded, and that the household servants, if they persisted in the profession of Christianity, be deprived of freedom. [2.5] Such was the first edict against us. But not long after, other decrees were issued, commanding that all the rulers of the churches in every place be first thrown into prison, and afterwards be forced by every method to offer sacrifice.

[3.1] Then indeed very many rulers of the churches eagerly endured terrible sufferings, and furnished examples of noble conflicts. But many others, numbed in spirit by fear, were easily weakened at the first onset. ...

[4.2] For though he who had received power was seemingly aroused now as from a deep sleep, yet from the time after Decius and Valerian, he had been plotting secretly and without notice against the churches. He did not wage war against all of us at once, but at first he tried only those in the army. ... [4.4] But as yet the instigator of this plot proceeded with moderation, and ventured so far as blood only in some instances; for the multitude of believers, as it is likely, made him afraid, and deterred him from waging war at once against all. [4.5] But when he attacked more boldly, it is impossible to relate how many and what sort of martyrs of God could be seen, among the inhabitants of all the cities and countries.

[5.1] Immediately on the publication of the decree against the churches in Nicomedia, a certain man, not obscure but very highly honoured with distinguished dignities, moved zealously toward God, and inspired by his ardent faith, seized the edict as it was posted openly and publicly, and tore it to pieces as a profane and impious thing; and this was done while two of the emperors were in the same city – the oldest of all, and the one who held the fourth place in the government after him. ...

[6.2] I will describe the manner in which one of them ended his life, and leave our readers to infer from his case the sufferings of the others. A certain man was brought forward in the above-mentioned city, before the rulers about whom I have spoken. He was then commanded to sacrifice, but as he refused, he was ordered to be stripped and raised on high and beaten with rods over his entire body, until, being conquered, he should, even against his will, do what was commanded. [6.3] But as he was unmoved by these sufferings, and his bones were already appearing, they poured vinegar mixed with salt upon the mangled parts of his body. As he scorned these agonies, a gridiron and fire were brought forward. And the remnants of his body, like flesh intended for eating, were placed on the fire, not at once, lest he should die immediately, but a little at a time. And those who placed him on the pyre were not allowed to stop until, after such sufferings, he should agree to the commands. [6.4] But he held his purpose firmly, and gave up his life in victory while the tortures were still going on. Such was the martyrdom of one of the servants of the palace, who was indeed well worthy of his name, for he was called Peter. ...

[6.8] Such things occurred in Nicomedia at the beginning of the persecution. But not long after, as persons in the country called Melitene, and others throughout Syria, attempted to usurp the government, a royal edict directed that the rulers of the churches everywhere should be thrown into prison and bonds. [6.9] What was to be seen after this exceeds all description. A huge mass were imprisoned in every place; and the prisons everywhere, which had long before been prepared for murderers and robbers of graves, were filled with bishops, presbyters and deacons, readers and exorcists, so that no room was left for those convicted of crimes. [6.10] And as other decrees followed the first, directing that if they would sacrifice those imprisoned should be permitted to leave in freedom, but that those who refused should be harassed with many tortures, how could any one tell the number of martyrs in every province, and especially of those in Africa, and Mauritania, and Thebais, and Egypt? From this last country many went into other cities and provinces, and became famous through martyrdom. ...

[7.2] I was present at Tyre myself when these things [martyrdoms] occurred, and have put on record the divine power of our martyred Saviour Jesus Christ, which was present and manifested itself mightily in the martyrs. ... [8.1] Such was the conflict of those Egyptians who contended nobly for religion in Tyre. But we must admire those also who suffered martyrdom in their native land; where thousands of men, women, and children, despising the present life for the sake of the teaching of our Saviour, endured various deaths. Some of them, after scrapings and rackings and most severe scourgings, and countless kinds of other tortures, terrible even to hear of, were committed to the flames; some were drowned in the sea; some offered their heads bravely to those who cut them off; some died under their tortures, and others perished with hunger. Still others were crucified, some according to the method commonly employed for malefactors, others yet more cruelly, being nailed to the cross with their heads downward, and being kept alive until they perished on the cross with hunger. ...

[9.3] In Thebais, sometimes more than ten, at other times more than twenty were put to death. Again not fewer than thirty, then about sixty, and yet again a hundred men with young children and women, were killed in one day, condemned to various and diverse tortures. ...

[12.1] Why need I mention the rest by name, or number them, or picture the various sufferings of the admirable martyrs of Christ? Some of them were killed with the axe – as in Arabia. The limbs of some were broken – as in Cappadocia. Some, raised on high by the feet, with their heads down, while a gentle fire burned beneath them, were suffocated by the smoke which arose from the burning wood – as in Mesopotamia. Others were mutilated by cutting off their noses and ears and hands, and cutting to pieces the other members and parts of their bodies – as in Alexandria. [12.2] Why need I revive the memory of those in Antioch who were roasted on grates, not so as to kill them, but so as to subject them to a lingering punishment? Or of others who preferred to thrust their right hand into the fire rather than touch the impious sacrifice? Some, shrinking from the trial, rather than be taken and fall into the hands of their enemies, threw themselves from lofty houses, considering death preferable to the cruelty of the impious. ...

[12.6] In Pontus, others endured sufferings horrible to hear. Their fingers were pierced with sharp reeds under their nails. Melted lead, bubbling and boiling with the heat, was poured down the backs of others, and they were roasted in the most sensitive parts of the body. [12.7] Others endured shameful and inhuman and unmentionable tortures on their bowels and private parts – torments which the noble and law-observing judges devised to show their severity, as more honourable manifestations of wisdom. And new tortures were continually invented, as if they were endeavouring, by surpassing one another, to gain prizes in a competition. ...

[13.9] What words could sufficiently describe the greatness and abundance of the prosperity of the Roman government before the war against us, while the rulers were friendly and peaceable toward us? Then those who were highest in the government, and had held the position ten or twenty years, passed their time in tranquil peace, in festivals and public games and most joyful pleasures and cheer. [13.10] While thus their authority was growing uninterruptedly, and increasing day by day, suddenly they changed their peaceful attitude toward us, and began an implacable war. But the second year of this movement was not yet past, when a revolution took place in the entire government and overturned all things. [13.11] For a severe sickness came upon the chief of those of whom we have spoken, by which his understanding was distracted; and with him who was honoured with the second rank, he retired into private life. Scarcely had he done this when the entire empire was divided, a thing not recorded as having ever occurred before. [13.12] Not long after, the emperor Constantius, who through his entire life was most kindly and favourably disposed toward his subjects, and most friendly to the Divine Word, ended his life in the common course of nature, and left his own son, Constantine, as emperor and Augustus in his stead. He was the first that was ranked by them among the gods, and received after death every honour which one could pay to an emperor. [13.13] He was the kindest and mildest of emperors, and the only one of those of our day that passed all the time of his government in a manner worthy of his office. Moreover, he conducted himself toward all most favourably and beneficently. He took not the smallest part in the war against us, but preserved the pious that were under him unharmed and unabused. He did not knock down the church buildings, nor did he devise anything else against us. The end of his life was honourable and thrice blessed. He alone at death left his empire happily and gloriously to his own son as his successor – one who was in all respects most prudent and pious. ... [13.14] But after this, Licinius was declared emperor and Augustus by a common vote of the rulers. [13.15] These things grieved Maximinus greatly, for until that time everyone called him only Caesar. Therefore, being very insolent, he seized the dignity [of power] for himself, and became Augustus, self-appointed. In the meantime he whom I have mentioned as having resumed the dignity [of power] after his abdication, being caught conspiring to kill Constantine, died a most shameful death. He was the first whose decrees and statues and public monuments were destroyed because of his wickedness and impiety.

[14.1] Maxentius his son, who obtained the government at Rome, at first feigned our faith, in complaisance and flattery toward the Roman people. On this account he commanded his subjects to cease persecuting the Christians, dissimulating faith so that he might appear more merciful and mild than his predecessors. [14.2] But he did not prove in his deeds to be such a person as was hoped, but ran into all manner of evil and held back from no impurity or licentiousness, committing adulteries and indulging in all kinds of corruption. ...

[14.6] It is impossible to tell the ways in which this tyrant at Rome oppressed his subjects, so that they were reduced to such an extreme dearth of the necessities of life as has never been known, according to our contemporaries, either at Rome or elsewhere. [14.7] But Maximinus, the tyrant in the east, having secretly formed a friendly alliance with the Roman tyrant as with a brother in wickedness, sought to conceal it for a long time. But being at last detected, he suffered merited punishment. [14.8] It was amazing how like he was in wickedness to the tyrant at Rome, or rather how far he surpassed him in it. ...

[15.1] During the entire ten years of the persecution, they [the emperors] were constantly plotting and warring against one another. For the sea could not be navigated, nor could men sail from any port without being exposed to all kinds of outrages; being stretched on the rack and lacerated in their sides, that it might be ascertained through various tortures, whether they came from the enemy; and finally being subjected to punishment by the cross or by fire. [15.2] In addition, shields and breastplates were prepared, and arrows and spears and other military equipment were manufactured, and galleys and naval armour were collected everywhere. And no-one expected anything else than to be attacked by enemies any day. ...

[16.1] Such was the state of affairs during the entire persecution. But in the tenth year, through the grace of God, it stopped altogether, having begun to wane after the eighth year. For when the divine and heavenly grace showed us favourable and propitious oversight, then truly our rulers, and the very persons by whom the war against us had been earnestly prosecuted, changed their minds most notably, and published a revocation, and by merciful proclamations and ordinances concerning us, extinguished the great fire of persecution which had been kindled. [16.2] But this was not due to any human agency. Nor was it the result, as one might say, of the compassion or philanthropy of our rulers – far from it, for every day from the beginning until that time they were devising more and more severe measures against us, and continually inventing outrages by a greater variety of instruments. But it was clearly due to the oversight of Divine Providence, on the one hand becoming reconciled to his people, and on the other, attacking him who instigated these evils, and showing anger toward him as the author of the cruelties of the entire persecution. [16.3] For though it was necessary that these things should take place, according to the Divine judgement, nevertheless the Word says, 'Woe to him through whom the offence comes.' Therefore punishment from God came upon him, beginning with his flesh, and proceeding to his soul. [16.4] For an abscess suddenly appeared in the middle of his genitals, and from it a deeply perforated sore spread irresistibly into his inmost bowels. An indescribable mass of worms sprang from them, and a deadly stench arose, as the entire bulk of his body had, through his greed, been changed, before his sickness, into an excessive mass of soft fat, which became putrid, and thus presented an awful and intolerable sight to those who came near. ...

[17.1] Wrestling with so many evils, he thought of the cruelties which he had committed against the pious. Turning his thoughts to himself, first he openly confessed to the God of the universe, and then summoning his attendants, he commanded that without delay they should stop the persecution of the Christians, and should by law and royal decree, urge them forward to build their churches and to perform their customary worship, offering prayers on behalf of the emperor. Immediately the deed followed the word. [17.2] The imperial decrees were published in the cities, containing the revocation of the acts.

[8. Appendix 1] Very shortly after this confession, [Galerius] the author of the edict was released from his pains and died. He is reported to have been the original author of the misery of the persecution, having endeavoured, long before the movement of the other emperors, to turn from the faith the Christians in the army, and first of all those in his own house, stripping some of their military rank, and abusing others most shamefully, and threatening still more with death, and finally inciting his partners in the empire to the general persecution. It is not proper to pass over the death of these emperors in silence. [2] As four of them held the supreme authority, those who were advanced in age and honour, after the persecution had continued not quite two years, abdicated the government, as we have already stated, and passed the remainder of their lives in a common and private position. [3] The end of their lives was as follows. He who was first in honour and age [Diocletian] perished through a long and most grievous physical infirmity. He who held the second place [Maximian] ended his life by strangling, suffering thus according to a certain demonic prediction, on account of his many daring crimes. [4] Of those after them, the last of whom we have spoken as the originator of the entire persecution, suffered such things as I have related. But he who preceded him, the most merciful and kindly emperor Constantius, passed all the time of his government in a manner worthy of his office. Moreover, he conducted himself towards all most favourably and beneficently. He took not the smallest part in the war against us, and preserved the pious that were under him unharmed and unabused. He did not pull down church buildings, or devise anything else against us. The end of his life was happy and thrice blessed. He alone at death left his empire happily and gloriously to his own son as his successor, one who was in all respects most prudent and pious. He entered on the government at once, being proclaimed supreme emperor and Augustus by the soldiers; [5] and he showed himself an emulator of his father's piety toward our doctrine.

[9.2.1] But he [Maximinus] indeed did not permit matters to go on in this way quite six months. Devising all possible means of destroying the peace, he first attempted to restrain us, under a pretext, from meeting in the cemeteries. [2.2] Then through the agency of some wicked men he had an embassy against us sent to himself, encouraging the citizens of Antioch to ask from him as a very great favour that he would by no means permit any of the Christians to dwell in their country; and others were secretly induced to do the same thing. ...

[4.2] As by a rescript the tyrant declared himself well pleased with their measures, persecution was rekindled against us. Priests for the images were then appointed by Maximinus himself in the cities, and besides them high priests. The latter were taken from among those who were most distinguished in public life and had gained celebrity in all the offices which they had filled; and who were imbued, moreover, with great zeal for the service of the idols they worshipped. [4.3] Indeed, the extraordinary superstition of the emperor, to speak briefly, led all his subjects, both rulers and private citizens, for the sake of gratifying him, to do everything against us, supposing that they could best show their gratitude to him for the benefits which they had received from him, by plotting murder against us and exhibiting toward us any new forms of malice. ...

[6.1] But we were obliged again to undergo exile and severe persecutions, and the governors in every province were once more stirred up against us fiercely; so that even some of those illustrious in the Divine Word were arrested and, without mercy, had the death sentence passed against them. ...

[6.4] Such trials were brought upon us in a brief time by Maximinus, the enemy of virtue, so that this persecution which was stirred up against us seemed far more cruel than the earlier one. ...

[7.2] It appears to me necessary to insert here this document of Maximinus which was posted on pillars, in order that there may be made manifest at the same time the boastful and haughty arrogance of the God-hating man. ...

[7.12] 'But if they still persist in their execrable vanity, let them, as you have desired, be driven far away from your city and territory, that thus, in accordance with your praiseworthy zeal in this matter, your city, being freed from every pollution and impiety, may, according to its native disposition, attend to the sacred rites of the immortal gods with becoming reverence.' ...

[7.15] This was published against us in all the provinces, depriving us of every hope of good, at least from men; so that, according to that divine utterance, 'If it were possible, even the elect would have stumbled' at these things. ...

[9.1] Thus when Constantine, whom we have already mentioned as an emperor, born of an emperor, a pious son of a most pious and prudent father, and Licinius, second to him – two God-beloved emperors, honoured alike for their intelligence and their piety – were stirred up by God, the absolute Ruler and Saviour of all, against the two most impious tyrants [Maxentius and Maximinus], they engaged in formal war against them, with God as their ally. Maxentius was defeated at Rome by Constantine in a remarkable manner, and the tyrant of the east did not long survive him, but met a most shameful death at the hand of Licinius, who had not yet become insane. ...

[10.7] Copy of the tyrant's edict in favour of the Christians, translated [into Greek] from Latin. 'The Emperor Caesar Gaius Valerius Maximinus, *Germanicus*, *Sarmaticus*, pious, fortunate, unconquered, Augustus. ... [10.8] When, before now, it came to our understanding that under pretext of the command of our most divine fathers Diocletian and Maximian, which prohibited Christians assembly, extortion and robbery had been practised widely by officials, and that increasingly those ongoing evils were harming our provincials whose interests are of particular concern to us, and whose possessions were dwindling away, letters were sent in the past year to the governors of each province, ordering that, if any one wished to follow such a practice or the same faith, he should be permitted without hindrance to pursue his purpose and should be obstructed and prevented by no-one, and that everyone should have licence to exercise their preference without any fear or suspicion. [10.9] But we have noticed that some of the judges have ignored our orders, causing our people to doubt the instructions, and making them reluctant to practise those religious acts which please them. [10.10] Therefore ... we have commanded that this edict be published, so that everyone can be clear that whoever wishes to practise this sect and religion is permitted to do so by virtue of this our indulgence; ... permission to build 'Lord's houses' is also granted. [10.11] But so that our indulgence may be greater, we have decided to order in addition that if any houses and property belonged by rights to the Christians before this time and according to the command of our fathers passed to the treasury's ownership, or were confiscated by any city council – whether they have been sold on or donated to anyone – all these should be restored to their original Christian owners, so that in this respect also everyone may know of our piety and care.'

## 9. John Malalas: *Chronicle* (after 574)
### Translated from the Greek original

[308.17] On the frontiers from Egypt to the Persian borders, the same Diocletian built camps, settling frontier troops in them; he chose generals and stationed one in each province behind the camps, with large numbers of men as a mobile reserve.

## 10. Zosimus: *New History* (fifth century)
### Translated from the Greek original

[2.34.1] In his providence, Diocletian safeguarded the empire by stationing all the army in cities, fortresses and towers on the frontiers; the barbarians could not cross the frontier, with troops everywhere to force them back. But Constantine ruined this security by withdrawing troops from the frontier to cities which did not need them.

## 11. *Panegyrici Latini* X(2) (21 April 289, Trier)
### (I Chapter 4.2)

[1.1] Since on all festival days, most sacred emperor [Maximian], your honour ought to be equated with divine affairs, then on this most celebrated day which is most joyful for you who are our emperors, worship of your godhead must be joined with the annual respect paid to the Sacred City. ... [3] For it is no story from poetic licence nor fancy from the rumours of long ago, but a clear and established fact, as the Great Altar of Hercules and the Pinaria family (guardians to the cult of Hercules) today bear witness that that founder of your family and name approached the walls of Pallanteum as victor and, although the palace was then only small, however when he was welcomed with such reverence, he made the beginnings of its future greatness, so that what had been the lodging house of Hercules could become the home of the emperors. ...

[2.2] Where should I begin? Indeed, shall I recall the services paid by your homeland to the state? ... [3] Or shall I recount the divine origin of your family, which you attest not only by your immortal deeds but also by the name you have inherited? [4] Or shall I speak of how you were raised and educated in that frontier, that seat of the most famous legions, amid the manoeuvres of energetic youth and the clash of arms echoing your infant cries? [5] These details are made up about Jupiter, but about you they are true, emperor. ...

[3.1] When you were called upon by your kindred godhead Diocletian to restore the state, you conferred more benefit than you received. ... [2] Your triumphal robes and consular *fasces*, your curule thrones, this retinue of attendants, the splendour, that light which rings your divine head in a clear orb, these are the trappings you have deserved, most beautiful indeed and most honoured. [3] But much greater by far is what you gave ... when you received power: to admit into your mind concern for so great a state, to assume responsibility for the destiny of the whole world, to forget yourself somehow and live for the people, to stand at the lofty pinnacle of human affairs, from where it is as if you look down on all land and sea, and you survey with eyes and mind in turn where calm is assured, where storms threaten, which judges copy your justice, which generals maintain the glory of your virtue, [4] to receive countless messengers from everywhere, to issue as many commands, to give thought to so many cities, nations and provinces, to spend all night and day in endless concern for the wellbeing of all. ...

[4.2] You [Maximian] came to the help of the Roman name, as it faltered, at the emperor's side, with that same opportune assistance as your Hercules once gave to your Jupiter, when he was beset with difficulties in his war with the Earthborn. Hercules then gained a great part of the victory, and proved that he had not so much received heaven from the gods as restored it to them. ...

[7.3] Formerly it seems that Nature herself had plotted the Rhine so that the Roman provinces would be protected from the savage barbarians by that frontier. [4] Before you became emperors, who ever failed to give thanks that Gaul was defended by that river? When did a period of good weather lower the level of the Rhine without causing us extreme fear? When did its floods increase without us feeling safe? [5] I believe the Euphrates protected the rich and fertile Syria in the same way, as if in an embrace, before the Persian kingdoms surrendered themselves to Diocletian. But he [Diocletian] executed this in the manner of his Jupiter, at whose paternal nod all things tremble, and by the majesty of your name. You, however, invincible emperor, have tamed those wild and untamed nations by ravaging, battles, massacres, with fire and sword. This is the lot of the race of Hercules, to owe what you claim to your virtue. [7] Let the Rhine dry up and struggle to push light pebbles with a weak current in its clear shallows – there is no fear there. Whatever I can see beyond the Rhine is Roman. ...

[9.1–2] In a recent fraternal summit meeting, you [emperors] exchanged shared examples of all the virtues, and in turn you increased them (apparently impossible!), Diocletian by showing you Persian gifts, you showing him German booty. ... [3] Both of you are now most bountiful, both most brave, and because of this very similarity of yours, you are more and more harmonious, and you are brothers in virtue, which is surer than blood kinship. ... [5] You [emperors] do this of your own accord, you whom not any similarity of features, but rather similarity of character has made equal in the highest affairs. ...

[11.1] Through your harmony, unconquered emperors, even fortune reacts to you with equally great success. For you rule the state with one mind, nor does the great distance which separates you hinder you from governing, so to speak, with right hands clasped. [2] And so, although you increase the royal majesty with your twinned godhead, by your unanimity you maintain the advantage of an undivided empire. [3] Therefore, if Greek poets do not vainly promise a twofold increase in their flocks and double yields from their trees to men who cultivate justice, now everything ought to be doubled for people throughout the world, whose masters you are, you who so scrupulously nurture justice and harmony. ... [6] For just as all useful things produced in the heavens or on land seem to come to reach us through the agency of different divinities, but nevertheless flow from the supreme creators, Jupiter, ruler of the heavens, and Hercules, pacifier of the Earth, so in all the most splendid exploits, even those carried out under the leadership of others, Diocletian makes the [*decisions/beginnings] and you [Maximian] fulfil them. ...

[14.1] Soon that day will dawn when Rome sees you victors, and alert at your right hand your son, born with every benefit of talent for most respected studies, for whom some lucky teacher waits. ... [4] And may you in particular light up these provinces (I believe that the east makes this very same request of Diocletian) and although they flourish in deepest peace, may you make the provinces happier by the arrival of your godhead. [5] Emperor, you see how great is the strength of your

---

* Unfortunately, at this key point, the Latin text is corrupt. It has been restored variously by editors (Nixon and Rodgers 1994: 71–2).

heavenly benefits to us: still we enjoy your presence, and already we long for your return.

## 12. *Panegyrici Latini* XI(3) (21 July 291, Trier)
### (I Chapter 4.2)

[2.2] Those very days on which you first took office are for that reason sacred and venerable because they declared such men emperors; but, for sure, your ... birthdays created those virtues with which you adorn your rule. [3] Most sacred emperor, every time they come round as the years revolve, we celebrate your birthdays with the same reverence for you as for your godheads, since you prove you are born of the gods both by your names but much more by your virtues. [4] The very force of divinity exercises the tireless movements and impulses of your virtues, a force which leads you in such journeys through the entire world which you rule. ... [4.1] For the reasons of your ancestry and native education, events often cause us surprise; now and then with the impatience of love we even feel fear because we cannot calculate your travels, because you refuse to linger for long in the same place, because neither the beauty of the regions nor the nobility of the cities nor even celebration of your victories detains you from your ceaseless course of achievements. ... [4] All your provinces, which you roam with godly speed, do not know where you are from one minute to the next; but they do know you have conquered everywhere.

[6.3] What age ever saw such harmony in the highest power? Which full or twin brothers enjoy an undivided inheritance as equally as you share the Roman world? ... [6] The Rhine and the Danube and the Nile and the Tigris with its twin the Euphrates and the two Oceans where the sun sets and rises again, and whatever lands and rivers and shores are between them, are as common to you, with ready goodwill, as the daylight in which the eyes take pleasure is common to them. [7] In this way, your sense of duty grants to you a double reward of divine power: each enjoys both his own empire and his colleague's. ... [7.5] You have mingled separate blood by your affections. [6] Your relationship is not of chance. [Your brotherhood] even conquers your difference in age, and with care for each other renders equals the older and younger ... . [7] For although you are different in age, most sacred emperors, we understand you have a twin accord. ... Neither of you favours his own nature more; each wishes to be what his brother is.

[10.4] Now however, as soon as your godhead shone forth from each summit of the Alps, a clearer light spread over all Italy. In equal measure wonder and uncertainty beset all who had gazed up – whether some gods were descending from those mountain tops, or by these steps they were coming down to earth from heaven. [5] But as you came closer and closer, and began to be recognised, all the fields were filled not only with men racing forward to see but even with flocks of animals leaving their distant pastures and groves; farmers rushed about amongst each other, announced to all what they had seen, altars were lit, incense placed upon them, wine libations were poured, sacrificial victims were slaughtered, everything was warm with joy, everything danced with applause, to the immortal gods praises and thanks were sung: not a Jupiter passed down by conjecture but a visible and present one was invoked near at hand, Hercules was adored not as a stranger but as the emperor.

[11.1] ... What a vision your piety granted when those who had been admitted into the palace at Milan to adore your sacred faces caught sight of you both, and your twinned godhead suddenly threw into confusion the customary practice of single veneration. ... [3] As if in an inner shrine, this private veneration stunned the minds only of those whose rank granted them access to you. When you crossed the threshold and were carried together through the middle of the city, I understand the buildings themselves almost moved as all men, women, children and elderly poured out from doorways onto the streets or leaned out of the windows of uppers storeys. [4] All shouted for joy, then without fear openly pointed at you: 'Do you see Diocletian? Do you see Maximian? They are both here! They are together! How closely they sit! How they chat in harmony! How quickly they pass by!'

[12.3] Meanwhile, however, while I bring before my eyes your daily conversations, your right hands joined at every conversation, the trivial and serious matters you shared, parties spent in contemplation of each other, the thought comes to me of the magnanimity with which you separated to revisit your armies and overcame your sense of duty for the benefit of the state. [4] What were your feelings at that time, what were your expressions! How incapable were your eyes of disguising the evidence of emotion! Of course, you looked back frequently, and this is not an empty fiction made up about you – [5] you exchanged such assurances since you intended soon to return to see each other. ...

[13.5] No part of the world lacks the presence of your majesty even when you seem to be absent. ... [14.3] [I proclaim that] wherever you are, although you may retire into one palace, your divinity is busy everywhere, all lands and all seas are filled with you. ...

[16.2] Sacred Jupiter and good Hercules, finally you have transferred civil war to the peoples who deserve that madness, and spread all that rage beyond the boundaries of this empire into enemy land. ...

[19.4–5] The stars which secure for you everlasting harmony, the affection of your families, and your enthusiasm to nurture the state likewise promise naval trophies in addition to the victories won all over the world, so that after the Punic Wars and the kings of Syria you may decorate the rostra of the Roman field with new spoils.

## 13. *Panegyrici Latini* VIII(4) (Spring 297, Trier)
### Anonymous (I Chapter 4.2)

[2.2] Let the divine birth of your majesty grant me my opening for today's rejoicing – an occasion brighter than the very beginning of spring which shone upon it. The day was calm and ... the summer sun was unseasonally warm, shining with a more honourable clarity of light than when it gave life to the beginning of the world. ...

[3.1] O spring, fertile and blessed with new growth, now joyful and venerable, not for the loveliness of your blossoms or the greenness of your crops or the jewels on the vines or the very Zephyr breezes and the light that is unlocked as much as for the origin of our greatest Caesars! O time at which everything is rightly believed to have been born, since we now see everything confirmed in the same season. O Kalends of March, just as you once were the beginning of the revolving years, so now you are the beginning of the eternal emperors. [2] Unconquered emperors, how many ages do you create for yourselves and the state by sharing the guardianship of your world? ...

[4.1] And, of course, in addition to the interests and concerns of the state, even that related majesty of Jupiter and Hercules, which is found in the emperors Iovius and Herculius, demanded a resemblance between the entire world and heavenly affairs. [2] Indeed, all the fundamentals rely on and rejoice in the number of your godhead: there are four elements and the same number of seasons of the year; and the world is divided fourfold by a double ocean; and the cycle of years returns after four revolutions of the sky; and the Sun's four-horse chariot; and Vesper and Lucifer added to the two lights of the sky. ...

[4] If I wanted to dwell on all these details, neither this day nor the next nor all thereafter would be enough, and I must take account of the time – Caesar is standing while I speak. ...

[6.1] Caesar you immediately conquered your Gaul by arriving there – your speed, by which you anticipated all reports of your elevation and arrival, caught the band of the piratical faction, who were trapped within the walls of Boulogne, stubborn in their wretched error, and denied access to the ocean which washes the city gates to those who once relied on the sea. ...

[9.3] And so, the Chamavian and the Frisian ploughs for me, and that vagabond and pillager labours at the cultivation of the neglected countryside, and attends my markets with livestock for sale; the barbarian farmer is bringing down the price of corn. ...

[11.1] [Britain] is so rich in crops, so fertile in the number of its pastures, so overflowing with streams of metals, so lucrative in tax-revenues, so girt with harbours, so vast in circumference. ...

[12.1] In that criminal banditry, first of all the fleet which had once protected Gaul was taken away by the pirate as he fled, and in addition, very many ships were built in our style, a Roman legion was seized, several divisions of foreign troops were intercepted, merchants of Gaul were gathered together for a levy, significant forces of barbarians were tempted by the booty from the provinces themselves, and they were all trained for naval service. ...

[13.1] Caesar, you so embarked upon this war which was so necessary, so difficult to approach, so long in the making and so well planned, that as soon as you stretched out the hostile thunderbolt of your majesty, everyone thought the war was over. ...

[14.5] For who would not dare to entrust himself to the sea, however adverse, when you were setting sail? It is said that when the news of your voyage was received, the united voice and encouragement was 'Why are we hesitating? Why do we delay? He himself has already set sail; he is moving forward; perhaps he has already arrived. Let us undergo everything, let us go through whatever waves there are. What is there for us to fear? We are following Caesar.' ...

[15.5] Why did the standard bearer of the criminal faction withdraw from the shore he held, why did he desert his fleet and harbour, unless because he feared your imminent arrival, unconquered Caesar, whose approaching sails he had seen? [6] He preferred to make trial of your generals than to receive in person the thunderbolt of your majesty – the fool who did not know that wherever he fled, the force of your divinity is everywhere that your images and standards are revered. [16.1] But in his flight he fell into the hands of your men, conquered by you he was crushed by your armies. ...

[17.2] O manifold victory of countless triumphs, in which Britain has been restored, the strength of the Franks completely routed, the obligation to obey imposed upon many peoples caught in the conspiracy of that crime, and finally the seas purged and returned to endless peace! [3] Boast yourself, indeed, invincible Caesar, that you have discovered another world, you who by restoring naval glory to Roman power have added to the empire an element greater than all lands. ...

[19.3] In addition to that reputation of yours for clemency and sense of duty which is celebrated by the common voice of nations, they saw the marks of all virtues in your face, Caesar; on the brow, dignity; in the eyes, gentleness; in the blush, modesty; in the speech, justice. [4] As they gazed and distinguished each of these, together they gave shouts of joy; to you they pledged themselves, to you they pledged their children, to your children they pledged all the future generations of their race. ...

[20.5] Everything which is worthy of you, I say, most invincible rulers, is yours, and as a result of this you may look after the interests of individual areas equally, since you hold them all. ...

[21.1] And so just formerly on your orders, Diocletian Augustus, Asia filled the deserts of Thrace by the transfer of its inhabitants, and as later, Maximian Augustus, at your command, the Laeti, restored by right of *postliminium*, and the Franks, granted access to our laws, have cultivated the empty fields of the Arvii and the Treveri, so now through your victories, unconquered Constantius Caesar, whatever land lay unused in the territory of the Ambiani, Bellovaci, Tricasses and Lingones turns green again under foreign cultivation.

## 14. *Panegyrici Latini* IX(5) Eumenius: 'On the Restoration of the Schools' (298, Trier ?) (I Chapter 4.2)

[4.1] Above all, therefore, your excellency, it is necessary to obey our Emperors' and Caesars' divine foresight and unusual kindness towards us in the restoration of this building too. They wanted to raise up and rebuild this city, which once gloried in the name of brother to the Roman people and was then finally struck by the most severe disaster when it was besieged by the banditry of a Batavian rebellion and called upon the aid of the Roman emperor, not only out of admiration for its merits but also from pity for its misfortunes; and they judged the very extent of its ruins worthy of everlasting memorials of their own generosity, so that the greater the task of rebuilding, the more illustrious the glory of the things rebuilt would be.

[6.1] But I cannot sufficiently admire the incredible concern and kindness toward the youth of his Gauls of our lord Constantius, truly the prince of youth. [2] He increased the honour of scholarship with this distinction too: when I was attempting to gain access to my former position for my son rather than for me, he ordered me to take up the teaching of oratory again. ...

[9.2] But what is situated more in the face and countenance of this city than these same Maenianae, which are placed right in the path of the most invincible rulers as they arrive here? ...

[18.4] Why should I number the camps of cavalry units and cohorts restored along the whole of the Rhine, Danube and Euphrates frontiers?

### 15. *Panegyrici Latini* VII(6) (307, Trier)
Anonymous (**I Chapter 4.2**)

[1.5] But we who are present in person to witness such a boon to the state ought to surpass all men in our rejoicing; and from consideration of your faces [Maximian and Constantine] we understand that you are so concordant that you have joined not only your right hands but even your feelings and minds, so that, if it were possible to be done, you would want to cross over into each other's hearts. ...

[6.2] For this, as I hear, is demonstrated by that picture in the palace at Aquileia, placed on view in the dining room. In it a young girl already adorable for her divine beauty, but as yet unequal to her burden, holds up and offers to you, then still a lad, Constantine, a helmet gleaming with gold and jewels, and conspicuous with its plumes of a beautiful bird, in order that her betrothal present might enhance your beauty, a result which scarcely any ornaments of clothing can produce. ...

[9.2] [You were] not led by lack of care for the state, nor by escape from work nor desire for idleness, but by brotherly duty and commitment to a plan long since agreed, as it happens, by both of you. ...

[14.2] So it will come about that you both have the counsel of a single heart and each the strength of two. ...

[3] Divine Constantius, fortunate during your reign and more fortunate afterwards, for you hear and see [this marriage] ... [4–6] How delighted will you be, how much pleasure will you enjoy when the same man as father, father-in-law and emperor has brought into possession of your empire such a son as yours, who first made you father! ... Maximian is not lacking a son such as you were, nor Constantine a father.

### 16. *Panegyrici Latini* VI(7) (310, Trier)
Anonymous (**I Chapter 4.2**)

[1.4] Although I look upon all of you with due reverence, most victorious emperors, whose majesty is harmonious and allied, however,

I shall address this speech, such as it is, to your godhead alone, Constantine. ...

[2.1] And so I shall begin with the first godhead of your family, about whom perhaps most people are still in ignorance, but those who love you most know. [2] For, there is in you an ancestral relationship from the deified Claudius [Gothicus] who first re-established the discipline of the Roman empire when it was dissolute and ruined. ... [3] Therefore although the anniversary of your accession was recently honoured with celebration as being most blessed, since that day first dressed you in your imperial robes, your imperial fortune had already come to you from that founder of the family. [4] Indeed, that ancient prerogative of your imperial house promoted your father himself, so that now you stand at the highest summit above the fate of human affairs, the third emperor after two rulers from your family. ... [3.1] No lucky consensus amongst men or any sudden outcome of favour made you emperor: you deserved power through your birth. ...

[5.1] Who cannot still see how and to what great extent [Constantius] embellished the state? On his first arrival on obtaining power he shut off the seething ocean from the countless enemy ships, and surrounded by land and sea alike that army which had settled on Boulogne's shore. ... [3] Not satisfied to have won, he brought [Frankish] people into Roman territory so that they were forced to put down not only their weapons but even their ferocity. ...

[7.5] For you were called to rescue the state by the vote of the gods when your father was crossing to Britain, and your arrival lit up the fleet as it set sail. ...

[14.5] When [Maximian] was about to come into the light of day and received a choice about his life, I believe he ran into an inescapable fate that would bring an unjust death to many men and finally, suicide to him. ... [15.4] But [Diocletian], that godlike man who was the first to share power and resign it, regrets neither his plan nor his action, and he does think he has lost what he transferred of his own accord.

## 17. *Panegyrici Latini* V(8) (311, Trier)
### Anonymous to Constantine (I Chapter 4.2)

[2.1] In this city which still enjoys your presence ... the whole contingent of your friends and the complete apparatus of empire stands by your side and ... all men from almost every city are here, either commissioned on public duty or to petition you on their own account. ...

[5.5] We were in possession of the fields which had been registered, and we were bound by the common formula of the Gallic census. ... [6.1] As I said, we have both the number of men who were recorded and the amount of land, but both are in vain because of the sloth of the men and the treachery of the land. ... [7.2] You did not see, as throughout the land of other cities, almost everything cultivated, cleared, flourishing, passable roads, navigable rivers washing the very gates of towns, but right from that turning-point where the road leads back into Belgica, everything devastated, uncultivated, neglected, silent, and dark. ...

[8.1] Emperor, you wondered from where such a crowd poured out to meet you, since from the neighbouring mountain-top you had seen the place deserted. For all men of all ages flew from the fields to see the one man they happily want to outlive them. ... [4] No doubt we decorated the streets which lead to the palace with wretched material, but we brought out the symbols of all the colleges and statues of all our gods and produced our very few decent musical instruments which, by means of short-cuts, greeted you on several occasions. ...

[9.3] For it is no light matter to make on one's own behalf a request of the emperor of the whole world, to put on a brave face at the sight of such a great majesty, to compose one's features, to reassure one's mind, to think of the words, to pronounce them confidently, to stop at the suitable place, to await a reply. ...

[10.5] Intent on reducing the burden of the census, you set the figure; intent on waiving our outstanding debts, you asked how great they were. ... [11.1] You remitted 7,000 *capita*, more than a fifth of our census.

## 18. *Historia Augusta* (c. 395)
### Translated from the Latin original (I Introduction I)

[Carus 13.1] When it was asked who would be the most just avenger of Numerian and who could be presented as a good leader of the state, with the gods' approval everyone proclaimed Diocletian Augustus, about whom many omens of imperial rule were said to have been made already. At the time, Diocletian was in charge of the imperial bodyguard, an outstanding man, wise, devoted to the state and his family, and ready for everything circumstances demanded. His counsel was always profound, though sometimes too bold, but he checked the impulses of his restless inclinations with prudence and great resolution.

[Elagabalus 35.4] ... Diocletian, father of a golden age, and Maximian, as is generally said, father of an iron one ...

## 19. *Edict of Maximal Prices* (November, 301)
Translated from the Latin text, itself reconstructed
from various inscriptions (**I Chapter 3.3**)

[Preface 1] The emperor Caesar Gaius Aurelius Valerius Diocletianus, pious, fortunate, unconquered, Augustus, *pontifex maximus*, *Germanicus maximus* for the sixth time, *Sarmaticus maximus* for the fourth time, *Persicus maximus* for the second time, *Brittanicus maximus*, *Carpicus maximus*, *Armenicus maximus*, *Medicus maximus*, *Adiabenicus maximus*, in the eighteenth year of his tribunician power and his seventh consulship, in the eighteenth year of his imperial power, father of his country, proconsul; [pr. 2] and the emperor Caesar Marcus Aurelius Valerius Maximianus, pious, fortunate, unconquered, Augustus, *pontifex maximus*, *Germanicus maximus* for the fifth time, *Sarmaticus maximus* for the fourth time, *Persicus maximus* for the second time, *Brittanicus maximus*, *Carpicus maximus*, *Armenicus maximus*, *Medicus maximus*, *Adiabenicus maximus*, in the seventeenth year of his tribunician power and his sixth consulship, in the seventeenth year of his imperial power, father of his country, proconsul; [pr. 3] and Flavius Valerius Constantius, *Germanicus maximus* for the second time, *Sarmaticus maximus* for the second time, *Persicus maximus* for the second time, *Brittanicus maximus*, *Carpicus maximus*, *Armenicus maximus*, *Medicus maximus*, *Adiabenicus maximus*, in the ninth year of his tribunician power, in his third consulship, most noble Caesar; [pr. 4] and Galerius Valerius Maximianus, *Germanicus maximus* for the second time, *Sarmaticus maximus* for the second time, *Persicus maximus* for the second time, *Brittanicus maximus*, *Carpicus maximus*, *Armenicus maximus*, *Medicus maximus*, *Adiabenicus maximus*, in the ninth year of his tribunician power, in his third consulship, most noble Caesar, declare: [pr. 5] Public virtue and Roman dignity and majesty will it that the fortune of our state be organised in good faith and elegantly adorned – second to the immortal gods, it is right to give thanks to the state as we remember the wars we have fought successfully, at a time when the world is in tranquillity, placed in the lap of deepest calm with the benefits of a peace which was earned with much sweat. Therefore, we who by the kind favour of the gods have crushed the burning havoc caused in the past by barbarian nations by slaughtering those people themselves, have protected the peace established for all time with the necessary defences of justice.

[pr. 6] If any restraint might curb those inclinations with which raging greed burns without end – avarice which without care for humankind hurries towards its own growth and gain, not by year or month or day, but almost by hour and minute – or if society's experience could with equanimity tolerate the licence to rage freely by which in its misfortune it is harmed most seriously day after day, perhaps there would be left an opportunity for dissimulation and reticence, since the communal patience in spirit would alleviate the hateful cruelty and wretched situation. [pr. 7] But because it is the single desire of untamed fury to give no account to the common need, and amongst wicked and extravagant people it is almost held a religion of greed, swelling and rising with violent emotions, to hold off harming the fortune of all through necessity rather than its own will, and since those whom extremes of poverty brought to a appreciation of their most wretched circumstances can no longer close their eyes to it, as we looked on, we who are the parents of the human race decided that justice should intervene as arbiter, so that a solution which has for a long time been desired but humankind has been unable to provide could, by the remedy of our foresight, be brought, for the general moderation of all.

[pr. 8] While we were devising plans or storing up remedies we had already discovered – in the hope that (as must be hoped for, through the laws of nature) when mankind is caught committing most serious crimes it might reform itself – thinking it far preferable for the stains of intolerable plundering to be removed, in sense and decision by the agreed judgement of the very men whom as they fell daily into worse offences and by some moral blindness inclined towards crimes against the state, serious guilt had identified as enemies of individuals and state, responsible for most vicious inhumanity, our provision for this situation comes almost too late, as the common knowledge of everyone realises, and the true reality of the situation proclaims [pr. 9]. Therefore, we rush to the remedies long required by circumstances, free from complaints that the intervention of our remedy might be thought untimely or unnecessary, or lenient or of no consequence amongst the wicked who, although aware that our silence of so many years was a lesson in restraint, have been unwilling to learn it [pr. 10]. For who is of such an unfeeling heart or is so removed from human sympathy that he cannot know, or rather has not sensed, that in the transactions conducted in the markets or effected in the daily exchange of the cities, liberties with prices are so widespread that uncurbed desire for profit is checked neither by plentiful supplies nor by fruitful harvests? [pr. 11] so that clearly, men of this type occupied in this line of work, always have it in mind to watch for the very breezes and weather by the movements of the stars, and in their iniquity they cannot bear it that fertile fields are watered from above to create hope for future harvests, since they consider it a loss to themselves if the moderation of the very heavens brings forth an abundance. [pr. 12] They are always keen to turn to profit the gifts of the gods, and to trim the affluence of general prosperity, and again, in years of poor harvest, to trade in losses and the services of pedlars – men who individually overflowing with the greatest riches, which could amply satisfy whole populations, go after small incomes and pursue damaging interest-rates. Common concern for humanity persuades us to set a limit on the greed of these men, O our provincials.

[pr. 13] But even now we must explain the causes whose necessity, long time postponed, has finally forced our patience to make provision, so that, although it is difficult to expose the greed which rages across the whole world with a specific argument or fact, however, the establishment of a remedy may be thought more just when the most un-restrained men are forced to recognise the untamed desires of their minds by some signs and tokens. [pr. 14] So who does not know that audacity, ambushing the public wellbeing, comes to the mind of the profiteer – wherever the common safety of all demands our armies be directed, not only through villages or towns, but throughout their entire journey – the audacity to extort a price for goods, not fourfold or eightfold but such that human speech cannot find words for the price and the act? Who does not know that sometimes a soldier is deprived of his donative and salary in the transaction of a single exchange, and that the whole world's entire tax contributions for the maintenance of armies is spent on the hateful profits of thieves, so that by their own hand our troops seem to transfer the hopes of their military career and their past efforts to universal profiteers, and those who ravage the state seize more day by day than they know how to hold?

[pr. 15] Since now humankind itself seems to be praying for help, justly and deservedly moved by all the matters outlined above, we have decided not that the prices of merchandise be fixed – for that would not be held just when occasionally many provinces celebrate the blessings of low prices and, as it were, the privilege of affluence – but that a ceiling should be fixed, so that when any violence of high prices appears (may the gods avert the omen!), the greed which could not be contained as if in the enormity of wide open spaces, should be restricted by the limits of our statute or the boundaries of law intended to restrain. [pr. 16] Therefore, it is decided that the prices set out in the text of the attached list be kept and observed by the whole world of ours, so that everyone may know that permission to exceed them has been denied, but without affecting the blessing of low prices in those areas where an abundant supply of goods is seen to flow – particular provision is made for this, when greed is restrained and suppressed. [pr. 17] And amongst buyers and sellers whose practice it is to visit ports and foreign provinces, this general decree should be a check, so that when they know in times of high prices that the prices fixed for goods cannot be exceeded, calculation of places, transportation and the entire business may be reckoned at the time of sale, whereby it is seen to have been justly decided that those who transport goods cannot sell them anywhere at a higher price.

[pr. 18] Therefore, since it is established that in the practice of passing laws even our ancestors suppressed insolence by prescribing a penalty to be feared – because it is unusual for a policy improving the human condition to be embraced of its own accord and as a guide, a most just fear is always found to govern responsibilities – it has been decided that if anyone works against this statute, for their boldness they will be subject to capital punishment. Let nobody consider this ruling harsh, as there is an immediate means of avoiding danger – by observing moderation. And he is subject to the same punishment who, in his desire to buy, conspires with the seller's greed against the statute. [pr. 19] And he will not rest immune from the same punishment who, in possession of goods necessary for life and business, thinks that after this regulation he must withdraw them [from the market], since punishment ought to be harsher for him who causes poverty than for him who aggravates it contrary to law.

[pr. 20] Therefore, we urge the sense of devotion in everyone to respect with calm obedience and due reverence the established ruling, particularly since a statute of this kind is seen not to provide for individual cities, peoples and provinces, but the whole world, to whose ruin a few people are known to have raged, people whose greed can be neither reduced nor satisfied by fullness of time nor riches, for which they are seen to strive.

*Prices for the sale of individual items which nobody can exceed are displayed below:*

**I**

| | | |
|---|---|---|
| wheat | army *modius* | 100 *denarii* |
| barley | 1 army *modius* | 60 *denarii* |
| rye | 1 army *modius* | 60 *denarii* |
| crushed millet | 1 army *modius* | 100 *denarii* |

| | | |
|---|---|---|
| whole millet | 1 army *modius* | 50 *denarii* |
| panic grass | 1 army *modius* | 50 *denarii* |
| hulled spelt | 1 army *modius* | 100 *denarii* |
| spelt | 1 army *modius* | 30 *denarii* |
| crushed beans | 1 army *modius* | 100 *denarii* |
| whole beans | 1 army *modius* | 60 *denarii* |
| lentils | 1 army *modius* | 100 *denarii* |
| chickling | 1 army *modius* | 80 *denarii* |
| crushed peas | 1 army *modius* | 100 *denarii* |
| whole peas | 1 army *modius* | 60 *denarii* |
| chickpeas | 1 army *modius* | 100 *denarii* |
| bitter vetch | 1 army *modius* | 100 *denarii* |
| oats | 1 army *modius* | 30 *denarii* |
| fenugreek | 1 army *modius* | 100 *denarii* |
| raw lupines | 1 army *modius* | 60 *denarii* |
| cooked lupines | 1 Italian pint | 4 *denarii* |
| dried kidney beans | 1 army *modius* | 100 *denarii* |
| flaxseed | 1 army *modius* | 150 *denarii* |
| cleaned rice | 1 army *modius* | 200 *denarii* |
| cleaned barley grits | 1 *modius* | 100 *denarii* |
| cleaned spelt grits | 1 *modius* | 200 *denarii* |
| sesame | 1 army *modius* | 200 *denarii* |
| hay seed | 1 army *modius* | 30 *denarii* |
| alfalfa seed | 1 army *modius* | 150 *denarii* |
| hemp seed | 1 army *modius* | 80 *denarii* |
| dried vetch | 1 army *modius* | 80 *denarii* |
| poppy | 1 army *modius* | 150 *denarii* |
| cleaned cumin | 1 army *modius* | 200 *denarii* |
| radish seed | 1 army *modius* | 150 *denarii* |
| mustard | 1 army *modius* | 150 *denarii* |
| prepared mustard | 1 Italian pint | 8 *denarii* |

…

## IV  Likewise for meat

| | | |
|---|---|---|
| pork | 1 Italian pound | 12 *denarii* |
| beef | 1 Italian pound | 8 *denarii* |
| goat or mutton | 1 Italian pound | 8 *denarii* |
| sow's womb | 1 Italian pound | 24 *denarii* |
| sow's udder | 1 Italian pound | 20 *denarii* |
| best fig-fed pig's liver | 1 Italian pound | 16 *denarii* |
| best salted pork | 1 Italian pound | 16 *denarii* |

| | | |
|---|---|---|
| best Menapic or Cerritane ham | 1 Italian pound | 20 *denarii* |
| Marsic ham | 1 Italian pound | 20 *denarii* |
| fat, fresh pork | 1 Italian pound | 12 *denarii* |
| pork fat ointment | 1 Italian pound | 12 *denarii* |
| The four feet and stomach are sold at the same price as the meat | | |
| pork sausage | 1 ounce | 12 *denarii* |
| beef sausage | 1 Italian pound | 10 *denarii* |
| smoked Lucanian pork sausage | 1 Italian pound | 16 *denarii* |
| smoked Lucanian beef sausage | 1 Italian pound | 10 *denarii* |
| fattened pheasant | | 250 *denarii* |
| wild pheasant | | 125 *denarii* |
| fattened hen pheasant | | 200 *denarii* |
| unfattened hen pheasant | | 100 *denarii* |
| fattened goose | | 200 *denarii* |
| unfattened goose | | 100 *denarii* |
| chickens | pair | 60 *denarii* |
| partridge | | 30 *denarii* |
| turtledove | | 16 *denarii* |
| wild turtledove | | 12 *denarii* |
| thrushes | 10 | 60 *denarii* |
| ringdoves | pair | 20 *denarii* |
| pigeons | pair | 24 *denarii* |
| francolin | | 20 *denarii* |
| ducks | pair | 40 *denarii* |
| hare | | 150 *denarii* |
| rabbit | | 40 *denarii* |
| songbird | 10 | 40 *denarii* |
| wild songbird | 10 | 20 *denarii* |
| figpeckers | 10 | 40 *denarii* |
| sparrows | 10 | 16 *denarii* |
| dormice | 10 | 40 *denarii* |
| peacock | | 300 *denarii* |
| peahen | | 200 *denarii* |
| quails | 10 | 20 *denarii* |
| starlings | 10 | 20 *denarii* |
| boar | 1 Italian pound | 16 *denarii* |
| venison | 1 Italian pound | 12 *denarii* |
| gazelle or wild goat or roe | 1 Italian pound | 12 *denarii* |
| suckling pig | 1 Italian pound | 16 *denarii* |
| lamb | 1 Italian pound | 12 *denarii* |
| kid | 1 Italian pound | 12 *denarii* |

| | | |
|---|---|---|
| suet, beef or mutton | 1 Italian pound | 6 *denarii* |
| butter | 1 Italian pound | 16 *denarii* |
| … | | |

## VII For wages

| | | |
|---|---|---|
| farm labourer, with maintenance | daily | 25 *denarii* |
| stone mason, with maintenance | daily | 50 *denarii* |
| cabinet maker, with maintenance | daily | 50 *denarii* |
| carpenter, with maintenance | daily | 50 *denarii* |
| lime burner, with maintenance | daily | 50 *denarii* |
| worker in marble paving and walls, with maintenance | daily | 60 *denarii* |
| wall mosaicist, with maintenance | daily | 60 *denarii* |
| worker in tessellated floors, with maintenance | daily | 50 *denarii* |
| wall painter, with maintenance | daily | 75 *denarii* |
| figure painter, with maintenance | daily | 150 *denarii* |
| wagonwright, with maintenance | daily | 50 *denarii* |
| blacksmith, for wagons, with maintenance | daily | 50 *denarii* |
| baker, with maintenance | daily | 50 *denarii* |
| shipwright, for seagoing vessels, with maintenance | daily | 60 *denarii* |
| shipwright, for rivergoing vessels, with maintenance | daily | 50 *denarii* |
| maker of bricks for firing, for 4 x 2ft bricks, and clay preparation, with maintenance | daily | 2 *denarii* |
| maker of sun-dried bricks, for 8 bricks, and clay preparation, with maintenance | daily | 2 *denarii* |
| camel, ass and hinny driver, with maintenance | daily | 25 *denarii* |
| shepherd, with maintenance | daily | 20 *denarii* |
| mule driver, with maintenance | daily | 25 *denarii* |
| veterinary, for clipping and preparing hoofs | per animal | 6 *denarii* |
| veterinary, for bleeding and cleaning the head | per animal | 20 *denarii* |
| barber | per man | 2 *denarii* |
| shearer, with maintenance | per animal | 2 *denarii* |

…

| notary, for writing a petition or legal documents | per 100 lines | 10 *denarii* |
|---|---|---|

…

| elementary teacher | per boy per month | 50 *denarii* |
|---|---|---|
| teacher of arithmetic | per boy per month | 75 *denarii* |
| teacher of shorthand | per boy per month | 75 *denarii* |
| copyist and antiquaries teacher | per pupil per month | 50 *denarii* |
| teacher of Greek or Latin and geometry | per pupil per month | 200 *denarii* |
| teacher of rhetoric or public speaking | per pupil per month | 250 *denarii* |
| advocate or jurist, for initiating a case | fee | 250 *denarii* |
| advocate or jurist, for pleading a case | fee | 1,000 *denarii* |
| architecture teacher | per boy per month | 100 *denarii* |
| supervisor of clothes | per bather | 2 *denarii* |
| keeper of a private bath | per bather | 2 *denarii* |

### 20.  *I.L.S.* 613 (Nicomedia)
Translated from the Latin

To the everlasting Gaius Aurelius Valerius Diocletian, the pious and fortunate Augustus, whose foresight ordered that the washroom of the Antonine Baths, utterly in ruins, be enlarged at his own expense and given to the public.

### *I.L.S.* 620 (town gates, Grenoble)
Translated from the Latin

When by their foresight the walls of Grenoble and the interior buildings had been built and finished, our lords the emperor Caesar Gaius Aurelius Valerius Diocletian, the pious and fortunate unconquered Augustus and the emperor Caesar Marcus Aurelius Valerius Maximian, the pious and fortunate unconquered Augustus ordered that the Roman gate be called the 'Iovian'.

When by their foresight the walls of Grenoble and the interior buildings had been built and finished, our lords the emperor Caesar Gaius Aurelius Valerius Diocletian, the pious and fortunate unconquered Augustus and the emperor Caesar Marcus Aurelius Valerius Maximian, the pious and fortunate unconquered Augustus ordered that the Viennese gate be called the 'Herculian'.

### I.L.S. 624 (Aquileia)
Translated from the Latin

The unconquered Augusti Diocletian and Maximian, to the god Sol.

### I.L.S. 640 (294, Vitudurum, Gaul)
Translated from the Latin

The emperor Caesar Gaius Aurelius Valerius Diocletian, *pontifex maximus, Germanicus maximus, Sarmaticus maximus, Persicus maximus*, with tribunician power for the eleventh time, emperor for the tenth, consul the fifth, father of his country, proconsul, and the emperor Caesar Marcus Aurelius Valerius Maximianus, *pontifex maximus, Germanicus maximus, Sarmaticus maximus, Persicus maximus*, with tribunician power for the tenth time, emperor for the ninth, consul the fourth, father of his country, proconsul, the pious and fortunate unconquered Augusti, and Valerius Constantius and Galerius Valerius the most noble Caesars, at their own expense built the wall at Vitudurum from the ground ...

### I.L.S. 646 (305, Rome)
Translated from the Latin

Having bought up the buildings for an enterprise of such size and all refinement, our lords Diocletian and Maximian the unconquered senior Augusti, fathers, emperors and Caesars, and our lords Constantius and Maximian [Galerius] the unconquered Augusti, and Severus and Maximinus the most noble Caesars, dedicated the completed fortunate Baths of Diocletian to their Roman people, baths which on his return from Africa in the presence of his majesty Maximian Augustus arranged and ordered to be built and consecrated to the name of his brother the Augustus Diocletian.

### A.E. 1933: 145 (Syria)
Translated from the Latin

Diocletian and Maximian Augusti and Constantius and Maximian Caesars ordered this stone to be set up to mark the boundary of the village of Mezze and Pamoioi, with most perfect Aelius Statutus supervising.

## 21. Panopolis Papyri
Translated from the Greek original (**I Chapter 2.4**)

### *P. Beatty Panop. 1. 53–9* (13 September 298)

[From the *strategos* of the *nome* of Panopolis] to the president:
With regard to the supplies of the *annona* ordered to be stored up in various places in preparation for the auspiciously impending visit of our ruler the emperor Diocletian, the senior Augustus, I have both a first and a second time instructed you with all speed to select receivers and overseers of provisions for the most noble soldiers who will enter the city, in order that no more delay may occur in regard to this most honourable duty. But since up to the present nothing requisite has been achieved by you, now for the third time I enjoin you to take the appropriate measures with regard to this honourable visitation, and also carry into execution the orders of Aurelius Isidorus, the procurator of the Lower Thebaid.
This letter is written by the clerk Leon, and signed by me.

### *1.167–79* (15 September 298)

[From the *strategos* of the *nome* of Panopolis] to the procurator.
Upon your orders, my lord, that the ships of the treasury requisitioned from the Upper Thebaid should be repaired and refitted from treasury funds for the service of the auspiciously impending visit of our ruler the emperor Diocletian, the ever-victorious senior Augustus, I have commanded the president of the city, Aurelius Plutogenes also called Rhodinus, to select a surveyor, so that the supervision of the aforesaid ships may be carried out honestly and for the profit of the most sacred treasury; and also to select an overseer of the same ships, to receive the money from the public bank and account for the expenditure incurred, so that by all means the true amount expended may be known to you in your diligence. But he, in contempt for this most honourable duty, had the audacity to reply that the city ought not to be troubled. How, then, is it possible, when this man shows such contempt for me in my mediocrity, for the repairs of the ships to be carried out and provision for their refitting to be made? And not only this, but there is the appointment of receivers and overseers of the supplies of the *annona* which have been ordered to be reviewed in different localities in readiness for those who are expected to arrive with our ruler Diocletian,

the senior Augustus. Concerning all these matters I have had to press him, and, not being satisfied with this, have also commanded the same president in writing, not only once but many times. And since he has not even yet nominated the receivers and overseers, I have found it necessary to report to you, in your concern for everything, enclosing copies, not only of my letters to him, but also of his replies, concerning both the surveyor and the overseer of the treasury ships. For if this man begins to disobey orders, others may try to do the same thing, and through this and his unparalleled insolence, the whole administration is endangered.

This letter is signed by me.

### *1.184–7* (15 September 298)

[From the *strategos* of the *nome* of Panopolis] to Polycrates, also called Petetriphis, son of Triadelphus, surveyor:

The most excellent senate, through its president in office, Aurelius Plutogenes also called Rhodinus, as he informs me, has signified its selection of you as surveyor of the treasury ships being constructed in accordance with the order of Aurelius Isidorus, procurator of the Lower Thebaid. In order therefore that you may be informed, and honestly enter upon the duties entrusted to you, I have sent you orders by my servant Colanthus.

This letter is signed by me.

### *1.213–6* (17 September 298)

[From the *strategos* of the *nome* of Panopolis] to the night police:

In his letters directed to me the most eminent governor of the Thebaid, Julius Athenodorus, has ordered that by all possible means search should be made for Nilus, a smith from the city of Hermonthis, who is required for work in the arsenal, and that he should be taken into custody and sent under escort, together with his tools, to his Highness; for this reason, I must hasten to order you to find and detain this man so that you do not place yourselves in jeopardy by disregarding these orders.

This letter is signed by me.

### *1.221–4* (17 September 298)

[From the *strategos* of the *nome* of Panopolis] to the senate:

Letters have just arrived from Aurelius Isidorus, procurator of the Lower Thebaid, in which he gives orders concerning both the preparation of the same *annona* of the most noble soldiers who are expected to arrive here with our ruler Diocletian, the invincible senior Augustus, and also the comestibles. Accordingly, enclosing a copy of what has been written concerning these same comestibles, I am obliged to order you to take measures for these provisions, and to select receivers and overseers for each dwelling and each kind of provision, and report to me; and also to appoint for the comestibles capable men who are able to execute the duty entrusted to them.

This letter is signed by me.

### *1.249–51* (17 September 298)

[From the *strategos* of the *nome* of Panopolis] to Hermias, son of Paniscus, overseer of vegetables:

In his communication to me, Aurelius Plutogenes, president in office, has notified me that you have been selected for the post of overseer of vegetables in preparation for the auspiciously impending visit of our ruler, the ever-victorious Diocletian, the senior Augustus. In order, therefore, that you may know and cause the necessary superintendence and disposition to be carried out by those responsible, this communication is sent to you by the hand of my servant Leon.

This letter is signed by me.

### *1.264–71* (18 September 298)

[From the *strategos* of the *nome* of Panopolis] to Aurelius Isidorus, procurator of the Lower Thebaid:

In accordance with the letters from you in your clemency, I have ordered the president of the city, Aurelius Plutogenes also called Rhodinus, to select the collectors, distributors, and receivers of the *annona* separately, so that the collection and distribution may be carried out smoothly by them. But he employed a different means, in order to confound and embarrass the military commissariat. For when he should have appointed the collectors of all kinds of provisions for each and every *toparchy* together and collectively, and not separately for each kind of provision, in order to speed up both the collection of the provisions and their transfer to the receivers or distributors, he nevertheless selected them for each and every kind of provision, and through this the whole organisation is, I fear, frustrated. For this reason, I request, if it pleases you, that you order that letters be written to him, so that collectors already nominated for each *toparchy* should make the collection of all kinds of provisions in concert, and that the receivers or distributors of each kind of provision should act together for the whole territory, both the city and the entire *nome*. For if this is done, the collection will run smoothly, and the distribution to the most noble soldiers will be facilitated. And, to avoid misinterpreting his communications to me, I enclose copies, referring them to you in your exactitude, my lord.

## *1.332–7* (19 September 298)

[From the *strategos* of the *nome* of Panopolis] to the president:
For the auspiciously impending visit of our master the emperor Diocletian, the senior Augustus, it is necessary that the other bakery near the theatre should be made ready so that the military supplies may be continuously maintained. As this requirement is now urgent, I hasten to order you to appoint after the usual manner a commissioner who will in all honesty undertake the repair of the bakery and will also provide for the bakers who will have to work there, so that by all means the most noble soldiers may receive their supplies.
This letter is signed by me.

## *1.353–64* (23 September 298)

[From the *strategos* of the *nome* of Panopolis] to the senate:
Immediately upon receipt of orders from Aurelius Isidorus, procurator of the Lower Thebaid, that preparation should be made of all kinds of provisions for the military commissariat, I ordered you, in accordance with the written instructions of his Grace, to select receivers or distributors separately, but collectors in a distinct category, so that both the collection and the distribution might proceed smoothly without endangering any of the interests of the military commissariat. But since, to judge from the information you have given me, it is your intention to nominate, by *toparchies*, two collectors for each and every type of provision, and distributors or overseers similarly, and thus the service is, I fear, likely to be endangered, and since, moreover, the soldiers stationed here are continually bothering me about the distribution of meat and other provisions, I am now forced to order you to bring together the collectors nominated by you for each of *toparchy* and each type of provision and appoint them collectively in each *toparchy* for all types of provisions of the military commissariat, and report to me; and similarly that the receivers or distributors for each type of provision for the entire *nome* should come together and carry out the distribution here, that is to say, of wine separately, of meat separately, of barley separately ... in order that the distribution may proceed smoothly. For if this is done, both the overseers will carry out the distributions with all possible smoothness by acting in unison, and in consequence no

interruption or delay will occur in the collection and distribution of the provisions.

This letter is signed by me.

### 1.365–8 (23 September 298)

[From the *strategos* of the *nome* of Panopolis] to the senate:

In his letters to me, Valerius Melas, the most excellent *procurator rei privatae* of the Thebaid, has ordered that in addition to the existing superintendents of the treasury estates, four others should be appointed so that nothing be lost from the present harvest of the estates. I must therefore hasten to order you to conform with these instructions, and to nominate the aforesaid four persons, who should be adequate both in property and in capability as has been ordered.

This letter is signed by me.

### 1.369–73 (23 September 298)

[From the *strategos* of the *nome* of Panopolis] to Valerius Melas, *procurator rei privatae*:

In accordance with the instructions of your excellency, my lord, concerning the four suitable and trustworthy men who are to be appointed additionally to the already existing superintendents of the treasury estates, I have ordered the most excellent senate, through Aurelius Plutogenes, president in office, to act in conformity with your instructions, my lord. But they have replied to the effect that orders by my lord the most eminent governor of the Thebaid, Julius Athenodorus, establish that no-one enjoying curial rank should be subjected to a treasury duty. Accordingly, I enclose a copy of their reply and refer it to you in your consideration for everything.

This letter is signed by me.

### 1.400–4 (24 September 298)

[From the *strategos* of the *nome* of Panopolis] to the most excellent senate:

The letter sent by you to me yesterday concerning the order given by my lord the most eminent governor of the Thebaid, Julius Athenodorus, that nobody enjoying curial rank should be subjected to a duty of the treasury I enclosed in a letter and referred to Valerius Melas the most excellent *procurator rei privatae* of the Thebaid, so that in his universal providence, he might be informed. On receiving this letter, he wrote in reply ordering that you should nominate four other responsible men, in addition to the posts already existing, for the supervision of the treasury lands. And to preclude misinterpretation of what he has written to me, I enclose a copy, enjoining you to act accordingly, for the profit of the most sacred treasury.

This letter is signed by me.

### 2.32–5 (25 January 300)

Aurelius Isidorus, procurator of the Lower Thebaid, to the *strategi* of the *nomes* of Hermopolis, Antinois, Cussis, Lycopolis, Antaeopolis and Panopolis:

Demand the arrears of corn owing from the harvest of the year 296–7 without any delay, and credit them to the accounts of the most sacred treasury – for both the time limit and the margin allowed to the taxpayers have expired. If you now neglect this, you should know that even without my bidding, you yourselves will be liable.

I bid you farewell.

### 2.61–4 (8 February 300)

Aurelius Isidorus, procurator of the Lower Thebaid, to Apolinarius, *strategos* of the Panopolite *nome*:

Understand from the observations of the enclosed letter about your failure, even up to the present time, to send in to the office the accounts for the period 28 December 299 until 26 January 300, and take care now both to pay the prescribed fine yourself and to exact the same amount from the assistant of your office, crediting the sums to the account of the most sacred treasury; also, send in the accounts immediately, so that the entire public accounts may not be held up any further through your slackness.

I bid you farewell.

### 2.68–71 (9 February 300)

Aurelius Isidorus, procurator of the Lower Thebaid, to Apolinarius, *strategos* of the Panopolite *nome*:

Well and truly, and continuing right up to the present time, you have been proved guilty, both by the accounts sent in to my office and by the second survey carried out before the *decemprimi* of the *nome* under your rule, of acting to the detriment of the most sacred treasury; and I have inferred the same from the reports drawn up in my office. At another time I might have pardoned what has occurred; but now, in order that you yourself and equally they may render accounts of such behaviour, imprison all the *decemprimi* in the city, and confine them there until the arrival of my lord Domnus, the most eminent *catholicus*.

I bid you farewell.

### 2.109–13 (mid-February 300)

Aurelius Isidorus, procurator of the Lower Thebaid, to Apolinarius, *strategos* of the Panopolite *nome*:

See that all the arrears of wine due for the year 298 and earlier years, complete to one *sextarius*, are lying in store in the harbours and suitable places in the *nome*, lest there be a delay in loading when the ships reach you. It will be necessary for the ships to load immediately and proceed on their voyage up river. For the most noble soldiers are short of their wine rations. And see to it that you inform me with all speed in what places and harbours the wine is stored.

I bid you farewell.

### 2.117–27 (15 February 300)

Aurelius Isidorus, procurator of the Lower Thebaid, to the *strategi* of the *nomes* of Cussis, Lycopolis, Hypselis, Apollinopolis, Antaeopolis, Panopolis, Thinis:

After I realised from my own observations the cause of the deficiency in the provisions of the most noble soldiers, which is increased by your own negligence, long ago I ordered you not to entrust your letters about the dispatch up river of the provisions of the commissariat to the overseers who convey them, but to send them by messenger to the distributors, or else to Philon, the procurator of the Upper Thebaid, in order that the quantities shipped may be demanded in full. But from what the same Philon writes to me, it appears you have paid no attention to these matters; due retribution for this is for the time being reserved for you together with the others. See now that you collect together all the overseers of the indictions, according to the types of provision, and demand from each of them accounts of the distribution in the Upper Thebaid of the supplies they had received on the spot, carrying your enquiry not merely to the point of checking figures but to the actual production of the receipts which they should have obtained from the recipients. Whosoever you find have handed over in full the quantities entrusted to them, give a clear discharge; but those who have made a deficient delivery send to me under guard of your servants, enclosing in your letters to me statements of your proceedings in each case. You must complete this enquiry within fifteen days so that I can determine each case and apply appropriate measures to prevent similar occurrences.

I bid you farewell.

## 2.145–52 (13 February 300)

Aurelius Isidorus, procurator of the Lower Thebaid, to the *strategi* of the procuratorial district:

Even though, with good reason, extreme peril awaited those who omitted to include their vineyards in the recent returns rendered in accordance with the divine decree before the arrival of the *censitores*, nevertheless ... I command you to make a comparison of all the returns, under each *nome* and locality, with the records compiled by the census, in order that those who neglected to make returns, either in whole or in part, may be detected; from whom, without the slightest delay, you should demand the wine due for the first and second indiction – they should, in fact, be well satisfied to have escaped a heavier penalty on this occasion – in order that this quantity of wine may benefit the military commissariat and not provide gain for the evil-doers. And since the survey clearly distinguishes the vineyard-land not yet planted at the time of the two indictions mentioned above, it is obvious that they do not have to endure any extraordinary inquisition. See also that you report to me by letter the quantity of wine which will be gained under this head, and all your relevant transactions, placing your own safety in this matter above any considerations of favour or gain.

I bid you farewell.

## 2.161–4 (8 February 300; delivered 19 February)

Aurelius Isidorus, procurator of the Lower Thebaid, to Apolinarius, *strategos* and the receivers of money of the Panopolite *nome*:

See that you pay out to the mounted archers under the command of Valerius, stationed in the fort of Potecoptus, on account of the *donative* for the accession of our ruler Diocletian the senior Augustus, on 20 November in the most blessed seventh and sixth consulate of our rulers Diocletian and Maximian the Augusti, thirty myriads of *denarii* and 2,500 *atticae*; and on account of the *donative* for the birthday of the same our ruler Diocletian, the senior Augustus, on 22 December in the same consulate, thirty myriads of *denarii* and 2,500 *atticae*, making a total altogether of sixty myriads of *denarii* and 5,000 *atticae*. And deliver these to Valerian ... and Maximus, cavalryman, the agents, and take written receipts from them at the counting of the money.

I bid you farewell.

### *2.211–14* (16 February 300)

Aurelius Isidorus, procurator of the Lower Thebaid, to the *strategi* of the procuratorial district:

Let each of you compile a detailed list of the persea and acanthus wood which has been sent to the most illustrious city of Alexandria and to the city of Nikiu, and let it be sent immediately to the office of the procurator, specifying how much of each kind of wood was sent down, and of what dimensions, and by which overseer or conductor, by which ship-captains, and on what day. For my lord Domnus, the most eminent *catholicus*, is anxious to have this information to compare with the production figures of the shipyards there.

I bid you farewell.

### *2.222–8* (16 February 300)

A public notice from the original of Aurelius Isidorus, procurator of the Lower Thebaid:

I have sent appropriate instructions in writing to the overseers of the embankments in each *nome* about their devoting so much zeal to the acre of the embankments and canals that not only may the customary operations be completed, but also that any other works which may appear useful for the irrigation of the fields, but in which in lapse of time have for various reasons been neglected, may now receive the necessary renovation, without prejudice to the authority of any of those responsible. I have now thought it appropriate in addition by public notice to appeal to the proprietors and farmers in all localities, and at the same time to the *decemprimi*, who are primarily exposed to the risks involved in tax-collection, asking that if they should consider any such measure profitable to them, they should apply to the *strategi* and overseers of embankments and surveyors, indicating those works which could usefully be undertaken but have hitherto suffered neglect; for I suppose that the latter, being mindful of my commands, will give first priority to such a duty. Furthermore I order the *strategi* to post up copies of this my public notice not only in the city, but also in each of the chief villages of the *nome*, so that all persons may be acquainted with these orders. Publish this.

### *2.229–44* (16 February 300)

A public notice from the original of Aurelius Isidorus, procurator of the Lower Thebaid:

I had supposed that every pretext for extortion of money had been wholly removed inasmuch as the divine decree has limited to a stated figure the amount of each tax liability. But when I heard a complaint in the Panopolite *nome* I learned that certain collectors of military supplies had so recklessly carried out their collection that some of them had dared, against the orders of their superiors, instead of the meat which should have been supplied, to accept money from those liable – and that too not equivalent to the amount laid down in the divine regulation, but many times greater, and completely intolerable to the tax-payers. Others, moreover, in the case of the barley and the chaff have been using not the authorised measures but larger ones, thereby inflicting no small loss upon the proprietors. And even though the requisite proceedings according to law have been taken against these persons, nevertheless, making it my aim that similar incidents do not occur in other *nomes* of the procuratorial district, I have thought it expedient to call upon all by means of this public notice, enjoining the collectors to abstain completely from such actions, understanding that should they be detected in such enormities they will not merely be visited with financial penalties, but will be facing the risk of capital punishment; and the contributors, on the other hand, must not submit to such demands, but furnish the provisions destined for the military commissariat precisely as laid down by regulation. Let the *strategi* also deprive the collectors of every excuse for extortion, and not allow the meat to be handed over to those due to receive it anywhere else than in the city itself, and that too by the fairest possible measure. And so that the delivery of chaff and barley may proceed in proper manner, publicly standardise the baskets to hold twenty-five pounds each, and also the measures, and sealing them with the public seal lock them up in each *toparchy*, or if possible each village, in order that the tax-payers may use these standard measures and no advantage may be taken of them. And let the country-dwellers abandon the practice which, it has come to my notice, they still dare to perpetrate in the Panopolite *nome*; for no-one ought to submit to charges for guards or for fodder for animals, or any other imposition of this kind, but should limit their payments to the amounts laid down in the divine regulations. And if after this exhortation of mine any of the collectors should decide to continue in their evil ways, or the *strategi* in collusion with them should permit any unlawful act to occur, on detection the guilty party will be sent under guard to my lord Domnus, the most eminent *catholicus*, to receive just retribution. Publish this.

## 22. Edict of Aristius Optatus (16 March 297) (P. Cair. Isidor. 1)
### Translated from the Greek original. (I Chapter 3.1)

Aristius Optatus, the most eminent prefect of Egypt, declares:

Our most provident emperors, Diocletian and Maximian the Augusti, and Constantius and Maximian [Galerius] the noblest Caesars have learnt that the levying of public taxes has occurred so that some people are affected lightly and others are oppressed; they have resolved to cut out this most evil and ruinous practice for the benefit of their provincials and to introduce a salutary system to which taxes must conform.

From the divine edict which has been published and the schedule attached to it (copies of which I have prefaced for public display with this edict of mine), everyone can know the levy on each *aroura* according to the quality of the land, and the levy on each of the peasants, and the lower and upper age limits for liability. And so, since in this matter too, the provincials have been treated very generously, let them take care to pay their tax contributions according to the imperial statutes with all speed, and in no way to wait for the collector to force them. For it is right for everyone to complete everything for payment most enthusiastically; and if anyone is caught doing otherwise after such beneficence, they will be in danger. The magistrates and presidents of each city have been ordered to send to every village and locality a copy of the divine edict's great schedule and of this edict so that the generosity of our emperors and Caesars can come to the attention of everyone as quickly as possible. Collectors of every kind of tax should remember to manage their activity with all their power; for if any of them is caught transgressing, he will risk capital punishment.

## 23. Land Declaration (11 September 299) (P. Cair. Isidor. 3)
### Translated from the Greek original (I Chapter 3.1)

From Aurelia Herois, the daughter of Chaeremon, from the village of Karanis in the first and sixth *toparchy* of the Heraclides division of the Arsinoite *nome*, to the *censitor* Julius Septimius Sabinus:

Conforming with the imperial edict of our lords the invincible kings the Augusti Diocletian and Maximian, and the most noble Caesars Constantius and Galerius, I declare to you that I own land near the above-mentioned village Karanis and that I have discovered the measurements of the *arouras* of my estate. The surveyors Aphrodisius and Paulinus measured the land in the presence of the *iuratores*

Apollonius, Kopres and Heron; present too were Syrus, the assistant to the *decemprimi* of the *toparchy*, and Pannes the *horiodeiktes*. All have signed below.

The land is arranged thus:

In the sixteenth section, in the hamlet called Kiamoul, three and twenty-nine thirty-seconds *arouras* of uninundated royal land, adjacent on the east to a canal (beyond which is waste-land of no ownership), and on the west to the estate of Maron.

Similarly, in the hamlet called ... nineteen sixty-fourths of an *aroura* of a productive olive-grove on private land, adjacent on the east to waste-land of no ownership, and on the west to a canal (beyond which is the estate of Kapeïs).

Similarly, in the same hamlet, twenty-six and nine-sixteenths *arouras* of uninundated royal land, adjacent on the east to the estate of Kapeïs, and on the west to a canal (beyond which is the estate of Panteris).

I swear by the fortune and victory of our lords the invincible kings that I declare this honestly.

[In 2nd hand] With an oath by the Augusti, I, Aurelia Herois, declare the above-mentioned *arouras*, and have discovered the measurements given above. I, Aurelius Horion, son of Heron, have written for her as she is illiterate.

[In 3rd hand] I, Aurelius Aphrodisius, surveyor, with my colleague Paulinus, have measured the above-mentioned *arouras* belonging to Herois.

[In 4th hand] I, Aurelius Paulinus, surveyor, with my colleague Aphrodisius, have measured the above-mentioned *arouras* belonging to Herois.

[In 5th hand] I, Aurelius Apollonius, councillor and *iurator*, attended the survey.

[In 6th hand] I, Aurelius Kopres, councillor and *iurator*, attended the survey.

[In 7th hand] I, Aurelius Heron, councillor and *iurator*, attended the survey.

[In 8th hand] I, Aurelius Syrus, assistant to the *decemprimi* of the toparchy, have verified the survey.

[In 9th hand] I, Aurelius Panous, *horiodeiktes*, have displayed all the above-mentioned *arouras*, and left nothing out.

[10th hand] Aurelius Herodes, *didaskalos*; this declaration was made in my office.

[11th hand] I, Julius Septimius Sabinus, *censitor*, have received and countersigned this declaration.

## 24. Legal Petition to the *strategos* of the Arsinoite *nome* (c. 298) (P. Cair. Isidor. 64)
### Translated from the Greek original

From Aurelia Taesis and Aurelia Kyrillous, daughters of Kopres, from the village of Karanis, to Aurelius Heron, the *strategos* of the Arsonoite *nome*:

O most noble *strategos*, when our father died, he left movable goods [consisting of sixty-one sheep, forty goats, a mill, silver, wheat and slaves]. But our uncle Chaeremon took all that had been left, and handed over to us women some *arouras* of public crop-land, although we cannot meet the rents on them. We approached the village chief Serenus, also known as Harpocras, who ordered Chaeremon to return to us all the goods left us by our father. But Chaeremon takes no account of us, so we ask you in your clemency to order him to return these things to us so that we can benefit from our own property.
Farewell.

## 25. *Notitia Dignitatum*
### Translated from the Latin original (I Chapter 1.2)

### EAST 1. List of civil and military dignitaries in the east
Praetorian prefect of the east.
Praetorian prefect of Illyricum.
Prefect of the city of Constantinople.
Two masters of cavalry and infantry in the [emperor's] presence.
[Master] of cavalry and infantry in Oriens.
[Master] of cavalry and infantry in Thrace.
[Master] of cavalry and infantry in Illyricum.
Provost of the sacred bedchamber.
Master of the offices.
Quaestor.
Count of the sacred treasuries.
Count of the private domains.
Two counts of the household troops: of cavalry; of infantry.

Superintendent of the sacred bedchamber.

Chief of the notaries.

Keeper of the sacred palace.

Masters of secretariats: of memorials, of correspondence, of petitions, of Greek.

Two proconsuls: of Asia; of Achaia.

Count of Oriens.

Augustal prefect.

Four vicars: of Asia; of Pontus; of Thrace; of Macedonia.

Two military counts: of Egypt; of Isauria.

Thirteen dukes:

> in Egypt two: of the Libyas; of Thebais.
>
> in Oriens six: of Phoenice; of Euphratensis and Syria; of Palestine; of Osroena; of Mesopotamia; of Arabia.
>
> in Pontus one: of Armenia.
>
> in Thrace two: of Moesia Secunda; of Scythia.
>
> in Illyricum two: of Dacia Ripensis; of Moesia Prima.

Fifteen consulars:

> in Oriens five: of Palestine; of Phoenice; of Syria; of Cilicia; of Cyprus.
>
> in Asia three: of Pamphylia; of Hellespontus; of Lydia.
>
> in Pontus two: of Galatia; of Bithynia.
>
> in Thrace two: of Europe; of Thrace.
>
> in Illyricum three: of Crete; of Macedonia; of Mediterranean Dacia.

Forty presidents:

> in Egypt five: of Libya Superior; of Libya Inferior; of Thebais; of Egypt; of Arcadia.
>
> in Oriens eight: of Palaestina Salutaris; of Palaestina Secunda; of Phoenice Libani; of Euphratensis; of Syria Salutaris; of Osrhoena; of Mesopotamia; of Cilicia Secunda.
>
> in Asia seven: of Pisidia; of Lycaonia; of Phrygia Pacatiana; of Phrygia Salutaris; of Lycia; of Caria; of the Islands.
>
> in Pontus eight: of Honorias; of Cappadocia Prima; of Cappadocia Secunda; of Helenopontus; of Pontus Polemoniacus; of Armenia Prima; of Armenia Secunda; of Galatia Salutaris.
>
> in Thrace four: of Haemimontus; of Rhodope; of Moesia Secunda; of Scythia.
>
> in Illyricum eight: of Thessalia; of Epirus Vetus; of Epirus Nova; of Dacia Ripensis; of Moesia Prima; of Praevalitana; of Dardania; of Macedonia Salutaris.

Two correctors: of Augustamnica; of Paphlagonia.

## EAST 2. The praetorian prefect of the east

Under the control of the illustrious praetorian prefect of the east are the dioceses below mentioned:

of Oriens; of Egypt; of Asia; of Pontus; of Thrace.

Provinces:

of Oriens fifteen: Palestine; Phoenice; Syria; Cilicia; Cyprus; Arabia; Isauria; Palaestina Salutaris; Palaestina Secunda; Phoenice Libanensis; Euphratensis; Syria Salutaris; Osrhoena; Mesopotamia; Cilicia Secunda.

of Egypt five: Libya Superior; Libya Inferior; Thebais; Egypt; Arcadia.

of Asia ten: Pamphylia; Hellespontus; Lydia; Pisidia; Lycaonia; Phrygia Pacatiana; Phrygia Salutaris; Lycia; Caria; Insulae.

of Pontus ten: Galatia; Bithynia; Honorias; Cappadocia Prima; Cappadocia Secunda; Pontus Polemoniacus; Hellenopontus; Armenia Prima; Armenia Secunda; Galatia Salutaris.

of Thrace six: Europa; Thrace; Haemimontus; Rhodope; Moesia Inferior, Scythia.

The staff of the illustrious praetorian prefect of the east:

Chief of staff.
Deputy chief deputy.
Chief assistant.
Custodian.
Record keeper.
Receivers of taxes.
Assistants.
Curator of correspondence.
Registrar.
Secretaries.
Aides.
Notaries.

## EAST 5. The master of the military in the [emperor's] presence

Under the control of the illustrious master of the military in the [emperor's] presence:

Five squadrons of palatine cavalry:

The senior promoted cavalry.
The companion cuirassiers.
The junior companion archers.
The companion Taifalians.
The Arcadian cavalry.

Seven squadrons of cavalry of the line:
    The Biturigensian cuirassiers.
    The senior Gallican heavy-armed cavalry.
    The fifth Dalmatian cavalry.
    The ninth Dalmatian cavalry.
    The first shield-bearers.
    The junior promoted cavalry.
    The first Parthian cuirassiers.

Six palatine legions:
    The senior lancers.
    The junior Jovians.
    The junior Herculians, The Fortenses.
    The Nervii.
    The junior Matiarii.

Eighteen palatine auxiliary units:
    The senior Batavians.
    The junior Brachiati.
    The Salians.
    The Constantians.
    The senior Mattiaci,.
    The senior Gallican archers.
    The junior Gallican archers.
    The third Valens archers.
    The Defenders.
    The Ractobarii.
    The Anglevarii.
    The Hiberi.
    The Visi.
    The fortunate junior Honorians.
    The Victors.
    The first Theodosians.
    The third Theodosians.
    The fortunate Isaurian Theodosians.

### EAST 13. The count of the sacred treasuries

Under the control of the illustrious count of the sacred treasuries:
    The counts of the treasuries in all the dioceses.
    The counts of the markets: in the East and Egypt; in Moesia, Scythia and Pontus, Illyricum.
    The provosts of the store-houses.

The counts of the metals in Illyricum.
The count and the accountant of the general tribute of Egypt.
The accountants of the general tribute.
The masters of the linen wardrobe.
The masters of the private wardrobe.
The procurators of the weaving-houses.
The procurators of the dye-houses.
The procurators of the mints.
The provosts of the goods despatch.
The procurator of the linen-weavers.

The staff of the count of the sacred treasuries includes:
The chief clerk of the whole staff.
The chief clerk of the secretariat of fixed taxes.
The chief clerk of the secretariat of records.
The chief clerk of the secretariat of accounts.
The chief clerk of the secretariat of gold bullion.
The chief clerk of the secretariat of gold for shipment.
The chief clerk of the secretariat of the sacred wardrobe.
The chief clerk of the secretariat of silver.

## EAST 14. The count of the private domain

Under the control of the illustrious count of the private domain:
The imperial estates.
The accountants of the private domain.
The private baggage train.
The provosts of the herds and stables.
The procurators of the pastures.

The staff of the illustrious count of the private domain:
A chief clerk of the whole staff.
A chief clerk of remitted taxes.
A chief clerk of the fixed taxes.
A chief clerk of receipts.
A chief clerk of the secretariats of private treasuries, and other, clerks of the secretariats.
A deputy chief clerk of the whole staff, who has charge of the documents of that staff, and other palatine officials.

## EAST 28. The count of the Egyptian frontier

Under the control of the worshipful military count of Egypt:
The fifth Macedonian legion, at Memphis.

The thirteenth twin legion, at Babylon.
The Stablesian cavalry, at Pelusium.
The Saracen Thamudene horse, at Scenae Veteranorum.
The third Diocletianic legion, at Andropolis.
The second Trajanic legion, at Parembole.
The Theodosian squadron, recently organised.
The Arcadian squadron, recently organised.
The second squadron of Armenians, in the lesser Oasis.

And these which are assigned from the lesser register:
The third squadron of Arabs, at Thenenuthis.
The eighth squadron of Vandals, at Nee.
The seventh squadron of Sarmatians, at Scenae Mandrorum.
The first squadron of Egyptians, at Selle.
The veteran squadron of Gauls, at Rinocoruna.
The first Herculian squadron, at Scenae without Gerasa.
The fifth squadron of Raetians, at Scenae Veteranorum.
The first Tangiers squadron, at Thinunepsi.
The Aprian squadron, at Hipponos.
The second squadron of Assyrians, at Sosteos.
The fifth squadron of Praelecti at Dionysias.
The third cohort of Galatians, at Cefro.
The second cohort of Asturians, at Busiris.

Of the province of Augustamnica:
The second Ulpian squadron of Africans, at Thaubastos.
The second squadron of Egyptians, at Tacasiria.
The first cohort of archers, at Naithu.
The first Augustan cohort of Pannonians, at Tohu.
The first cohort of Epirotes, at Castra Judaeorum.
The fourth cohort of Juthungians, at Aphroditopolis.
The second cohort of Ituraeans, at Aiy.
The second cohort of Thracians, at Muson.
The fourth cohort of Numidians, at Narmunthi.

The staff is as follows:
A chief of staff from the school of secret agents of the first class, who
proceeds with insignia, after offering worship to the emperor in his
clemency.
Receivers of taxes.
A custodian.
An assistant.

A receiver of requests, or under-secretary.
Secretaries and other officials.

### WEST 1. List of civil and military dignitaries in the west

Praetorian prefect of Italy.
Praetorian prefect of the Gauls.
Prefect of the city of Rome.
Master of infantry in the [emperor's] presence.
Master of cavalry in the [emperor's] presence.
Master of cavalry in the Gauls.
Provost of the sacred bedchamber.
Master of the offices.
Quaestor.
Count of the sacred treasuries.
Count of the private domains.
Count of the household cavalry.
Count of the household infantry.
Superintendent of the sacred bedchamber.
Chief of the notaries.
Governor of the sacred palace.
Masters of secretariats: of memorials; of correspondence; of petitions.
Proconsul of Africa.
Six vicars: of the city of Rome; of Italy; of Africa; of Spain; of the Seven Provinces; of Britain.
Six military counts: of Italy; of Africa; of Tingitania; of the tractus Argentoratensis; of Britain; of the Saxon shore of Britain.
Thirteen dukes: of the frontier of Mauritania Caesariensis; of the Tripolitan frontier; of Pannonia Prima and Noricum Ripense; of Pannonia Secunda; of Valeria; of Raetia Prima and Secunda; of Sequanica; of the Armorican and Nervican tract; of Belgica Secunda; of Germania Prima; of Britannia; of Mogontiacensis.
Twenty-two consulars:
    of Pannonia.
    in Italy eight: of Venetia and Histria; of Emilia; of Liguria; of Flaminia and Picenum Annonarium; of Tuscia and Umbria; of Picenum Suburbicarium; of Campania; of Sicilia.
    in Africa two: of Byzacium; of Numidia.
    in Spain three: of Baetica; of Lusitania; of Gallaecia.
    in the Gauls six: of Viennensis; of Lugdunensis Prima; of Germania Prima; of Germania Secunda; of Belgica Prima; of Belgica Secunda.
    in the Britains two: of Maxima Caesariensis; of Valentia.

Three correctors:
  in Italy two: of Apulia and Calabria; of Lucania and Brittii.
  in Pannonia one: of Savia.
Thirty-one presidents:
  in Illyricum four: of Dalmatia; of Pannonia Prima; of Noricum Mediterraneum; of Noricum Ripense.
  in Italy seven: of the Alpes Cottiae; of Raetia Prima; of Raetia Secunda, of Samnium; of Valeria; of Sardinia; of Corsica.
  in Africa two: of Mauritania Sitifensis; of Tripolitana.
  in Spain four: of Tarraconensis; of Carthaginensis; of Tingitana; of the Balearic Isles.
  in the Gauls eleven: of Alpes Maritimae; of Alpes Graiae et Poeninae; of Maxima Sequania; of Aquitanica Prima; Aquitanica Secunda; of Novem Populi; of Narbonensis Prima; of Narbonensis Secunda; of Lugdunensis Secunda; of Lugdunensis Tertia; of Lugdunensis Senonica.
  in the Britains three: of Britannia Prima; of Britannia Secunda; of Flavia Caesariensis.

### WEST 9. The illustrious master of the offices

Under the control of the illustrious master of the offices:
  The first school of shield-bearers.
  The second school of shield-bearers.
  The senior light-armed school.
  The school of senior clansmen.
  The third school of shield-bearers.
  The school of secret agents.
  The bureau of memorials.
  The bureau of assignments.
  The bureau of correspondence.
  The bureau of petitions.
  The doorkeepers.
  The court ushers.

The arsenals mentioned below:
  In Illyricum:
      of shields, saddle-cloths and weapons, at Sirmium;
      of shields, at Acincuin;
      of shields, at Carnuntum;
      of shields, at Lauriacum;
      of weapons, at Salona.

In Italy:
    of arrows, at Concordia;
    of shields and weapons, at Verona;
    of leather corselets, at Mantua;
    of shields, at Cremona;
    of bows, at Ticinum;
    of broadswords, at Luca.
In Gaul:
    of all weapons, at Argenton;
    of arrows, at Macon;
    of leather corselets, catapults, and mail, at Autun;
    of shields, at Autun;
    of [indecipherable], at Soissons;
    of broadswords, at Rheims;
    of shields, at Trier;
    of catapults, at Trier;
    of broadswords and shields, at Amiens.

The staff of the aforesaid illustrious master of the offices is constituted
from the school of confidential agents as follows:
    A chief assistant.
    A deputy to the chief assistant.
    Assistants for the various arsenals.
    An inspector of the public post in the presence.
    Inspectors for all the provinces.
    Interpreters for all people.

### WEST 17. The master of the secretariats

The master of the secretariat of memorials formulates all rescripts and
issues them, and also responds to petitions.
The master of the secretariat of correspondence deals with legations
from cities and consultations and petitions.
The master of the secretariat of petitions deals with the hearing of cases
and petitions.

### WEST 43. The consular of Campania

Under the control of the right honourable consular of Campania:
    The province of Campania.

His staff is as follows:
    A chief of staff from the staff of the praetorian prefect of Italy.
    A chief deputy.

Two accountants.
A chief assistant.
A custodian.
A keeper of the records.
An assistant.
Secretaries and other *cohortalini*, who are not allowed to pass to another service without the permission of the imperial clemency.

## WEST 45. The president of Dalmatia

Under the jurisdiction of the honourable president of Dalmatia:
The province of Dalmatia.

His staff is as follows:
A chief of the same staff.
A chief deputy.
Two accountants.
A custodian.
A chief assistant.
A keeper of the records.
An assistant.
Secretaries and other *cohortalini*, who are not allowed to pass to another service without the permission of the imperial clemency.

## 26. *Notitia Dignitatum.* The *insignia* for the Count of the Saxon Shore
### (I Chapter 1.2)

## 27. *Verona List*
### Translated from the Latin original (**I Chapter 2.1**)

The list of names of all the provinces begins:

The diocese of Oriens has eighteen provinces:
Libya Superior.
Libya Inferior.
Thebais.
Aegyptus Iovia.
Aegyptus Herculia.
Arabia Nova.
Arabia.
Augusta Libanensis.
Palestine.
Phoenicia.
Syria Coele.
Augusta Euphratensis.
Cilicia.
Isauria.
Cyprus.
Mesopotamia.
Osrhoene.

The diocese of Pontica has seven provinces:
Bithynia.
Cappadocia.
Galatia.
Paphlagonia.
Diospontus.
Pontus Polemoniacus.
Armenia Minor.

The diocese of Asia has nine provinces, written below:
Pamphylia.
Phrygia Prima.
Phrygia Secunda.
Asia.
Lydia.
Caria.
Insulae.
Pisidia.
Hellespontus.

The diocese of Thrace has six provinces:
Europa.
Rhodope.
Thrace.
Haemimontus.
Scythia.
Moesia Inferior.

The diocese of Moesia has eleven provinces:
Dacia.
Dacia Ripensis.
Moesia Superior/Margensis.
Dardania.
Macedonia.
Thessaly.
Achaea.
Praevalitana.
Epirus Nova.
Epirus Vetus.
Crete.

The diocese of Pannonia has seven provinces:
Pannonia Inferior.
Savensis.
Dalmatia.
Valeria.
Pannonia Superior.
Noricum Ripense.
Noricum Mediterranea.

The diocese of Britannia has six provinces:
Britannia Prima.
Britannia Secunda.
Maxima Caesariensis.
Flavia Caesariensis.

The diocese of Gallia has eight provinces:
Belgica Prima.
Belgica Secunda.
Germania Prima.
Germania Secunda.
Sequania.
Lugdunensis Prima.

Lugdunensis Secunda.
Alpes Graiae et Poeninae.

The diocese of Viennensis has seven provinces:
Viennensis.
Narbonensis Prima.
Narbonensis Secunda.
Novem Populi.
Aquitanica Prima.
Aquitanica Secunda.
Alpes Maritimae.

The diocese of Italia has sixteen provinces:
Venetia.
Histria.
Flaminia.
Picenum.
Tuscia.
Umbria.
Apulia.
Calabria.
Lucania.
Corsica.
Alpes Cottiae.
Raetia.

The diocese of Hispania has six provinces:
Baetica.
Lusitania.
Carthaginiensis.
Gallaecia.
Tarraconensis.
Mauretania Tingitania.

The diocese of Africa has seven provinces:
Africa Proconsularis.
Byzacena.
Tripolitana.
Numidia Cirtensis.
Numidia Militiana.
Mauretania Caesariensis.
Mauretania Sitifensis.

### 28. Manichaean rescript. Collation of the Laws of Moses and Rome 15.3 (31 March 302(?), Alexandria) (I Chapter 5.2)

The emperors Diocletian and Maximian [and Constantius] and [Galerius] to dearest Julianus, proconsul of Africa:

[1] Excessive leisure sometimes provokes ill-suited people to cross natural limits and encourages them to introduce false and outrageous forms of superstitious doctrine, so that many others are persuaded to recognise the authority of their mistaken beliefs. [2] In their foresight, the immortal gods have deigned to insist that the principles of virtue and truth be acknowledged and confirmed by the counsel and thoughts of many good, great and wise men. It is wrong to oppose or resist these principles; and no new belief should criticise the religion of old. It is highly criminal to discuss doctrines established and defined by our ancestors, which still have their acknowledged place and role. [3] For this reason we are absolutely determined to punish the stubborn madness of these worthless people. [4] We have heard all those matters relating to the Manichaeans which in your wisdom you reported to us in our serenity – that against the older beliefs they establish new and unknown sects, wickedly intending to overthrow the doctrines confirmed for us long ago by divine favour; that recently they have advanced or emerged from their native homes in Persia – an enemy of ours – like strange and monstrous portents, and have settled in this part of the world, where they commit many evil acts, upsetting the peace of the people and seriously damaging towns. There is a danger that in time they will try, as usual, to contaminate with the Persians' criminal habits and insane laws the innocent, orderly and peaceful Roman people, and the whole empire as well, as if with the poison of an evil snake. [5] Because everything you in your prudence explained in your report about their religion demonstrates that what our laws see as their crimes are born of a wild and false imagination, we have set deserved and suitable penalties for these people. [6] We command that the authors and leaders of these sects receive severe punishment and be burnt in the flames with their detestable books. We order that if they prove defiant, their followers suffer capital punishment, and their possessions pass to the imperial treasury. [7] If those people who have crossed to that unknown, outrageous and disreputable belief, or to the Persians' belief, are in public office or are of any rank or higher social status, you must confiscate their estates and send the offenders to the Phaeno [quarry] or the Proconnesus mines. [8] In your devotion, hurry to execute our

orders and commands so that this iniquitous disease is completely cleansed from our most happy age.

### 29. *Theodosian Code*
Translated from the Latin original, compiled in the fifth century

#### 7.22.1

From Constantine Augustus to Octavianus [governor of Lucania and Bruttium]:

Some of the veterans' sons who are for military service lazily refuse to fulfil their obligatory military duties, and others of them are so cowardly they wish to avoid the obligation by mutilating themselves. If they are considered unsuitable for military service because they have cut their fingers off, we order them to be allocated, without hesitation, to the obligatory public services and responsibilities of decurions.

### 30. *Justinianic Code*
Translated from the Latin original, compiled in the sixth century

#### 5.4.17

1 May 295 at Damascus. The emperors the Augusti Diocletian and Maximian and their Caesars:

Nobody may contract a marriage with their daughter, granddaughter or great-granddaughter, or likewise with their mother, grandmother or great grandmother, or with their paternal or maternal aunt, or with their sister, sister's daughter or granddaughter, or with their brother's daughter or granddaughter, or likewise with their step-daughter, step-mother, daughter-in-law, mother-in-law or the others related by marriage forbidden by ancient law; we wish everyone to abstain from such practice.

#### 7.35.2

February 286. The emperors the Augusti Diocletian and Maximian to Aurelius the court physician:

You insist that those people about whom you complain rushed into matters which were yours by law and that you are away from our court on medical business; because you are absent, the affair cannot be considered face to face. Those whom this case affects have been summoned, and my praetorian prefect will investigate. You need not seek to forestall an order against you on the grounds of lengthy absence, since the good reason for your absence and your duty to the public need defend you against prejudice of this sort.

### 9.20.7

8 December 287. The Augusti Diocletian and Maximian to Maximus the urban prefect:
Since you point out that slaves are being taken from the city by kidnappers, and you write occasionally it happens that freeborn men are carried off in this crime, we have decided we must meet the lawlessness of these criminals with greater severity. If you arrest anyone in this sort of crime, do not hesitate to behead him, so that by this manner of punishment the rest may be deterred from taking or transferring from the city slaves or freemen with audacity of that kind.

### 9.41.8

292 (?). The Augusti to the governor Sallustianus:
We grant that in criminal cases, soldiers should not be subjected to torture or ordinary penalties, even if they do not seem to have been discharged with their veteran's stipend (with the obvious exception of those who have been dismissed in disgrace). This ruling shall prevail for the sons of soldiers and veterans as well. When investigating the truth in cases at the public courts, judges ought not to take their lead from evidence given under torture, but in the first instance to use evidence which is probable and likely. And if they are led by this evidence as if it were certain to think that in the interests of investigating the truth torture is necessary, they should turn to this finally, if the status of the individuals allows it. By this procedure, all our provincials will enjoy the benefit of our innate kindness.

### 31. *Act of St Crispina*
Translated from the Latin original (**I Chapter 5.3**)

[1] In the colony of Thebestina, on 5 December when the Augusti were consuls, Diocletian for the ninth time, Maximian for the eighth [304], the proconsul Anullinus sat in judgement on the tribunal in the council chamber, and the court clerk said,
'If you consent, Crispina, from Toura, is to be tried – she has spurned the law of our lords the emperors.'
    The proconsul Anullinus said, 'Bring her in.'
    When Crispina had come in, the proconsul Anullinus said, 'Do you know the meaning of the sacred command?'

Crispina replied, 'I do not know what has been commanded.'

Anullinus said, 'That you should make sacrifice to all our gods for the wellbeing of the emperors, according to the law issued by our lords the pious Augusti Diocletian and Maximian and the most noble Caesars Constantius and Maximian [Galerius].'

Crispina replied, 'I have never made sacrifice, and shall not sacrifice unless to the only true God and our Lord his son Jesus Christ, who was born and died.'

The proconsul Anullinus said, 'Cut out this superstition, and bow your head to the sacred rites of the Roman gods.'

Crispina replied, 'Every day I worship my omnipotent God; I know no God other than him.'

Anullinus said, 'You are stubborn and defiant, and you will begin to feel the force of the law against your will.'

Crispina replied, 'Whatever happens, I will gladly suffer it for the sake of my faith which I hold.'

Anullinus said, 'It is your mind's vanity that you will not dismiss your superstition and worship the sacred gods.'

Crispina replied, 'I worship every day – but the living and true God, who is my Lord, besides whom I know no other.'

Anullinus said, 'I am showing you the sacred command, which you should obey.'

Crispina replied, 'I will obey the command, but that of my Lord Jesus Christ.'

The proconsul Anullinus said, 'I will order your beheading unless you obey the commands of our lords the emperors – subdued, you will be forced to serve them. As you are in no doubt, all of Africa has made sacrifice.'

Crispina replied, 'May they never succeed in making me sacrifice to demons, but only to God "who has made heaven and earth, the sea and all things within them" [Acts 4:24].'

[2] Anullinus said, 'So are the gods not acceptable to you? You will be forced to demonstrate your enslavement to them if you wish to stay alive for any worship at all!'

Crispina replied, 'That is no worship which forces unwilling men to be oppressed.'

Anullinus said, 'But we ask that you worship, that in the sacred temple with bowed head you sacrifice incense to the gods of the Romans.'

Crispina replied, 'I have never done this, from the time I was born; I do not know how; I shall not do it as long as I live.'

Anullinus said, 'But do it, if you wish to evade unharmed the severity of the laws.'

Crispina replied, 'I do not fear what you say; this is nothing; but if I agree to commit sacrilege, God who is in heaven will destroy me immediately, and I will not be found in Him in days to come.'

Anullinus said, 'You will not be committing sacrilege if you obey the sacred orders.'

Crispina replied, 'May the gods who did not make heaven and earth perish! I sacrifice to the eternal God, who will remain for ever, who is the true God and to be feared, who made the sea and the green grass and the dry earth; what can men who were His creation offer to me?'

The proconsul Anullinus said, 'Honour the religion of Rome, which our lords the most unconquered Caesars and we ourselves practise.'

Crispina replied, 'By now I have said to you very often, I am ready to sustain any tortures you wish to subject me to rather than pollute my soul with idols, which are stones and creations made by the hand of men.'

Anullinus said, 'You speak blasphemously, for you do not proceed in a way which contributes to your wellbeing.'

[3] The proconsul Anullinus said in addition to the court clerk, 'Let her be reduced to complete disfigurement, with her hair cut and her head made bald with a razor, so that her appearance will first be brought to ignominy.'

Crispina replied, 'Let the gods speak, and I will believe in them. If I were not seeking my own wellbeing, I would not now be on trial before your tribunal.'

Anullinus said, 'Do you wish to live a long life, or to die amid punishments, just like your sister companions?'

Crispina replied, 'If I wished to die and to give my soul to destruction in the eternal fire, I would now surrender my will to your demons.'

Anullinus said, 'I will order your beheading if you show contempt for the adoration of the venerable gods.'

Crispina replied, 'I give thanks to my God if I achieve this. Most happily I wish to lose my head on my God's behalf; for I will not sacrifice to those most false, mute and deaf idols.'

The proconsul Anullinus said, 'Do you absolutely persist in this foolish attitude of yours?'

Crispina replied, 'My God, who is and who remains for ever, Himself ordered me to be born; He Himself granted me salvation through the salutary water of baptism; He Himself gives me succour and in everything gives strength to me as His handmaid, so that I will not commit sacrilege.'

[4] Anullinus said, 'Why should we tolerate this impious Christian any more? Read the records of the trial, as they were said.'

When they were read, the proconsul Anullinus read the sentence from a notebook: 'Crispina persists in the disgraceful superstition and is unwilling to sacrifice to our gods; according to the heavenly orders of the Augustan law, I order her to be put to the sword.'

Crispina replied, 'I bless God who thus sees fit to free me from your hands. Thanks be to God.'

Making the sign of the cross on her forehead and stretching out her neck, she was beheaded for the name of our Lord Jesus Christ whose honour is for ever. Amen.

### 32.  *Act of Felix the Bishop*
Translated from the Latin original (**I Chapter 5.3**)

[1] In the eighth consulship of Diocletian and the seventh of Maximian [303], the Augusti, an edict from the emperors and their Caesars went out over the earth's entire face; throughout colonies and cities, leaders and magistrates were instructed in their own locality to wrest holy books from the hands of bishops and presbyters. The edict was posted in the city of Tibiuca on 5 June. ... The next day, the city magistrate Magnilianus ordered the bishop Felix to be brought to him by his officials.

The magistrate said to him, 'Are you bishop Felix?'

Bishop Felix said, 'I am.'

The magistrate Magnilianus said, 'Hand over whatever books or parchments you own.'

Bishop Felix said, 'I have them but I will not hand them over.'

The magistrate Magnilianus said, 'Hand over the books to be burned in the fire.'

Bishop Felix said, 'It is better for me to be burned in the fire than the holy books; for it is good "to give obedience to God rather then to men" [Acts 5:29].'

The magistrate Magnilianus said, 'The emperors' orders come before what you say.'

Bishop Felix said, 'God's command comes before man's.'

Magnilianus said, 'Think this over for three days, because if you neglect to fulfil commands in my city, you will go to the proconsul, and at his court you will account for what you are saying here.'

After three days, the magistrate ordered the bishop Felix to be brought to him, and he said to him, 'Have you thought this over?'

Bishop Felix said, ' What I said before and I say again now, I shall say before the proconsul.'

The magistrate Magnilianus said, 'Therefore you will go to the proconsul and render an account there.' ... at the fourth hour of night bishop Felix was brought out from prison in chains, before the proconsul Anullinus.

Anullinus said to him, 'Why will you not hand over the useless scriptures?'

Bishop Felix replied, 'I will not hand them over.'

Then, on 15 July, Anullinus ordered him to be put to the sword.

Bishop Felix lifted his eyes to heaven and said in a clear voice, 'God I give you thanks. I have been fifty-six years on earth; I have preserved my virginity, I have observed the Gospels, I have preached faith and truth. Jesus Christ, Lord God of heaven and earth, who will remain for ever, I bend my neck in sacrifice to you.'

His prayer over, he was led away by soldiers and beheaded.

### 33. *Act of Julius the Veteran* (Spring 304)
Translated from the Latin original (**I Chapter 5.3**)

[1] During the persecution, when the glorious struggles confronting the Christian faithful were looking to receive the eternal promises, Julius was arrested by officials and brought to the prefect Maximus.

'Who is this?' asked Maximus.

One of the officials said, 'This man is a Christian who is not willing to obey the legal orders.'

The prefect said, 'What is your name?'

'Julius,' he replied.

'What do you say, Julius? Are the reports about you true?'

Julius replied, 'Yes. For I am a Christian. I do not deny I am what I am.

The prefect said, 'Surely you know the emperors' edicts, which order sacrifice be made to the gods?'

Julius replied, 'I know them; but I am a Christian and I cannot do what you want; for I must not forget my true and living God.

[2] The prefect Maximus said, 'What is serious about offering sacrificial incense and departing?'

Julius replied, 'I cannot despise the heavenly edicts and show myself unfaithful to my God. In my twenty-seven years of military service, in vain since I seem to have been in error, I was never brought before a judge as if I were criminal or troublesome. Seven times I went out on campaign, and I never sheltered behind anyone or was inferior to anyone in battle. My officer never saw me at fault, and do you think that when I was always found faithful in the past, I could now be found faithless to superior orders?'

The prefect Maximus replied, 'What was your military service?'

Julius replied, ' I was in the army, and after my term I campaigned as a veteran, always in fear of "God who made heaven and earth" [Acts 4:24], to whom even now I dedicate my service.'

The prefect Maximus said, 'Julius, I see you are a wise and serious man; so be persuaded by me, sacrifice to the gods, and receive a large payment.'

Julius replied, 'I cannot do what you want, in case I incur everlasting punishment.'

The prefect Maximus said, 'If you think it is a sin, let me take the consequences. I am forcing you, so that you will not be seen to acquiesce willingly. Afterwards you can go home in peace with your ten-year bonus, and nobody will trouble you again in future.'

Julius replied, 'Neither Satan's money nor your underhand inducements can deprive me of eternal light. For I cannot deny God. So pass sentence against me, as against a Christian.'

[3] Maximus said, 'Unless you show respect to the imperial edicts and offer sacrifice, I shall have you beheaded.'

Julius replied, 'Good thinking! I ask you, good prefect, by the well-being of your emperors, to fulfil your plan and pass sentence on me, so that my wishes can be realised.'

The prefect Maximus replied, 'Unless you change your mind and sacrifice, you will be delivered to your wishes.'

Julius replied, 'If I deserve to suffer this, eternal praise will await me.'

Maximus said, 'Be persuaded. For if you suffered for the sake of your country's laws, you would have eternal praise.'

Julius replied, 'I certainly suffer this for the sake of laws – heavenly laws.'

Maximus said, 'Laws which a man dead and crucified has given to you? See how foolish you are when you fear a dead man more than living emperors.'

Julius replied, 'He "died for our sins" [1 Cor. 15:3] to give us eternal life. This same Christ is God who will remain for time to come. He who confesses Him will have eternal life; he who denies Him has everlasting punishment.'

Maximus said, 'Out of sorrow for you, I advise you to sacrifice and continue to live amongst us.'

Julius replied, 'If I live with you, I will die; if I die in sight of God, I live for ever.'

Maximus said, 'Listen to me and sacrifice, so that I will not have to kill you, as I threatened.'

Julius replied, 'I have chosen to die for now so that I shall live with the saints for ever.'

Thus the prefect Maximus passed sentence, saying, 'Let Julius receive capital punishment, as he is unwilling to obey the imperial edicts.'

[4] When he had been taken to the usual place, everyone kissed him. Blessed Julius said to them, 'Let each man see what sort of kiss this is.' … He took the blindfold, covered his eyes, stretched out his neck and said, 'Lord Jesus Christ, in whose name I suffer this, I pray You deign to accept my spirit with Your holy martyrs.'

And so the servant of the devil brandished his sword and brought death to the most blessed martyr, in Jesus Christ our Lord, whose honour and glory are for ever. Amen.

## 34. Sketch of Luxor fresco, Gardner Wilkinson

## 35. Plan of Diocletian's Palace, Split

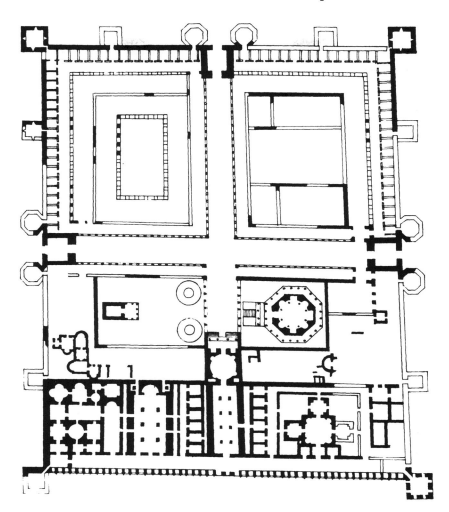

## 36. Plan of Tetrarchic Palace, Gamzigrad

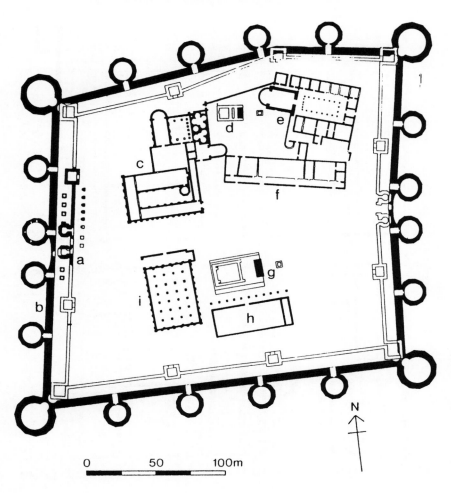

## 37. Plan of the Baths of Diocletian, Rome

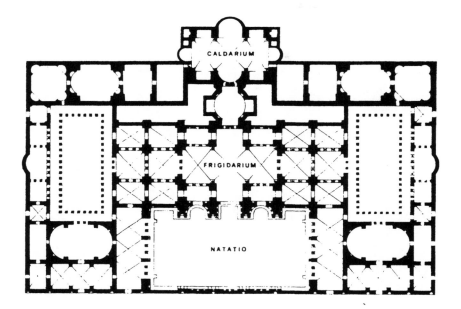

## 38.  Portchester Fort, Saxon Shore

## 39.  Senate House, Rome

## 40. Arch of Galerius, Thessalonica, detail

## 41.  Constantinian Basilica, Trier

## 42.  Maxentian Basilica, Rome

## 43a, b.  *Decennalia* Base, Rome, details

## 44. Coin of Carausius, obverse

## 45. Arras Medallion

## 46. Porphyry Group, Venice

## 47.  Porphyry Group, Vatican Library

## 48.  Porphyry Bust of Diocletian (?), Worcester Museum, Massachusetts

## 49.  Porphyry Bust of Licinius (?), Egyptian Museum, Cairo

## 50. Porphyry Bust of Galerius (?), Gamzigrad

# Chronology

| | |
|---|---|
| November 284 | Diocletian became emperor |
| Spring 285 | Diocletian defeated Carinus at the battle of Margus |
| 285 | Dyarchy ('rule of two') created<br>Maximian appointed Caesar by Diocletian |
| 286 | Maximian appointed Augustus |
| c. 287–93 | Carausius 'Roman emperor' in Britain |
| c. 288 | Imperial *signa* adopted<br>Diocletian *Jovius* and Maximian *Herculius* |
| 293 | Carausius assassinated and replaced by Allectus<br>Tetrarchy ('rule of four') created |

Diocletian Augustus *Iovius*        Maximian Augustus *Herculius*
              |                                      |
Galerius Caesar *Iovius*        Constantius Caesar *Herculius*

| | |
|---|---|
| 294 | Reform of the Mints |
| 296 | Allectus defeated by Constantius |
| 297 | Galerius suffered reverse against Persians |
| 297–8 | Egypt rebelled under Achilleus and Domitius Domitianus.<br>Diocletian crushed the rebellion. |
| 298 | Galerius defeated Persians |
| 301 | Currency reform<br>The Edict of Maximal Prices |
| February 303 | Beginning of the 'Great' Persecution |
| May 305 | Diocletian and Maximian retired from office<br>The 'Second' Tetrarchy |

Galerius Augustus                Constantius Augustus
              |                                      |
Maximinus Daia Caesar        Severus Caesar

| | |
|---|---|
| July 306 | Constantius died. His son Constantine proclaimed Augustus |

by his troops. Galerius promoted Severus to Augustus and recognised Constantine as Caesar.

| | |
|---|---|
| October 306 | Maximian's son Maxentius proclaimed emperor at Rome. Maximian left retirement to join his son as emperor again. Severus invaded Italy but was put to death. |
| 307 | Constantine married Maximian's daughter<br>Galerius invaded Italy unsuccessfully |
| 308 | Imperial conference at Carnuntum<br>Licinius proclaimed Augustus |
| 310 | Death of Maximian |
| 311 | End of 'Great' Persecution<br>Death of Galerius |
| 312 | Constantine defeated Maxentius<br>Death of Diocletian (?) |
| 313 | Edict of Milan<br>Death of Maximinus Daia |

# Further Reading

## Part I  Debates

### Introduction

Cameron (1993), Garnsey and Humfress (2001) and Brown (1971) are very accessible introductions to Late Antiquity, the latter with good illustrations. The monumental survey by Jones (1964) is not always sympathetic to the reader, but useful narrative chapters are complemented by more detailed thematic discussions. A second edition of the *Cambridge Ancient History vol. 12* is due out soon. The early pages of Barnes (1981) offer a clear, scholarly narrative. Williams (1985) is an uncomplicated and influential work; it remains an excellent example of narrative and analysis balanced to persuasive effect, but it has a marked tendency to oversimplify. There is not a scholarly work in English to compare with the unfinished project of Seston (vol. 1, 1946, in French) or the colossal overview of Kuhoff (2001, German, with good bibliography). There are interesting articles, in various languages, in volumes 2 and 3 of the journal *Antiquité Tardive*. Srejovic (1995) gathers an assorted collection. The Tetrarchs are not well served by biographers; Castritius (1969) on Maximinus Daia, Pasqualini (1979) on Maximian and Cullhed (1994) on Maxentius are three dedicated works. Constantine has received much more attention: Alfoldi (1948) remains a classic work, and Lieu and Montserrat (1998) is a collection of more recent approaches. The entries on individual emperors and sources in *O.C.D.*[3] are very useful; *P.L.R.E.* can be useful on emperors and others.

Discussions of Eutropius and Aurelius Victor preface Bird's translations (1993, 1994); likewise Eadie (1967) for Festus. Bird (1993 xlvii–xlix, 1994 xii–xiv) briefly surveys modern scholarship on the lost *Kaisergeschichte*. The *Historia Augusta* has been the subject of countless disparate studies; Syme (1971, 1983) was one of its most observant critics; Honoré (1987) provides a different approach to the perennial question of its authorship; see also the dedicated issue of the journal *Literary and Linguistic Computing* 13.3 (1998). For Ammianus Marcellinus, see Matthews (1989). For Lactantius' *On the Deaths of the Persecutors*, the introduction and commentary of Creed (1984) are indispensable; Barnes (1973) discusses the circumstances of authorship;

Africa (1982) offers a memorable interpretation. For consideration of Eusebius, Barnes (1981) is excellent.

## Chapter 1: The Military

Sources for the Late Antique military sometimes make it difficult to distinguish between Tetrarchic and later Constantinian developments; this is reflected in much of the secondary works in monograph form, which tend to be broad in thematic or chronological scope. Jones (1964: 52–60) has some concise observations to make. Nicasie (1998) covers a great deal of ground including recruitment, organisation and strategy; on the last point, he defends Luttwak (1976) against his critics, prominent amongst whom are Mann (1979), Isaac (1992) and Whittaker (1994).

On the eastern frontier Blockley (1992) complements the source material collected by Dodgeon and Lieu (1991). Schönberger (1969) considers Germany. Petrikovits (1971) analyses fortifications. Johnston (1977) is a very useful collection of short discussions of the Saxon Shore. For military equipment, Bishop and Coulston (1993) is the standard work. Brennan (1995, 1998) has made several penetrating studies of the *Notitia Dignitatum*. A new translation is being prepared for the Translated Texts for Historians series (Liverpool University Press).

## Chapter 2: Administration

Jones (1964: 42–52) makes important but brief remarks about Diocletian's administrative changes; see also some of his articles reprinted in 1974. A key study of the culture of imperial administration is Millar (1977, 1992[2]), but his thematic organisation can confound attempts to identify changes over time. Barnes (1982) is a focused, eclectic and endlessly useful collation of various administrative and prosopographical details from the period. Corcoran (1996, 2000[2], with good bibliography) introduces and catalogues legal sources from 284 to 324 and offers important and far-reaching conclusions about government procedures.

Curran (2000) includes consideration of the Tetrarchs' attitude to Rome; Cullhed (1994) focuses on Maxentius there. Lançon (2000) looks to Constantine and beyond in engaging style. Ward-Perkins (1981, Chapter 15) considers the architecture of Tetrarchic capitals; see also Sear (1982, Chapter 12). There are several specific studies on Tetrarchic capitals and palaces: on Trier, Wightman (1970), on Antioch, Liebeschuetz (1972), on Split (Wilkes 1986), on Cordoba, Haley (1994), on Gamzigrad-Romuliana, Srejovic (1995), on Milan, Krautheimer (1983). The controversy surrounding the Piazza Armerina has not been raised here, but Wilson (1983) is a standard work.

Bagnall (1993) provides a welcome survey of late Roman Egypt; he has also written a guide to the use of papyri in ancient historical research (1995). Rowlandson (1996) is an important book on the complexities and efficiencies of land ownership in Egypt. Although occasionally very technical, the introduction and notes in Skeat (1964) offer useful insights into the Panopolis archive. Adams (forthcoming 2004) provides a wider perspective.

## Chapter 3: Economics

General studies of Roman economics include Frank (1933–40), Rostovsteff (1957²) and Duncan-Jones (1994). On more specific issues, to Jones (1964: 61–8) should be added his collection of papers (1974).

On coinage, *R.I.C.* 5.2 and 6 remain vital, although the former in particular is now dated. Howgego (1995) discusses the use of coins in historical enquiry. Ermatinger (1996) is unusual as a book-length study of Diocletian's economy. Of specific studies, the following are good examples: on tax, Thomas (1978), Barnes (1982: 226–34); on military pay, Duncan-Jones (1978, revised 1990); on mints, Hendy (1972); on coinage, Sutherland (1955, 1956, 1961), Sperber (1966); on the Prices Edict, Corcoran (1996, 2000²: Chapter 8).

## Chapter 4: Ceremonial

On *adventus*, in literary and artistic representation, the publications of MacCormack are essential reading (1972, 1981 with good bibliography). The discussion by L'Orange (1965) of late third- and fourth-century artistic forms is an important forerunner. McCormick (1986) traces the representation of leadership beyond Late Antiquity.

MacCormack (1975) is the first study in English to consider the social context of the *Panegyrici Latini*; Nixon (1983, 1993) and Nixon and Rodgers (1994) further contextualise the speeches. See the introduction of Russell and Wilson (1981) for the dating of Menander Rhetor; and Russell (1998) for rhetorical style and training in Late Antiquity. Seager (1983) considers the canon of virtues in the *Panegyrici Latini*, and Rees (1998) the emperors' private lives. Rees (2002, 2003) focuses on the speeches up to 307; Warmington (1974) and Rodgers (1989) on those delivered to Constantine.

There have been few studies in English of the *signa*: Mattingly (1952), Nixon and Rodgers (1994: 48–51) and Rees (forthcoming 2004).

## Chapter 5: Religion

Beard, North and Price (1998) provide an expansive approach to the religious culture of Rome; for Late Antiquity in particular, see Liebeschuetz (1979). Frend (1984) and Chadwick (1967) offer chronological accounts of the early church, including the Tetrarchic period.

There is no single work on Tetrarchic religion; for secondary material, see the recommended works for specific sources.

On the Manichaeans, see Bruce (1983). For the causes of the persecution, see de Ste Croix (1963); on the Martyr Acts, Frend (1965), Musirillo (1972), Tilley (1996). Eusebius' *Martyrs of Palestine* is available online (see below for his *History of the Church*).

## Chapter 6: Unity, Succession and Legitimacy

For *concordia* in panegyrics, see Nixon and Rodgers (1994) and Rees (2002). The porphyry groups have been much discussed: for a range of interpretations, see Berenson (1954), L'Orange (1965), Hannestad (1986), Kleiner (1992), Rees (1993) and Smith (1997).

On legitimacy, Casey (1977, 1994) and Shiel (1977) discuss Carausius; see also Lyne (2003). Cullhed (1994) and Barnes (1996) provide different perspectives on Maxentius; Leadbetter (1998b) focuses on Constantine.

## Part II Documents

Translations of texts are available as follows:

1.  Aurelius Victor: *Book of the Caesars* – Bird (1994)
2.  Eutropius: *Breviarium* – Bird (1993)
3.  Festus: *Breviarium* – Eadie (1967)
4.  *Epitome about the Caesars* – Latin text in Pichlmayr (1970)
5.  *Anonymous Valesianus* – Rolfe (1939)
6.  Lactantius: *On the Deaths of the Persecutors* – Creed (1984); www.newadvent.org; www.ccel.org
7.  Ammianus Marcellinus: *Histories* – Rolfe (3 vols. 1935–9); abridged version, Hamilton (1986)
8.  Eusebius: *History of the Church* – Williamson (1965, 1989$^2$); www.newadvent.org; www.ccel.org
9.  Malalas: *Chronicle* – Jeffreys, Jeffreys, Scott (1986)
10. Zosimus: *New History* – Ridley (1982)
11–17. *Panegyrici Latini* – Nixon and Rodgers (1994)
18. *Historia Augusta* – Magie (1932)
19. Edict of Maximal Prices – Frank (1940)
21. Panopolis Papyri – Skeat (1964)
22. Edict of Aristius Optatus – Boak and Youtie (1960)
23. Land Declaration – Boak and Youtie (1960)
24. Legal Petition – Boak and Youtie (1960)
25. *Notitia Dignitatum* – www.fordham.edu/halsall/source/notitiadignitatum.html; a new translation is in preparation with Liverpool University Press
27. *Verona List* – Barnes (1982: 205–8)
28. Manichaean rescript – Hyamson (1913); Dodgeon and Lieu (1991: 135–6)
29. Theodosian Code – Pharr (1952)
30. Justinianic Code – Birks and McLeod (1987)
31–3. Martyr Acts – Musirillo (1972)

# Essay Questions and Exercise Topics

## The Military

### Questions

1. What made Tetrarchic military exploits successful?
2. Were military considerations at the heart of all of Diocletian's policy decisions?
3. Who defeated the Persians, Diocletian or Galerius?
4. What challenges did Constantine face when confronting Maxentius, and why did he succeed where Severus and Galerius had failed?

### Topics

5. Create a map of the empire which includes frontier archaeology and physical geography. Can a unifying strategy be identified?
6. Relate a map of the Saxon Shore to the dates for each fort. Was there a strategy and can the Saxon Shore be described as Tetrarchic?

## Economics and Administration

### Questions

7. How did Diocletian make use of the law as a mechanism for social order?
8. How efficient were Diocletian's administrative reforms?
9. Were Diocletian's fiscal measures successful?
10. Was the Edict of Prices a failure, and, if so, why?

### Topics

11. Use *R.I.C.* to draw a map indicating the locations of mints between 284 and 313. Consider when each mint was operating and relate that information to changes in the constitutional and political scene. What conclusions can be drawn about the importance of money supply and the role of coinage in imperial ideology?
12. Take the Lower Thebaid and one other Tetrarchic province, and use

sources such as the Panopolis Papyri, the *Verona List*, and the *Notitia Dignitatum* to establish a picture of how they were administrated and governed. Include, as far as possible, details of territory and administrative and military hierarchies. How radical a change did this represent from earlier practice, and what, if any, are the main differences between the administrative structures in the two provinces?

## Ceremonial and Religion

### Questions

13. Did the Tetrarchs have a coherent and considered religious policy?
14. What were Tetrarchic *signa* for?
15. Was the Tetrarchic persecution 'Great'?
16. What role did the Tetrarchs play in the evolution of ceremonial?

### Topics

17. Read Lactantius, Eusebius and the Martyr Acts and identify rhetorical techniques and other literary strategies they share. Do these compromise their reliability?
18. Use Suetonius' biographies of Augustus and Nero to compare the Julio-Claudian culture of imperial accessibility with Tetrarchic practice. What were the essential differences between how frequently and why in these two periods Roman emperors made themselves available to the ordinary public?

## Unity, Succession and Legitimacy

### Questions

19. Was Tetrarchic government ever harmonious?
20. How important were relationships by blood and marriage in Tetrarchic imperial ideology?
21. Was there a system of centralised control over sculptural images of the Tetrarchs?
22. Do the remains of his palace complexes at Gamzigrad and/or Thessaloniki support the claim (made by Lactantius) that Galerius had monarchical ambitions?

### Topics

23. Compile a list of internal challenges to the Tetrarchy (perhaps starting with Barnes 1982: 10–16). How were they mounted, sustained and defeated? Are there any patterns to account for their rejection by the central government? Can a typology for legitimacy be constructed?
24 Look at Constantine's coins (*R.I.C.* 6), panegyrics (Nixon and Rodgers 1994) and edicts and letters (Corcoran 1996, 2000[2]) for the years 306–13.

Are the different media consistent in their projection of Constantine's break with collegiate government?

## General Questions

25. What position did the city of Rome have in Diocletian's imperial ideology?
26. Why was the Tetrarchic experiment so short-lived?
27. Was the Tetrarchy a revolution or evolution in constitutional government?
28. For the poor of the empire, was the Tetrarchy a time for celebration?
29. Did the Tetrarchy redefine *Romanitas*?
30. Was Diocletian either a careful strategist or an adept improvisor?

# Bibliography

C. E. P. Adams, forthcoming 2004: Transition and Change in Diocletian's Egypt: Province and Empire in the Late Third Century, in S. Swain and M. Edwards (eds), *Aspects of Late Antiquity*, Oxford: Oxford University Press.

T. Africa, 1982: Worms and the Deaths of Kings: A Cautionary Note on Disease and History, *Cl.A.* 1, 1–17.

A. Alföldi, 1948: *The Conversion of Constantine and Pagan Rome*, Oxford: Oxford University Press.

G. Alföldy, 1974: The Crisis of the Third Century as seen by Contemporaries, *G.R.B.S.* 15, 89–111.

J. G. C. Anderson, 1932: The Genesis of Diocletian's Provincial Reorganisation, *J.R.S.* 22, 24–32.

R. S. Bagnall, 1993: *Egypt in Late Antiquity*, Princeton, NJ: Princeton University Press.

— 1995: *Reading Papyri, Writing Ancient History*, London: Routledge.

T. D. Barnes, 1973: Lactantius and Constantine, *J.R.S.* 63, 29–46.

— 1980: The Editions of Eusebius' *Ecclesiastical History*, *G.R.B.S.* 21, 191–201.

— 1981: *Constantine and Eusebius*, Cambridge, MA: Harvard University Press.

— 1982: *The New Empire of Diocletian and Constantine*, Cambridge, MA: Harvard University Press.

— 1996: Emperors, Panegyrics, Prefects, Provinces and Palaces (284–317), *J.R.A.* 9, 532–52.

— 1999: The Wife of Maximinus, *C.Ph.* 94, 459–60.

M. Beard, J. North and S. Price, 1998: *The Religions of Rome*, 2 vols, Cambridge: Cambridge University Press.

B. Berenson, 1954: *The Arch of Constantine or the Decline of Form*, London: Chapman and Hall.

H. W. Bird, 1993: *Eutropius: Breviarium*, Liverpool: Liverpool University Press.

— 1994: *Aurelius Victor: De Caesaribus*, Liverpool: Liverpool University Press.

P. Birks and G. McLeod, 1987: *Justinian's Institutes*, London: Duckworth.

M. Bishop and J. C. N. Coulston, 1993: *Roman Military Equipment*, London: Batsford.

R. C. Blockley, 1984: The Romano-Persian Treaties of 299 and 363, *Florilegium* 6, 28–49.

— 1992: *East Roman Foreign Policy: Formation and Conduct from Diocletian to Anastasius*, Leeds: Francis Cairns.

A. E. R. Boak and H. C. Youtie, 1960: *The Archive of Aurelius Isidorus in the Egyptian Museum, Cairo*, Ann Arbor, MI: University of Michigan Press.

A. K. Bowman, 1978: The Military Occupation of Upper Egypt in the Reign of Diocletian, *B.A.S.P.* 15, 25–38.

P. Brennan, 1995: The *Notitia Dignitatum*, in *Entretiens sur l'Antiquité Classique* 42, 147–78.

— 1998: The Users' Guide to the *Notitia Dignitatum*: The Case of the *Dux Armeniae ND*. Or 38, *Antichthon* 32, 34–49.

P. Brown, 1971: *The World of Late Antiquity*, London: Thames and Hudson.

L. D. Bruce, 1983: Diocletian, the Proconsul Iulianus and the Manichaeans, in C. Deroux (ed.), *Studies in Latin Literature and Roman History* 3 (*Collection Latomus* 180), Brussels: Latomus, 336–47.

P. Bruun, 1976: Portrait of a Conspirator. Constantine's Break with the Tetrarchy, *Arctos* 10, 5–25.

A. Cameron, 1993: *The Later Roman Empire*, London: Fontana.

P. J. Casey, 1977: Carausius and Allectus – Rulers in Gaul?, *Britannia* 8, 283–301.

— 1994: *Carausius and Allectus: The British Usurpers*, London: Batsford.

H. Castritius, 1969: *Studien zu Maximinus Daia*, Kallmünz: M. Lassleben.

H. Chadwick, 1967: *The Early Church*, Harmondsworth: Penguin.

S. Corcoran, 1996, 2000²: *The Empire of the Tetrarchs. Imperial Pronouncements and Government AD 284–324*, Oxford: Oxford University Press.

J. C. N. Coulston, 2002: Arms and Armour of the Late Roman Army, in D. Nicolle (ed.), *A Companion to Medieval Arms and Armour*, Woodbridge: Boydell Press, 3–24.

J. L. Creed, 1984: *Lactantius: De Mortibus Persecutorum* (ed. and commentary), Oxford: Oxford University Press.

B. Croke and A. M. Emmett (eds), 1983: *History and Historians in Late Antiquity*, Sydney and New York: Pergamon Press.

M. Cullhed, 1994: *Conservator Urbis Suae: Studies in the Politics and Propaganda of the Emperor Maxentius*, Stockholm: P. Aström.

B. Cunliffe, 1977: The Saxon Shore – Some Problems and Misconceptions, in D. E. Johnston (ed.), *The Saxon Shore* (C.B.A. Research Report 18).

J. Curran, 2000: *Pagan City and Christian Capital: Rome in the Fourth Century*, Oxford: Oxford University Press.

P. S. Davies, 1989: The Origin and Purpose of the Persecution of AD 303, *J.Th.S.* 40, 66–94.

M. H. Dodgeon and S. N. C. Lieu, 1991: *The Roman Eastern Frontier and the Persian Wars AD 226–363*, London: Routledge.

R. P. Duncan-Jones, 1978: Pay and Numbers in Diocletian's Army, *Chiron* 8,

541–60.

— 1990: *Structure and Scale in the Roman Army*, Cambridge: Cambridge University Press.

— 1994: *Money and Government in the Roman Empire*, Cambridge: Cambridge University Press.

J. W. Eadie, 1967: *The Breviarium of Festus*, London: Athlone.

D. E. Eichholz, 1953: Constantius Chlorus' Invasion of Britain, *J.R.S.* 43, 41–6.

K. T. Erim, J. Reynolds and M. H. Crawford, 1971: Diocletian's Currency Reform; A New Inscription, *J.R.S.* 61, 171–7.

J. W. Ermatinger, 1990: Diocletian's Economic Revolution, *Münsterische Beiträge zur Antiken Handelsgeschichte* 9, 45–9.

— 1996: *The Economic Reforms of Diocletian*, St Katharinen: Scripta Mercaturae.

T. Frank, 1933–40: *An Economic Survey of Ancient Rome*, Baltimore, MA: Johns Hopkins University Press.

W. H. C. Frend, 1965: *Martyrdom and Persecution in the Early Church*, Oxford: Oxford University Press.

— 1984: *The Rise of Christianity*, London: Darton, Longman and Todd.

P. Garnsey and C. Humfress, 2001: *The Evolution of the Late Antique World*, Cambridge: Orchard Academic.

E. Gibbon, 1776, 1781, 1788: *The Decline and Fall of the Roman Empire*, 6 vols, London.

E. W. Haley, 1994: A Palace of Maximianus Herculius at Cordoba?, *Z.P.E.* 101, 208–14.

W. Hamilton, 1986: *Ammianus Marcellinus*, Harmondsworth: Penguin.

N. Hannestad, 1986: *Roman Art and Imperial Policy*, Jutland Archaeological Society, Aarhus: Aarhus University Press.

J. Harries, 1999: *Law and Empire in Late Antiquity*, Cambridge: Cambridge University Press.

M. F. Hendy, 1972: Mint and Fiscal Administration under Diocletian, his Colleagues and his Successors, *J.R.S.* 62, 75–82.

A. Higham, 1995: *Diocletian. The Tale of a Singular Man*, Chichester: Whyke Road Press.

T. Honoré, 1987: *Scriptor Historiae Augustae*, *J.R.S.* 77, 156–76.

M. K. Hopkins, 1978: *Conquerors and Slaves*, Cambridge: Cambridge University Press.

— 1980: Taxes and Trades in the Roman Empire, *J.R.S.* 70, 62–80.

C. Howgego, 1995: *Ancient History from Coins*, London: Routledge.

M. Hyamson, 1913: *Mosaicarum et Romanarum Legum Collatio*, London: Oxford University Press.

A. Isaac, 1992: *The Limits of Empire: The Roman Army in the East*, Oxford: Oxford University Press.

E. Jeffreys, M. Jeffreys and R. Scott, 1986: *The Chronicle of John Malalas* (*Byzantina Australiensa* 4), Melbourne: Australian Association for Byzantine

Studies.

D. E. Johnston (ed.), 1977: *The Saxon Shore (C.B.A. Research Report 18)*.

S. Johnston, 1983: *Late Roman Fortifications*, London: Batsford.

A. H. M. Jones, 1953: Census Records of the Later Roman Empire, *J.R.S.* 43, 49–64.

— 1964: *The Later Roman Empire 284–602. A Social, Economic and Administrative Survey*, 3 vols, reprinted in 1973, Oxford: Blackwell.

— 1974: *The Roman Economy: Studies in Ancient Economic and Administrative History*, Oxford: Oxford University Press.

I. Kalavrezou-Maxeiner, 1975: The Imperial Chamber at Luxor, *D.O.P* 29, 225–51.

P. Keresztes, 1983: From the Great Persecution to the Peace of Galerius, *Vigiliae Christianae* 37, 379–99.

D. E. E. Kleiner, 1992: *Roman Sculpture*, New Haven and London: Yale University Press.

F. Kolb, 1987: *Diokletian und die Erste Tetrarchie: Improvisation oder Experiment in der Organisation monarchischer Herrschaft?*, Berlin and New York: Walter de Gruyter.

R. Krautheimer, 1983: *Three Christian Capitals: Topography and Politics*, Berkeley, CA: University of California Press.

W. Kuhoff, 2001: *Diokletian und die Epoche der Tetrarchie*, Frankfurt: Peter Lang.

B. Lançon, 2000: *Rome in Late Antiquity* (translation from 1995 French original), Edinburgh: Edinburgh University Press.

R. Lane-Fox, 1986: *Pagans and Christians*, Harmondsworth: Penguin.

W. Leadbetter, 1996: Imperial Policy and the Christians in the Late Third Century, in M. Dillon (ed.), *Religion in the Ancient World: New Themes and Approaches*, Amsterdam: Hakkert, 245–55.

— 1998a: *Patrimonium Indivisum*? The Empire of Diocletian and Maximian, 285–289, *Chiron* 28, 213–28.

— 1998b: The Illegitimacy of Constantine and the Birth of the Tetrarchy, in S. N. C. Lieu and D. Montserrat (eds), *Constantine. History, Historiography and Legend*, London: Routledge, 71–85.

— 2000: Galerius and the Revolt of the Thebaid in 293–4, *Antichthon* 34, 82–94.

N. Lewis, 1991: In the World of P. Panop. Beatty, *B.A.S.P.* 28, 163–78.

J. H. W. G. Liebeschuetz, 1972: *Antioch: City and Imperial Administration in the Later Roman Empire*, Oxford: Oxford University Press.

— 1979: *Continuity and Change in Roman Religion*, Oxford: Oxford University Press.

S. N. C. Lieu and D. Montserrat (eds), 1998: *Constantine. History, Historiography and Legend*, London: Routledge.

H. P. L'Orange, 1965: *Art Forms and Civic Life in the Late Roman Empire*, Princeton, NJ: Princeton University Press.

A. Louth, 1990: The Date of Eusebius' *Historia Ecclesiastica, J.Th.S.* 41, 111–23.

E. Luttwak, 1976: *The Grand Strategy of the Roman Empire*, Baltimore and London: Johns Hopkins University Press.

M. Lyne, 2003: Some New Coin Types of Carausius and Allectus and the History of the British Provinces AD 286–296, *N.C.* 163, 147–68.

S. G. MacCormack, 1972: Change and Continuity in Late Antiquity: The Ceremony of *Adventus, Historia* 21, 721–52.

— 1975: Latin Prose Panegyrics, in T. A. Dorey (ed.), *Empire and Aftermath: Silver Latin II*, London: Routledge & Kegan Paul, 143–205.

— 1981: *Art and Ceremony in Late Antiquity*, Berkeley, CA: University of California Press.

R. MacMullen, 1976: *Roman Government's Response to Crisis*, New Haven, CN: Yale University Press.

M. McCormick, 1986: *Eternal Victory: Triumphal Rulership in Late Antiquity, Byzantium and the Early Mediaeval West*, Cambridge: Cambridge University Press.

D. Magie, 1932: *Scriptores Historiae Augustae*, London: Heinemann.

J. C. Mann, 1977: *Duces* and *Comites* in the Fourth Century, in D. E. Johnston (ed.), *The Saxon Shore* (C.B.A. Research Report 18) 11–15.

— 1979: Force and the Frontiers of the Empire, *J.R.S.* 69, 175–83.

J. F. Matthews, 1989: *The Roman Empire of Ammianus*, London: Duckworth.

H. Mattingly, 1952: Jovius and Herculius, *H.Th.R.* 45, 131–4.

F. Millar, 1977, 1992²: *The Emperor in the Roman World*, London: Duckworth.

S. Mitchell, 1988: Maximinus and the Christians in AD 312: A New Latin Inscription, *J.R.S.* 78, 105–24.

A. Momigliano (ed.), 1963: *The Conflict between Paganism and Christianity in the Fourth Century*, Oxford: Oxford University Press.

H. Musirillo, 1972: *The Acts of the Christian Martyrs*, Oxford: Oxford University Press.

M. J. Nicasie, 1998: *Twilight of Empire: The Roman Army from the Reign of Diocletian until the Battle of Adrianople*, Amsterdam: Gieben.

C. E. V. Nixon, 1983: Latin Panegyrics in the Tetrarchic and Constantinian Period, in B. Croke and E. M. Emmett (eds), *History and Historians in Late Antiquity*, Sydney and New York: Pergamon Press, 88–99.

— 1993: *Constantius Oriens Imperator*: Propaganda and Panegyric. On Reading Panegyrics 7 (307), *Historia* 42, 229–46.

C. E. V. Nixon and B. S. Rodgers, 1994: *In Praise of Later Roman Emperors: The Panegyrici Latini*, Berkeley, CA: University of California Press.

H. M. D. Parker, 1933: The Legions of Diocletian and Constantine, *J.R.S.* 23, 175–89.

A. Pasqualini, 1979: *Massimiano 'Herculius' per un' interpretazione della figura e dell' opera*, Rome: Istituto italiano per la storia antica.

H. von Petrikovits, 1971: Fortifications in the North-Western Roman Empire from the Third Century to the Fifth Century, *J.R.S.* 61, 178–218.

A. Pharr, 1952: *The Theodosian Code*, Princeton, NJ: Princeton University Press.

Fr Pichlmayr, 1970: *Sextus Aurelius Victor*, Leipzig: Teubner.

M. S. Pond Rothman, 1975: The Panel of the Emperors Enthroned on the Arch of Galerius, *Byzantine Studies* 2, 19–40.

— 1977: The Thematic Organisation of the Panel Reliefs on the Arch of Galerius, *A.J.A.* 81, 427–54.

D. W. Rathbone, 1996: Monetisation, Not Price Inflation, in Third Century AD Egypt, in C. King and D. Wigg (eds), *Coin Finds and Coin Use in the Roman World*, Proceedings of the 13th Oxford Symposium on Coinage and Coinage History (*Studien zu Fundmünzen der Antike* 10), Berlin: Mann, 321–39.

R. D. Rees, 1993: Images and Image: A Re-examination of Tetrarchic Iconography, *G.&R.* 40, 181–200.

— 1998: The Private Lives of Public Figures in Latin Prose Panegyrics, in M. Whitby (ed.), *The Propaganda of Power: The Role of Panegyric in Late Antiquity* (*Mnemosyne Supplements* 183), Leiden: Brill, 77–101.

— 2002: *Layers of Loyalty in Latin Panegyric AD 289–307*, Oxford: Oxford University Press.

— 2003: Talking to the Tetrarchs: The Dynamics of Vocative Address, in C. Deroux (ed.), *Studies in Latin Literature and Roman History XI* (*Collection Latomus* 272) Brussels: Latomus, 447–92.

— forthcoming 2004: The Emperors' New Names: Diocletian Jovius and Maximian Herculius, in L. Rawlings and H. Bowden (eds), *Herakles/Hercules in the Ancient World*, Swansea: Classical Press of Wales.

R. T. Ridley, 1982: *Zosimus. New History*, Canberra: Australian Association for Byzantine Studies.

B. S. Rodgers, 1986: Divine Insinuation in the *Panegyrici Latini*, *Historia* 35, 69–104.

— 1989: The Metamorphosis of Constantine, *C.Q.* 39, 233–46.

J. C. Rolfe, 1935–9: *Ammianus Marcellinus*, 3 vols, London: Heinemann.

M. Rostovsteff, 1957[2]: *Social and Economic History of the Roman Empire*, Oxford: Oxford University Press.

J. Rowlandson, 1996: *Landowners and Tenants in Roman Egypt. The Social Relations of Agriculture in the Oxyrhynchite Nome*, Oxford: Oxford University Press.

D. A. Russell, 1998: The Panegyrists and their Teachers, in M. Whitby (ed.), *The Propaganda of Power: The Role of Panegyric in Late Antiquity*, (*Mnemosyne Supplements* 183) Leiden: Brill, 17–50.

D. A. Russell and N. G. Wilson, 1981: *Menander Rhetor*, Oxford: Oxford University Press

G. E. M. de Ste Croix, 1954: Aspects of the 'Great' Persecution, *H.Th.R* 47, 75–113.

— 1963: Why Were the Early Christians Persecuted?, *Past and Present* 26, 6–38.

M. Salzman, 1990: *On Roman Time: The Codex Calendar of 354 and the*

*Rhythms of Urban Life in Late Antiquity*, Berkeley, BA: University of California Press.

H. Schönberger, 1969: The Roman Frontier in Germany: An Archaeological Survey, *J.R.S.* 59, 144–97.

R. Seager, 1983: Some Imperial Virtues in the Latin Prose Panegyrists. The Demands of Propaganda and the Dynamics of Literary Composition, *P.L.L.S.* 4, 129–65.

F. Sear, 1982: *Roman Architecture*, London: Batsford.

W. Seston, 1946: *Dioclétian et la Tétrarchie I: Guerres et Réformes*, Paris: E. de Boccard.

N. Shiel, 1977: *The Episode of Carausius and Allectus: The Literary and Numismatic Evidence, British Archaeological Reports* 40, Oxford.

T. C. Skeat, 1964: *Papyri from Panopolis in the Chester Beatty Library, Dublin*, Dublin: Hodges Figgis.

R. R. R. Smith, 1997: The Public Image of Licinius I, *J.R.S.* 87, 170–202.

D. Sperber, 1966: *Denarii* and *Aurei* in the time of Diocletian, *J.R.S.* 56, 190–5.

D. Srejovic, 1994, The Representations of the Tetrarchs in *Romuliana, A.T.* 2, 143–52.

— (ed.), 1995: *The Age of the Tetrarchs* (Serbian Academy of Sciences and Arts, Scientific Meetings 74: Historical Sciences 24), Belgrade.

C. H. V. Sutherland, 1955: Diocletian's Reform of the Coinage: A Chronological Note, *J.R.S.* 45, 116–18.

— 1956: Flexibility in the 'Reformed' Coinage of Diocletian, in R. A. G. Carson and C. H. V. Sutherland (eds), *Roman Coinage. Essays Presented to Harold Mattingly*, Oxford: Oxford University Press, 174–89.

— 1961: *Denarius* and *Sestertius* in Diocletian's Coinage Reform, *J.R.S.* 51, 94–7.

— 1963: Some Political Notions in Coin Types between 294 and 313, *J.R.S.* 53, 14–20.

— 1967: *Roman Imperial Coinage 6: From Diocletian's Reform (294) to the Death of Maximinus (313)*, London: Spink.

R. Syme, 1971: *Emperors and Biography*, Oxford: Oxford University Press.

— 1983: *Historia Augusta Papers*, Oxford: Oxford University Press.

J. D. Thomas, 1976: The Date of the Revolt of L. Domitius Domitianus, *Z.P.E.* 22, 253–79.

— 1978: Epigraphai and Indictions in the Reign of Diocletian, *B.A.S.P.* 15, 133–45.

M. Tilley, 1996: *Donatist Martyr Stories. The Church in Conflict in Roman North Africa*, Liverpool: Liverpool University Press.

J. B. Ward-Perkins, 1981: *Roman Imperial Architecture*, Harmondsworth: Penguin.

B. H. Warmington, 1974: Aspects of Constantinian Propaganda in the *Panegyrici Latini, T.A.P.A.* 104, 371–84.

A. Watson, 1999: *Aurelian and the Third Century*, London: Routledge.

C. R. Whittaker, 1994: *Frontiers of the Roman Empire: A Social and Economic Study*, Baltimore and London: Johns Hopkins University Press.

E. M. Wightman, 1970: *Roman Trier and the Treveri*, London: Hart-Davis.

J. J. Wilkes, 1986: *Diocletian's Palace, Split*, Sheffield: University of Sheffield.

S. Williams, 1985: *Diocletian and the Roman Recovery*, London: Batsford (paperback edition, 1997, London and New York: Routledge).

G. A. Williamson, 1965, 1989[2]: *Eusebius. The History of the Church*, Harmondsworth: Penguin.

R. J. A. Wilson, 1983: *Piazza Armerina*, London: University of Texas Press.

# Glossary

*adventus*   ceremony of arrival
*annona*   tax in goods, especially grain
*aroura*   unit of land
*atticae*   see *denarius*
Augustus   senior imperial rank (see Caesar)
*aureus*   gold coin
Caesar   junior imperial rank (see Augustus)
*capita*   fiscal unit (the precise details of which are unknown)
*catholicus*   financial overlord of Egypt
*censitor*   census official
*cohortalini*   imperial bodyguard
*comitatus*   imperial court
*consecratio*   deification
*damnatio memoriae*   decree condemning the memory of a deceased person
*decemprimi*   official tax collectors
*decennalia*   tenth anniversary (of accession)
*denarius*   silver coin
*didaskalos*   instructor
diocese   administrative unit consisting of several provinces
Dyarchy   college of two emperors (usually denoting Diocletian and Maximian)
*fasces*   symbolic rods of office
*fasti*   list or register (of dates, consuls, etc.)
*follis*   copper coin
*frumentarius*   collectors of grain-tax with secret police powers
*genius*   (guardian) spirit
Germanicus   victory title taken after a defeat of the Germans
*haruspex*   diviner
*horiodeiktes*   official appointed to determine boundaries
*iugum*   unit of land productivity
*iuratores*   assistants to the *censitor*
*modius*   measure of corn; a peck

*nome*   administrative area in Egypt, usually consisting of a metropolis and surrounding countryside, divided into toparchies

*nummus*   coin with silver wash

*Pontifex Maximus*   chief of the state college of priests

*postliminium*   return to one's condition and privileges

praetorian prefect   emperor's deputy

*princeps*   prince

*procurator rei privatae*   controller of state land revenues

*sextarius*   pint

*signum*   appellation

*strategos*   official in charge of the administration of a *nome*

Tetrarchy   college of four emperors

*toparchy*   local administrative area in Egypt

*vicarius*   official responsible for a diocese

*vicennalia*   twentieth anniversary (of accession)

# Internet Resources
# for Diocletian

Inevitably, the internet provides a mixed bag of sites relating to Diocletian and the Tetrarchy, ranging from online sources in text and image format to surveys, usually brief and uncomplicated. The following list is not exhaustive; nor does the inclusion of any site constitute particular recommendation.

**General**
http://www.perseus.tufts.edu/
http://perseus.esad.ox.ac.uk
http://www.roman-emperors.org
http://campus.northpark.edu/history/WebChron/Mediterranean/Diocletian.
   html
http://www.roman-empire.net/decline/diocletian.html
http://www.ualberta.ca/~csmackay/CLASS_379/Diocletian.html
http://www.electriciti.com/garstang/emperors/tetofdiocletian.htm

Some source material is available at
www.fordham.edu/halsall/ancient/

Many early Christian sources in translation, including Lactantius and Eusebius, are available at
www.newadvent.org and www.ccel.org

On currency,
http://www.tulane.edu/~august/H303/currency/Diocletian.htm

For coins,
http://www.wildwinds.com/coins/ric/diocletian/i.html

Archaeological resources feature on
www.ancientsites.com

On Split in particular
http://www.ibiblio.org/expo/palace.exhibit/intro.html
http://archive.ncsa.uiuc.edu/SDG/Experimental/split/builder.html
http://www.st.carnet.hr/split/diokl.html

On the Baths of Diocletian
http://www2.siba.fi/~kkoskim/rooma/pages/TDIOCLET.HTM

# Index